D0984524

Growth, Innovation and Reform in Eastern Europe

The Economics of Technological Change
Edwin Mansfield, *General Editor*

The economics of technological change is, without question, one of the most rapidly growing fields of economics. The National Science Foundation has been supporting considerable research of this sort, and it has helped to finance conferences and other outlets for research findings. As a researcher, teacher, and consultant, as well as a member of various advisory committees, I see a considerable amount of very good work taking shape. This work deals with topics ranging from econometric studies of the determinants and effects of industrial R and D spending to policy research concerned with the implications of robotics for employment and unemployment. At present, much of this material is scattered among a wide variety of journals, here and abroad. The University of Wisconsin Press, through its series on the Economics of Technological Change, is doing a valuable service by providing a focus for work in this field.

Stanislaw Gomulka is Senior Lecturer in Economics at the London School of Economics and a well-known analyst of socialist economies. His book covers a wide variety of topics that are of great interest to economists and others dealing with technological change. In particular, his book sheds light on the fundamental questions concerning the effects of economic systems (like socialism and capitalism) on the rate of innovation. There is a strong emphasis on the role of *systemic* factors—that is, economic-system-related factors—in innovation, resource allocation, foreign trade, and growth.

Dr. Gomulka's book is the second in this series. Franco Malerba's *The Semiconductor Business: The Economics of Rapid Growth and Decline* was concerned with the decline of the European semiconductor industry, relative to that in the United States and Japan. While superficially Malerba's book may seem quite remote from the present volume, this is not really the case. Both are attempts to understand why some organizations are more successful than others in promoting and accepting new technologies. This is an extremely important question, both from the point of view of economic analysis and public policy, and one that will be the concern of future books in this series.

August 1985

Edwin Mansfield
Director, Center for
Economics and Technology
University of Pennsylvania

Growth, Innovation and Reform in Eastern Europe

Stanislaw Gomulka

Senior Lecturer in Economics
London School of Economics

The University of Wisconsin Press

Published in 1986 in the United States of America by
The University of Wisconsin Press
114 North Murray Street
Madison, Wisconsin 53715

338,947
G634

Published in Great Britain by
Wheatsheaf Books Ltd
A Member of the Harvester Press Publishing Group
16 Ship Street, Brighton, Sussex

First printing
Printed in Great Britain

ISBN   0-299-10660-8
LC Number   85-40774

Contents

Introduction

This book is concerned with various aspects of the economies of
Eastern Europe and the USSR. It comprises essays that are highly
interrelated, providing pieces of evidence and theory which reinforce each other and which together form a distinct way of interpreting socialist economies. It was this close interrelation and the
concern to make this distinct interpretation more apparent which
persuaded me to collect them into one book. All fourteen studies
in this collection have been written over the last eight years, five
being published for the first time.

The essays focus primarily on economic growth, efficiency and
innovation, and on the mutual interrelationships between these
three aspects and the institutional and ideological factors which
differentiate these socialist economies from market-based capitalist
economies. Some of the studies are policy-oriented or deal with
specific problems. Others are more theoretical and general. The
analytical methods which have been used also vary: some are
institutional and historical, while others are mathematical and
econometric.

There are three parts in the book. Part A, entitled *Socialism,
Capitalism and Innovation*, deals primarily with innovation,
growth and efficiency under capitalism and socialism. Chapters 1
and 3 offer elements of a general theory of long term economic
growth and institutional change. Chapter 1 includes also a criticism
of Brus's thesis on the link between economic efficiency and
political democracy under socialism. Professor Brus's response to
this criticism forms Chapter 2. Another debate in Part A is with
Professor Janos Kornai. An evaluation and a re-statement of his
theory of shortages and inefficiency under socialism are presented
in Chapter 5. Part A gives also an empirically-based analysis of the
inventive and innovative activities in centrally-planned economies
(Chapter 3) and in Yugoslavia (Chapter 4).

Part B, entitled *Industrialisation, Growth and Growth Slowdown*,
is more technical and specific, dealing with major aspects of
economic growth, especially industrial growth, in the USSR and
Eastern Europe in the postwar period. Two Chapters, 7 and 8, and

an Afterword are devoted to the slowdown in Soviet industrial growth. Alternative interpretations are presented, but the emphasis is on contrasting the author's own theory with that of Martin Weitzman and Padma Desai. Chapter 6 discusses industrialisation in Eastern Europe as a whole and Chapter 9 in Poland. The latter is an instructive case study of industrialisation under Soviet-type socialism. An important aspect of economic growth in Eastern Europe has been the so-called import-led growth. Chapter 10 presents both a theoretical model intended to capture the economic relations underlying this type of growth and an empirical computation of the potential growth effect.

Part C of the book, *Crisis and Reform*, is intended to explain why the import-led growth strategy has plunged most of Eastern Europe into an economic depression and Poland into a deep and politically destabilizing economic crisis. All three chapters of this Part focus on Poland, the country-laboratory in which the major economic and political problems associated with socialism of the Soviet type may be seen particularly clearly.

The book is not intended to cover all the ground in a comprehensive way. However, the reader will find in it a body of general theory and methods used in the field of comparative economics and, above all, detailed analysis of some of its central and most debated topics.

Most of this book was written in the stimulating and exciting environment of the London School of Economics. It would be impossible to list all of my colleagues and students who have influenced me and to whom I remain much in debt. Some of these influences will be evident in the acknowledgements and citations in the individual papers. However, I would like to mention Michal Kalecki and Oskar Lange, my teachers and colleagues before my leaving Poland in 1969, and Michio Morishima and Peter Wiles, my colleagues at the LSE since 1970, as those who in their rather different ways have made particularly significant impact on my choice of research interests in economics and ways of pursuing those interests.

The material in this book was prepared for publication in Philadelphia where I was with the Economics Department of the University of Pennsylvania in the academic year 1984/85. I wish to thank Herb Levine and the Department in general for being most helpful and understanding during that fine year.

London, January 1985   Stanislaw Gomulka

Part A

SOCIALISM, CAPITALISM AND INNOVATION

1 Economic Factors in the Democratisation of Socialism and the Socialisation of Capitalism[1]*

The immediate stimulus to write this paper came from reading *The Economics and Politics of Socialism* (1973) and *Socialist Ownership and Political Systems* (1975), both published by Włodzimierz Brus. The main ideas of these two books are presented and discussed in Part I of this chapter. In the course of the discussion attention is also drawn to a number of socioeconomic phenomena which, it is argued, cannot be interpreted convincingly within either the original Marxian theory of social change or its modification developed by Brus. Two of these phenomena are thought to be especially important: (1) the large variation in the rate of economic development between countries with approximately the same social systems; and (2) the clear preference for socialism in relatively less-developed countries at the time when the capitalist system still prospers in the most advanced countries.

In Part II the aims are twofold. One is to outline a model of long-run growth, which was developed elsewhere, and which I find useful in reinterpreting the empirical material defined by (1) and (2). The other is to argue that this reinterpretation, which in this chapter is only briefly sketched, implies economic requirements for socialism and democracy that are different from those suggested by Brus in his books.

I

1. BRUS'S THEORY

The primary concern of Brus (1975) is the relationship between

* Reprinted with permission from Stanislaw Gomulka (1977), *Journal of Comparative Economics* 1 pp. 389–406, with the omission of sections 1 and 2. The numbering of sections is changed accordingly. © by Academic Press, Inc.

economic efficiency and the form and operation of the central political and economic institutions in the countries of Eastern Europe and the USSR. The generalisations which the author formulates on these matters may be spelled out as follows:

(i) It is meaningful to make a distinction between public ownership (of the state or cooperative-type) of the means of production and their social ownership. Public ownership is the result of an act of law (nationalisation) while social ownership, which presupposes nationalisation, is really the result of a social process (political democratisation).

(ii) In the countries of Eastern Europe and the USSR the political system continues to be authoritarian; hence the degree of socialisation of the means of production remains low. This applies especially to the countries of the Soviet bloc, where an 'etatist model' has been adopted, but to a large extent also to Yugoslavia, despite her 'self-management model'.

(iii) Marx's chain of causation—production potential → production relations → institutions—should, in the case of the USSR and Eastern Europe, be replaced by the chain: production potential → institutions → production relations.[2] In particular, the Marxian thesis of the unceasing recurrence of contradictions between historically-formed production relations and society's need for further economic development, and Marx's resolution of these contradictions through class struggle, should be replaced by (1) the unceasing recurrence of contradictions between the form and operation of the institutional set-up and the needs of economic progress; and (2) the resolution of these contradictions through the process of struggle between the ruling elite and the workers and intellectuals.

(iv) A positive correlation exists between the degree of socialisation of the means of production (public ownership plus political democracy) and the level of economic efficiency. This correlation is especially powerful in societies where public ownership dominates.

(v) Capitalism is unable to meet several of the important requirements of our time, such as a more equitable distribution of incomes and wealth; more effective national and global planning, especially in the area of environmental protection and in the use of non-reproducible natural resources; reduction of unemployment; increase of job security; and price stability. On the other hand, socialism in its present totalitarian form is wholly unacceptable. Hence the increasing obsolescence of capitalism and the continuing unacceptability of the existing forms of socialism is a major dilemma of our time. A way out of this dilemma is through a slow transformation of capitalism into a democratic socialism in the West and in a gradual democratisation of totalitarian socialism in the East.

(vi) In the economic field, the present Soviet system of controlling from the centre prices and quantities should be replaced by a system in which only prices, including wages and interest rates, and some macroquantities would remain controlled, while the micro decisions about what, how and in what quantities to produce would be left for individual producers to make, in response to the signals coming from the 'regulated market'.[3]

In connection with (v) the basic question is, What might democratise totalitarian socialism? What 'objective necessity' will cause the principle of 'the leading role of the communist party', i.e. 'the effective control of the entire political life of the country by the political leadership' (1975, p. 169), to be no longer maintainable in the future? In his answer Brus refers to the work of some western industrial sociologists, notably to Douglas McGregor's *Leadership and Motivation*. One of the premises adopted by Brus (p. 189) is the notion that

people are by nature active and ambitious, capable of integrating their aims with those of organisations, inclined to accept responsibility and display initiative—while indications to the contrary should be ascribed principally to the long refusal to give them an active goal.

This notion is thought to apply to economic organisations as well. The extent to which the above-mentioned 'natural inclinations' of individual workers are respected and taken advantage of influences the motive to work. This is thus Leibenstein's 'X-efficiency factor' which influences the organisation's current performance as well as its dynamic, long-run performance (by increasing the workers' interest and zeal in assimilating innovations).

Hence it follows that considerations of economic efficiency create the need for further democratisation of the political system. No empirical work is produced that would indicate the practical relevance of this rule. But Brus believes that it is relevant, especially under central planning, where to motivate employees requires their meaningful participation in forming economic policy at higher levels of the decision-making structure, particularly at the central level. A higher degree of political democracy is also thought to increase the probability that the policies adopted are close to the social optimum, and that the cadres employed are better selected to carry these policies out.

Using economic terminology, Brus treats political democracy as a 'factor of production' (1975, p. 180). And while, of course, he is well aware of the fact that democracy is also a 'consumption good' in itself, it is exclusively its production role to which he refers to justify the proposition that 'considerations of economic efficiency are creating a need for democratization of the political system of the socialist countries, a need which is long-term and has no substitute' (p. 180). This economic role of democracy is to be the main driving force of the 'historical process' of the democratisation of socialism.[4]

2. INTERPRETATION AND CRITICAL REMARKS

Although distinction (i) was first introduced by the Polish economist E. Lipiński in 1948, its role has been much enhanced by the use to which it was put by Brus. Proposition (ii) also seems acceptable. There is now a vast amount of evidence that makes it reasonable to say that the changes introduced in the post-Stalin period, such as the replacement of massive-scale preventive terror by terror directed against selected groups and individuals, the gradual transition from total to selective control in the area of science and the arts, the employment in that area of censorship rather than command, and the controlled relaxation of isolation from the outside world, 'have not infringed the ruling *political system*; on the contrary—they were to serve to maintain it, as more effective, more adequate instruments for "dynamic petrification"' (1975, p. 140).

Proposition (iii) implies, I think, that the contradiction between the practically unchanged form and operation of the institutional set-up and the needs of economic development in Eastern Europe and the USSR has been systematically increasing in the post-war period. However, if one takes gross material domestic product per man-hour (that is, aggregate labour productivity) as an index of economic development, and if proper adjustments are made for the impact of the second world war, then one finds that the index for each of these countries was increasing at a more or less constant rate. In the USSR, a very high and declining growth rate of in-dustrial labour productivity in the period 1947–52, a high stable growth rate in the years 1955–61, a 'jump-down' in that rate in the period 1962–63, followed by a recovery in the years 1968–75, can all be explained without recourse to the notion that over time the Soviet system has had an *increasingly* adverse influence on the 'joint (capital and labour) productivity residual'.[5] A certain decline in the productivity residual in Poland and Czechoslovakia in the 1960s, which appeared to support (iii), and in terms of which it was often interpreted, has been made up by an upswing in growth after 1970. Moreover, this upswing probably has been associated with a decline, not an increase, in the extent of political democracy.

Proposition (vi) is of course the core of Brus's economic ideas, developed primarily in 1961, and modified in 1973 and 1975 by placing a much stronger emphasis on the economic role of democracy. These ideas have often been misinterpreted as representing a model of 'market socialism' of the Lange-type. It may be recalled that in Lange's model, wages and prices of consumer goods are determined directly in the market. Only the prices of producer goods, including interest rates, are decided by the centre. Moreover, these latter prices are being changed in response to quantity signals coming from the market (the size of excess demand for goods and money), ultimately to become not only approximately market clearing, but also reflecting the preferences of the individual consumers (except for investments). Thus, as far as prices are concerned, Lange's planners play the passive role of the Walrasian auctioneer. The only substantive decision to be taken at the centre concerns the distribution of profits derived from the use of the socially-owned capital and natural resources, and the production and distribution of public goods. Lange's system is truly decentralised. The aim of Brus's model is 'not decentralization but the provision of suitable means of attaining superior public ends, formulated and achieved under the guidance of the central level using methods different from the centralised model' (1973, p. 12). Thus Brus's system is a close relative of the models developed by Arrow and Hurwicz, Malinvaud, Weitzman, Heal, and others. In these models consumers are not really active players, and producers operate within an environment (of prices and decision criteria, such as profit-maximisation) carefully devised by the centre to deprive them of any effective counter-strategy: the allocation of resources is, to use Ellman's phrase 'perfectly indirectly centralised'. It is centralised because social preferences dominate. The market is merely an instrument for planners thought to be more effective than direct orders, if, as is usual, the centre has very poor knowledge about producers' production possibilities. As under the Soviet model, which is imperfectly directly centralised, consumers would continue to make their preferences felt only through the political process, with the exception of cases, or periods of time, when the planners choose to refrain from imposing their own preferences. The theoretical difficulties associated with identifying social preferences (Arrow's impossibility theorem) and the potential practical difficulties associated with translating these preferences, however imperfectly arrived at, into millions of 'socially optimal' prices are of course well known, and they are acknowledged by Brus to be serious. In any practical application of Brus's model, the planners would probably have to limit the control of prices to priority products and, by applying the method of trial and error, hope to learn about the correspondence between prices and quantities. Judging from the experience with Poland's agricultural sector, which as far as prices and outputs are concerned operates on rules similar to those advocated by Brus, the method may well be effective. However, his idea of full wage control seems both impractical and, in a democratic society, difficult to implement. Unfortunately, the potentially serious economic implications of these practical and political limits to parametric planning remain largely unexplored.

The case for the far-reaching alteration in the respective roles of institutions and social relations under socialism, claimed by (iii), rests on the fact that the socialist state is playing a dual role, of which the new one is that of the dominant owner of the means of production. This role enables the political superstructure to exert a major influence on the relations between, say, managers and workers. More importantly (for Brus anyway) it influences the extent to which the 'working man ceases to treat his production task as a private affair' (E. Lipiński, after Brus, 1973, p. 66). Brus's modification of the original doctrine stresses the 'inseparability of the economic and political factors' under socialism (p. 89) which makes the traditional distinction between base and superstructure 'more and more inadequate' (p. 87). But historical change, including democratisation, is still to take place as a result of societies trying to make good use of the opportunities offered to them by technological innovations. However, the exact origin of the pressure for such democratisation is not immediately clear. It is here also that I find Professor Brus's views not very convincing.

Since those views are inspired by Marxian theory, it may be appropriate to first make two observations about this theory.

3. TWO CHARACTERISTIC FEATURES OF MARXIAN THEORY

One key feature of the Marxian model is the identification of technological innovation as being ultimately the stimulus that causes economic, institutional and eventually cultural change to take place. But while the history of major innovations received a great deal of Marx's attention, no serious attempt was made to develop a coherent model of technical change itself. Innovation is treated, essentially, as if it were exogenously given, as a result of 'interaction' between man and nature. A theory based on such an assumption may be said to be incomplete, and to be so at its very foundation. One consequence of this incompleteness is that Marx has something definite to say only about the mechanism and the direction of economic and social change, and has relatively little to say about the rate of change. The only major endogenous factor influencing this rate in his model is the extent to which production relations and institutions are 'progressive'. Such an approach is clearly not good enough if we are to explain the observed large variation in the rate of economic development between countries where approximately the same socioeconomic systems operate, as, for instance, between Japan and the United Kingdom, France and the United States, Romania and Poland, etc. Nor is the theory particularly strong in explaining changes in that rate over time, such as the upswing in economic development in Spain, Portugal, Turkey and South Korea by the end of the 1950s, the marked acceleration in Brazil and Taiwan over the last twenty years or, generally, the post-war acceleration in Western Europe and Japan, the scale and firmness of which have been such a surprise for the post-war generation of Marxists (as well as for everyone else!). It is this experience which has led Marxists in the USSR and Eastern Europe gradually to abandon the once standard interpretation of the rate of economic growth as an indicator of the progressiveness of the socioeconomic system.

The other characteristic feature of Marx's theory is its 'materialism'. Here I have in mind the preference of Marx the economist to address himself to the problem of the social conditions of production and distribution of material goods more or less exclusively. Today, however, modern societies appear to devote increasingly more time and attention to creating and consuming a wide variety of 'non-material' goods as well. These are things that satisfy or can satisfy non-material human needs, e.g.

information, sensation or experience. The sphere of non-material goods includes the mass media, political, religious and tourist activities, science and education, the arts and literature, etc. Some non-material goods may actually be 'bads' (i.e. they may have an adverse effect on one's happiness), including lies of the mass media, activities of the secret (political) police and national humiliation by an outside power.

Expressions of this change away from the old emphasis on material goods can be found in the popular demand for a higher 'quality of life', or in the movement in favour of an 'alternative technology' and an 'alternative culture'. Moreover, science and the mass media have brought about a dramatic increase in the competition among ideas. This increase is causing a flattening of hierarchical social groups and structures, and is associated with a call for consensus and with an increase in the diversity of opinion. As a result, societies are probably becoming more pluralistic, and so also increasingly conducive to creating and enjoying non-material goods.

These are all relatively new phenomena, which, of course, Marx was not concerned with, but which it would seem that a modern macro theory of economic and social change can no longer afford to ignore. In particular, Brus's notion that political democracy is a 'non-substitutable factor of production' must not be limited to the sphere of material goods alone, where its role is doubtful anyway.[6] The avenue of associating the prospects of the democratisation of socialism with the increasing social need to expand activities 'producing' non-material goods, and thereby also with the notion of economic and political democracy becoming increasingly a non-substitutable good in itself, is possibly the more promising one.[7]

II

4. VARIATION IN THE RATE OF ECONOMIC GROWTH AND THE POSSIBILITY OF INNOVATION LIMITS TO GROWTH

As recalled above, the Marxian model locates the heart of economic and social development in perpetual technological change; but it treats this heart as if it were exogenously given. It was also noted that the observed wide variation in the rates of economic growth over time and between nations, including those with approximately the same social systems, suggests that the rate of technological change must depend too, and in a crucial way, upon non-systemic factors. Identification of these factors and the underlying causal relations is in fact the subject of research that has recently been attracting increasing attention.

The theory of technological change and long-run growth remains still at an early stage of development. Nevertheless, I would like to draw attention to one particular approach, since certain social implications appear to flow from it that are relevant to the subject matter of this paper.

(i) This approach considers, first, the area of the technological frontier—once a part of Western Europe and now mainly the United States. Empirical evidence indicates that for such an area technological diffusion from the rest of the world is a relatively minor factor compared with the innovational output of the area's technological sector. Edmund Phelps (1966) proposed a model of this sector that implies that the trend rate of technological change is a positive function of the growth rates of inputs engaged in that sector, capital M and employment R, that is $g_T = \beta g_M + \gamma g_R$, where β and γ are both positive.[8] At between 4 and 6 percent, g_R over the last two centuries has been about five times greater than g_L, the growth rate of total employment.[9] As a result, the ratio R/L has been doubling approximately every 20 years. But since it cannot exceed unity, there must, sooner or later, come a decline in g_R to g_L, which must approach zero. Similarly, g_M has so far been much higher than g_Y. Again this unbalanced growth must come to an end. Hence both $g_R \rightarrow g_L$ and $g_M \rightarrow (g_L + g_T)$. Consequently, $g_T \rightarrow [(\beta + \gamma)/(1 - \beta)]g_L$, and g_T may be expected to decline gradually to zero when the size of the technological sector finally stops growing (assuming $g_L \rightarrow 0$). (Since in the past g_M in the US technological sector is estimated to have been several times greater than the US g_T, it follows from $g_T = \beta g_M + \gamma g_R$ that parameter β is significantly less than unity, possibly not more than 0.1.)

(ii) Countries that found themselves behind the technological frontier can obtain innovations from abroad through one of several forms of diffusion. The evidence that diffusion for those countries is in fact the dominant determinant of g_T is both direct and indirect. The direct evidence concerns particular countries of this category, such as Japan in the 1960s, and suggests that nearly all new products and processes adopted there are either of foreign origin or represent extensions of imported technology (OECD, 1967, pp. 142–3).

Another piece of evidence of this type concerns the international trade in technology. In the 1960s Japan imported about ten times more innovations, in terms of dollars paid, than it exported. The analogous ratio for Western Europe was approximately 2, and for the United States only about 0.1.[10]

The indirect evidence originates from comparing the expansion of the technological sector in various parts of the world. For instance, in Western Europe this sector has been expanding less rapidly than in the United States. Yet in the post-war period g_T has been significantly higher in Europe than in the United States. Denoting $\dot{T} = \dot{T}_h + \dot{T}_d$, where $\dot{T}_h$ is the home output of new technology and $\dot{T}_d$ is diffusion, we have:

$$g_T = \eta g_{T,h} + (1 - \eta)g_{T,d} \qquad 0 < \eta < 1,$$

where $\eta = T_h/T$, while $g_{T,h}$ and $g_{T,d}$ are the growth rates of T_h and T_d, respectively. Assuming that the US weights β and γ apply universally, the West European $g_{T,h}$ has been less than the US $g_{T,h}$, and the latter is less than the Western European g_T. Therefore in post war Western Europe $g_{T,d}$ has been greater than g_T. Moreover, when $g_{T,h} < g_{T,d}$ then η is declining,[11] so that $g_T \rightarrow g_{T,d}$, pointing to an increasing role of diffusion in determining growth.

A model of technical change with diffusion (Gomulka, 1971) generates g_T that depends strongly on the relative technological gap x. Namely, g_T is relatively low when x is either very high or very low. That is to say, the model expects the countries in the range of medium-sized x's to exhibit the highest growth rates of labour productivity (at a given capital/output ratio). This property of the model is in fact found to be partly corroborated by the growth data for 55 countries covering the period 1950–68 (Gomulka, 1971, Chapter IV). These data give rise to what is termed the 'Hat-shape Relationship'. This is a relationship of the hat-like shape between the growth rate of GDP per capita (a proxy for g_T) and the ratio of the US income per capita to that of a given country (a proxy for x).

However, the data also show that variations in g_T at a given x can still be quite considerable; the 'hats' can be of different heights. These variations might be interpreted as a corroboration of the view, expressed often in empirical studies on diffusion at a micro level, that technological advance in the area behind the frontier is also under the powerful influence of non-economic factors, such as drive and determination of technical and managerial personnel in finding out and adopting new innovations (their, as it were, innovational spirits), degree of resistance to technical change by workers, degree of exposure of the home producers to the pressure of domestic and international competition etc. A combination of these cultural, political and institutional factors appears to differentiate strongly the technologically less-advanced countries with respect to the tempo at which they catch up with the United States. An example of this differentiation is the industrial sectors of the United Kingdom, France, the USSR and Japan with their average rates of growth of output per man-hour, respectively, of 3, 6, 7, and 9 per cent per annum in the period 1951–75.

Possibilities of a very rapid growth, typically in the range between 5 and 10 per cent, come to an end, however, when the technological gap to the frontier is substantially reduced or completely eliminated, and then the regularities described under (i) above begin to operate. This purely technical constraint on economic growth applies equally to capitalist and socialist countries, to democracies and to dictatorships. Moreover, as a result of the increasing influence of that constraint, a gradual fall in the rate of economic growth can be expected to begin in about 10–15* years in West Germany, France and Japan, and in about 15–30 years in the USSR and Eastern Europe. By the beginning of the next century the growth rate in all these countries should, according to this scenario, reach more or less the present US level of about 2–3 per cent per head, and subsequently to continue to decline still more.

(iii) From (i) and (ii) above it follows that the technological revolution in each country, and indeed in the world as a whole, may evolve according to a certain characteristic sequence. Namely, after the initial period of transition from nearly zero growth to a state where both labour productivity and consumption per head grow at an annual rate of, say 1–2 per cent, and after the still contemporary period of rapid growth at a trend rate in the range between 3 and 10 per cent, there may come a period of strong deceleration of growth, to about 2–3 per cent, to be followed by a gradual and a relatively slow transition back to nearly zero growth. Hence the industrial (or technological, or scientific and technical) revolution may be viewed, according to this model, as a transitory phenomenon that has been generating, and indeed still continues to generate, a perturbation, or a fluctuation, in the dynamics of the

* Calculated from date of original publication, in 1977.

economic development of humanity: a powerful, yet by historical standards short-lived, deviation from a nearly zero rate of growth. This prediction, it should be emphasised, is independent of any anticipated shortages of the non-reproducible natural resources; these shortages, should they actually come about, would only reinforce the process of growth slowdown and bring forward the stage of 'touchdown'.

On the other hand, if the technological factors described above begin to slow down growth before shortages of natural resources may develop, the Club of Rome-type predictions of economic chaos, socially explosive disorder and political dictatorships should be less likely to materialise.

5. STAGES OF ECONOMIC GROWTH AND THE SYSTEM OF VALUES

If the model outlined above is essentially correct, or if the limits to growth are instead social (Hirsch, 1977) or physical (lack of minerals and space), the initial and the end 'points' of the technological revolution would be identical with respect to the rate of economic growth. But during the intermediate period there would take place, of course, a very substantial and eventually radical improvement in the level of satisfying people's needs, especially perhaps their material needs. During that period, by opening up the possibilities of improving human well-being, the technological revolution becomes also a factor changing the system of values and attitudes so that they are instrumental in implementing the superior aim of translating these historically unique possibilities into a real improvement. Hence the social position of an enterprising person rises in esteem compared to someone merely well born; a far-reaching division of labour and strong work discipline acquire social acceptance; great inequality of wealth and massive use of material incentives to reward effort, initiative and professional skills are regarded as being not essentially contradictory with social justice and human dignity; more often than at any time before, people are evaluating their own and other persons' virtues in terms of money; ideals of competition, competitiveness and economic efficiency are strongly emphasised and widely cultivated.

The so-called capitalist or bourgeois system of social values is possibly quite close to the ideal of the 'culture of growth'. This ideal does not catch on everywhere to the same extent. Depending upon long-lived cultural traditions and historical experience, various societies respond to the pressure created by the possibilities of rapid growth with a greater or lesser degree of assimilation of the culture of growth. Apart from the size of the technological gap between a given country and the frontier, and apart from the stage of development of the frontier itself, the cultural traditions become a third major factor influencing the rate of economic growth, thereby differentiating this rate among countries. Social relationships in production and the form and operation of the institutional superstructure are two further such contributing factors.

6. PURSUIT OF THE FRONTIER AND THE PARADOX OF 'NEGATIVE CORRELATION'

The Marxian theory is known to have great difficulty in supplying a satisfactory interpretation of the fact that the 'socialist revolutions' so far have all taken place in economically less-advanced countries at the time the capitalist system is still alive and doing reasonably well in the countries that are most advanced. This apparently negative correlation between economic advance and the social system is clearly an important socioeconomic phenomenon of the twentieth century.

The traditional explanation of the phenomenon (developed soon after the Russian Revolution of October 1917) that has been used to invoke the interpretation of Marxian 'objective regularities' of development, which predict the arrival of socialism only after capitalism is no longer able to function as a viable system, is that these are 'statistical tendencies' and not deterministic relationships. This interpretation was supplemented with the hypothesis of a 'weak link'. All this meant to convey was that the Russian Revolution was just an exception to the rule that still applies.

Now the above explanation has lost much of its initial appeal, since it is only such exceptions that have been recorded since October 1917.

Let us now consider briefly an alternative interpretation of the paradox. This interpretation rests on the following two propositions (we continue the numbering of section 4).

(iv) The natural social system of the historical epoch of the industrial revolution is the capitalist system. With its specific human values and attitudes and with built-in strong economic competitiveness, the capitalist system represents a socioeconomic environment well designed to press both for high inventiveness in the technological sector and for speedy translation of the possibilities created there into rapid economic growth.

(v) For various reasons, some of which are mentioned in section 4 above, economic development has been highly non-uniform among countries. Hence variation in the distance from the most advanced frontier, and division into countries of the First, Second, Third and Fourth Worlds. Countries of the first category became a standard of progress for all countries, as well as a model to be copied, an object of aspiration, and often also a source of military threat.[12] This is the so-called demonstration effect. The strength of the effect is selective: probably more powerful among the intelligentsia and relatively weak among peasants. It is also differentiated among countries, depending on cultural factors as well as on the historically-achieved level of development and the current tempo of pursuit.

In some of the less-developed countries the reaction to their relative backwardness may take yet another form. It may bring into existence various revolutionary groups. In their infancy, these groups usually comprise members of the intelligentsia. They aim to reorganise economic relationships and social institutions. Whatever their ideological colours, their common economic goal is to accelerate the tempo of pursuit of the technological frontier. The revolutionary groups may use either peasants (China, Vietnam, Cuba), the military (Iraq, Egypt, Ethiopia), workers and peasants (Russia, Yugoslavia), or the military and the bureaucracy (pre-revolutionary Iran, Indonesia) as a medium to power. The revolution may also be imposed, as in Eastern Europe. The latter case apart, all the above countries either made a late start in their development, were developing too slowly to transform increasing numbers of unemployed peasants into industrial workers quickly enough, or both. Conditions created during the two world wars, or (alternatively) anti-colonial and nationalistic movements in some countries, provided the 'revolutionary group' with circumstances favourable to the launching of a successful revolution.

While the combination of the demonstration effect and favourable circumstances has been decisive in deciding where and if the revolutionary group comes to power, it was the low level of social and economic development that has 'determined' the totalitarian form of the political system after the revolution.[13]

Irrespective of the initial ideas and motivations—communist, socialist, or merely nationalistic—the revolutionary group, in its role as a manager of the pursuit of the technological frontier, begins immediately after the revolution to acquire the characteristics of a capitalist class; it begins to turn from a revolutionary into a 'leading' group. Organising a less or more drastic form of state-run economy, the group takes over the role of capitalist not only in the area of decision-making, but also as an agent of the 'culture of growth', propagating its values. Indeed, in the USSR and Eastern Europe strong material incentives dominate; relatively large income inequalities are maintained, ideals of competition, promotion, success, power and economic efficiency are cultivated. A similar political and cultural model is adopted in other less-developed countries where state ownership prevails, for example, in Algeria, Egypt, Iraq, Iran, Nigeria and Tanzania.[14] Only in China and possibly in Vietnam and Cuba may the inequality in the level of consumption (both private and state-financed taken together) be relatively smaller. But even in these three countries the differences in money incomes and in private consumption are apparently also high.

7. ON THE ECONOMIC REQUIREMENTS FOR SOCIALISM AND DEMOCRACY

It seems reasonable, and I believe appropriate, to say that apart from a high degree of political democracy and socialisation of the means of production, 'true socialism' presupposes also human relations and attitudes based on a certain system of values. While it is not easy and may even be impossible to define the system precisely, the popular perception of the socialist idea suggests that social justice, specifically understood, is one of its basic principles. The degree to which the principle actually operates depends, however, on the scope and measure of voluntary acceptance of the system of value that protects the weak, the unpractical, the poor and the less talented against the strong, the resourceful, the rich and the more capable, and that also protects man as an individual against the power of institutions, traditions, myths and so forth. Such values must to a large extent, though not entirely, be a negation of the values prevailing in the period of rapid economic growth that promote (as was mentioned above) competitiveness, competition, power and efficiency.

However, as long as there is a strong social demand to improve material standards of living and as long as the technological means to meet this demand are present, the socialist value system is not likely to acquire a high measure of acceptance. It is this view that leads me to suggest that while capitalism (competitive or mixed) and state-dominated socialism (whether of the Soviet or, say, of the [pre-1979] Iranian-type) are both natural sociocultural systems for relatively poor people faced with large possibilities of improving their material standard of living rapidly, 'true' socialism may gain a greater measure of acceptance in the period after the growth explosion brought about by the industrial revolution has come to an end.

The above statement is of course an extreme, black-and-white formulation of the relationship between economic conditions and systems of values and attitudes. In fact the transformation of capitalism into socialism appears to proceed in a gradual way. The welfare state in the West, especially in Western Europe, is an attempt to eliminate the 'unacceptable face of capitalism'. As a result, there has developed a mixed system: capitalist and socialist together, in which the share of typically socialist values and attitudes is quite large, though possibly not dominant.

In this respect there is also not much difference to be found between the West and the USSR and Eastern Europe, except that the pressure of the 'culture of growth' remains greater in the West, notably in the United States, and that the individual under authoritarian socialism remains much weaker, and (in case of conflict) much more defenceless against the power of the state.

Finally, there is the question of the exact origin of the pressure for democratization in the USSR and Eastern Europe. The evidence presented in this paper, and the wider framework within which it was interpreted, is suggestive rather than definitive. It may be summarised as follows. The Adelman–Morris (1967) finding—that the direct, short-term link between political democracy and economic growth, whether positive or negative, is weak or non-existent—applies also to the USSR and Eastern Europe. But there may well operate an indirect, long-term link between democracy and the level of economic advance. As economic development proceeds, the intelligentsia rise in numbers, the shortage of material goods abates, the demand for non-material goods rises, and the need for democracy may well tend to increase. The sharpness of that need and the tempo of the increase are, however, likely to vary strongly from one country to another, depending on the historically formed tastes for goods of the nonmaterial type.

The USSR is for obvious reasons the country on which the tempo of democratisation in the whole of Eastern Europe depends. At present, catching up with the United States in each field of importance, especially perhaps in the military field and in material standard of living, appears to be the dominant goal of the Soviet nation, not just of its 'leading group'. As long as this continues to be the case, the prospects for democratisation in Eastern Europe must in my view remain poor.

NOTES

1. The paper greatly benefited from critical comments and helpful suggestions received at various stages in its preparation. The author is especially grateful to Włodzimierz Brus, Milića Barać, Antoni Chawluk, Michael Ellman, Malcolm Falkus, Joanna Gomulka, Fred Hirsch, Michael Montias, Jan Rostowski, Walter Stern, and Tadeusz Nadel-Turoński.
2. *Productive forces,* or the total productive potential of society, comprise physical capital, technology, people and their skills, and natural resources; *production relations,* or the *base,* refer to conscious or unconscious social relations that develop between people in connection with their economic activities; the *superstructure* covers institutions and culture.
3. Wiles (1975) gives the following summary of Brus's economic ideas: '(i) Macro decisions, especially about large investment projects and the broad structure of the economy, must, under socialism, be taken at the centre; (ii) such decisions will be taken by political authorities, but they are political anyway; this is unavoidable; (iii) micro decisions must with equal inevitability be taken at the periphery; there is no other administratively tolerable solution; (iv) but we can easily make a virtue of this necessity, since otherwise the workers will not get codetermination—they must have something to co-determine directly, and without it they become explosively alienated; (v) there must therefore be a regulated market; (vi) we need not merely co-determination in small things, but widespread public discussion in large matters too; its absence makes for great inefficiency and eventually, again great explosions.' And further, 'Brus rejects public ownership without (i) as commodity fetishism, the deification of the market and not socialism at all. Macro calculations must be in rational prices, but he expects externalities, distributive and purely political considerations to be uppermost. He rejects pure self-administration because the maximand, net value-added per head, restricts employment and wastes capital. (iv) is to be preferred, largely because it is democratic, and constitutes a feedback for the planners: Brus has no Illyrian illusions.'
4. Brus acknowledges the presence of several factors, such as high and increasing degrees of technical complexity of economic problems,

public disinterest in long-term considerations, etc. which point to a negative association between economic efficiency and democracy. He argues that these factors, while weakening, do not reverse the overall positive association.

5. For discussion of alternative interpretations of the slow-down, see Gomulka (1976, 1977): Chapters 7 and 8, this volume.

6. In an imaginative application of factor analysis to the study of the relationship between non-economic and economic variables, Adelman and Morris (1967) found that as much as 70 per cent of variations in the level of per capita GNP in 1961 among the 74 less-developed countries they studied was 'associated' with differences in 24 social and political characteristics. Underlying the characteristics were four independent 'factors', one of which was the degree of political democracy. This factor was found to be positively associated with the level of per capita GNP, and was estimated to 'explain' about 10 per cent of the inter-country variance in that level. But the same factor was also found to have a mild negative association with the change in per capita GNP in the years 1950/51–1963/64. The form of government, the authors concluded, whether democratic or authoritarian, has little or no systematic effect on economic performance at any level of development. For the sub-group of countries at a relatively high level of development, to which the USSR and Eastern Europe in 1961 belonged, the most important political variable affecting growth was found to be the 'extent of leadership commitment to economic development'. This factor was estimated to account for close to 60 per cent of cross-country differences in growth rates.

7. If Marx's category of social forces of production is widened to include the non-material sphere, then the Brus-type contradictions between institutions and the needs of development, affirmed by (iii), would cease to be characteristic, as Brus wants them to be, for totalitarian socialism alone or, generally, for the post-capitalist societies. Indeed, defence of Polish culture and national uprisings in the period when Poland was under foreign domination could then validly be interpreted also as an expression of such contradictions.

8. Phelps assumes technical progress to be neutral in the Harrod–Kalecki sense, so that $Y = F(K, TN)$, where T is the level of technology. The technological sector is described by an embedded two-level production function: $\dot{T} = E^{\alpha}T^{1-\alpha}$, $0 \leqslant \alpha \leqslant 1$, and $E = M^{\beta}R^{\gamma}, \beta, \gamma > 0$, where E is the flow or research output. Assuming α, β, γ constant, the model implies that $g_T = \beta g_M + \gamma g_R - (1/\alpha)\dot{g}_T/g_T$. Hence if g_M and g_R are constant over time, then $g_T \to g_T^*$, where $g_T^* = \beta g_M + \gamma g_R$.

9. According to de Solla Price (1963, Figure 1), the total world number of scientific journals in the period 1750–1950 was rising at an almost constant rate of 4.6 per cent per year. Approximately the same figure applies presumably to the number of published scientific papers and to scientific manpower.

10. The source of these data on the payment receipt ratio in technology trade is Freeman and Young (1965), Table 6, p. 74.

11. By definition $\eta = T_h/T$, so that $\dot{\eta}/\eta = \dot{T}_h/T_h - \dot{T}/T \equiv g_{T,h} - g_T$. But $g_T = \eta g_{T,h} + (1 - \eta)g_{T,d}$. Therefore $\dot{\eta}/\eta = g_{T,h} - \eta g_{T,h} - (1 - \eta)g_{T,d} =$

$(1 - \eta)(g_{T,h} - g_{T,d})$ where $0 < \eta < 1$. Thus if $g_{T,h} < g_{T,d}$ then $\dot{\eta} < 0$, so η is declining.

12. Morishima (1975), in his analysis of the ideas and events leading up to the Meiji Restoration of 1867–68, draws attention to the threat posed at the beginning of the nineteenth century by the arrival on Japanese waters of the naval fleets of Britain, Russia and America. It was then that 'the ruling classes and the intelligentsia realised that the isolation policy which had been devised for the purpose of maintaining the centralised feudal system ... might lead to the destruction of Japan. Such a contradiction is not attributable to the autonomous self-evolution of productive capacity, as orthodox Marxists would claim, but to the external pressure caused by the technology gap between the West and Japan. Therefore it was the intelligentsia who displayed the most sensitive desire to know the West' (p. 59). An important role of the military factor is also emphasised by Seton-Watson (1967) in his interpretation of the ideas underlying the reforms of Peter the Great, undertaken at the beginning of the eighteenth century and intended to increase Russia's capacity to assimilate Western European technology. These reforms were later abandoned, but the military factor came to play a role again in the second half of the nineteenth century, leading up to reforms which finally allowed industrial revolution to take firm roots in Russia (Gerschenkron, 1962, Chapter 6).

13. The connection between backwardness and dictatorship became quite clear to Russian revolutionary socialists before 1917. Out of this connection two interrelated ideas were born with which later the whole communist movement was to be associated. One was the doctrine of permanent revolution (Trotsky, 1905, adopted by Lenin in 1917), which asserted that 'for the backward countries the road to democracy leads through the dictatorship of the proletariat' (Trotsky, 1930, pp. 27–8; I owe this quotation to M. Ellman). The other idea, sketched by Marx but developed fully by Lenin, asserted that ordinary people, including workers, were prone to succumb to bourgeois economism (which Lenin saw as natural to them) and were unable to develop, by their own effort, a 'revolutionary and socialist consciousness.' Hence the historical need for an enlightened revolutionary vanguard that must take the lead and convert the proletarian masses to socialism and eventually communism (cf. Sweezy, 1971).

14. A similar approach is suggested by Petras (1977). The paper is based on the post-war experiences of several less-developed countries; it argues that, faced with widening income and wealth gaps between their countries and the 'North', the impatient state bureaucracies increasingly take over the role traditionally exercised by private capitalists and themselves conduct the process of modernisation and industrialisation. Petras calls the bureaucracies 'state-capitalist regimes', but in so far as public ownership in those countries dominates and political democracy is limited, the regimes are clearly close relatives of the Soviet- or Chinese-type state socialism.

REFERENCES

Adelman, I. and Morris, C. T. *Society, Politics and Economic Development: A Quantitative Approach,* Baltimore: Johns Hopkins Press, 1967.

Brus, W., *The Market in a Socialist Economy, 1961,* English translation. London: Routledge & Kegan Paul, 1972.

Brus, W., *The Economics and Politics of Socialism,* London: Routledge & Kegan Paul, 1973.

Brus, W., *Socialist Ownership and Political Systems,* London: Routledge & Kegan Paul, 1975.

Freeman, C. and Young, A. J., *The Research and Development Effort in Western Europe, North America and the Soviet Union,* Paris: OECD, 1965.

Gerschenkron, A., *Economic Backwardness in Historical Perspective,* New York: Praeger, 1962.

Gomulka, S., 'Extensions of the "Golden Rule of Research" of Phelps' *Review of Economic Studies,* **37**, January 1970, pp. 73–93.

Gomulka, S., *Inventive Activity, Diffusion, and the Stages of Economic Growth,* Monograph of the Institute of Economics, Aarhus, Denmark, 1971.

Gomulka, S., 'Soviet Postwar Industrial Growth, Capital–Labour Substitution and Technical Change: A Re-examination', in Fallenbuchl Z. (ed.), *Economic Development in the Soviet Union and Eastern Europe,* Vol. 2, *Sectoral Analysis.,* New York: Praeger, 1976 (Chapter 7, this volume).

Gomulka, S., 'Slowdown in Soviet Industrial Growth 1947–1975 Reconsidered' *European Economic Review,* **10**, 1, 1978, pp. 37–49 (Chapter 8, this volume).

Hirsch, F., *Social Limits to Growth,* London: Routledge & Kegan Paul, 1977.

Kuznets, S., *Modern Economic Growth,* New Haven and London: Yale University Press, 1966.

Morishima, M., 'A Historical Resolution of the Technological Gap; Japan and the West', *Economic Notes* **4**,1, 1975, pp. 49–74.

Organisation for Economic Cooperation and Development, *Reviews of National Science Policy, Japan.* Paris: OECD, 1967.

Petras, J., 'State Capitalism and the Third World', *Development and Change* **8**, January 1977, pp. 1–18.

Phelps, E. S., 'Models of Technical Progress and the Golden Rule of Research', *Review of Economic Studies,* **33**, April 1966, pp. 133–45.

Price, D. J. de Solla, *Science since Babylon,* New Haven and London: Yale University Press, 1961.

Price, D. J. de Solla, *Little Science, Big Science,* New York: Columbia University Press, 1963.

Rosenberg, N., *Perspectives on Technology,* esp. Chapter 7, 'Karl Marx on the Economic Role of Science', Cambridge: Cambridge University Press, 1976.

Rostow, W. W., *The Stages of Economic Growth; A Non-Communist Manifesto,* Cambridge: Cambridge University Press, 1960.

Seton-Watson, G. H. N., *The Russian Empire 1801–1917.*, Oxford: Oxford University Press, 1967.

Sweezy, P. M., 'The Transition to Socialism', *Monthly Review,* **23**, May 1971, pp. 1–15.

Trotsky, L., *Die Permanente Revolution,* Berlin: 1930.

Wiles, P. J. D., Review of W. Brus's *The Economics and Politics of Socialism. Economica;* **42**, May 1975, pp. 232–3.

2 Political System and Economic Efficiency: The East European Context[1]*

1. DEMOCRATISATION OF SOCIALISM—THE CHALLENGE AND THE ANSWER

The basic propositions of my book *Socialist Ownership and Political Systems* (1975) have met with a comprehensive challenge in Stanislaw Gomulka's article (chapter 1). A number of stimulating points have been raised which undoubtedly will be taken up in the future. My purpose here is a limited one: to argue, without denying the weight of some of Gomulka's objections, that the case for the link between democracy and efficiency under socialism can by no means be regarded as lost.

In his article, Gomulka has given a fair summary of my books, thus there is no need to repeat the basic line of argument here; I start therefore with a presentation of his challenge to my position.

Gomulka first invokes the findings of Irma Adelman and Cynthia T. Morris (1967) that in the 74 less developed countries they investigated, political democracy as an independent factor was positively associated only with the *level* of per capita GNP ('explaining' about 10 per cent of the inter-country variance in that level) and not at all (or even mildly negatively) associated with the *change* in per capita GNP 1950/51–1963/64. Gomulka considers this finding to be valid for East European socialist countries as well. He argues that the rate of technological change, which is at the heart of economic and social development, depends in a crucial way on non-systemic factors. In the technologically leading areas (the 'technological frontier' now being predominantly in the USA) the rate of technological change depends on the *growth rates of inputs in the R & D sector* (both capital and labour engaged in this

*Reprinted with permission from W. Brus (1980), *Journal of Comparative Economics* 4 (1), pp. 40–55. © by Academic Press, Inc.

sector have been growing at a much faster rate than total capital and employment; hence at some stage in the future, growth of this sector must decrease and eventually may cease). In the countries that are not on the technological frontier, the main factor is the *diffusion of technologies* obtained from abroad. Among non-economic factors of utilisation (and promotion) of technological opportunities—both created and diffused—not the degree of political democracy is essential but 'the extent of leadership commitment to economic development' (Adelman and Morris) and what Gomulka calls the 'culture of growth': a system of values close to the one regarded as capitalist or bourgeois, i.e. values promoting competition, initiative and skills, and rewarding them accordingly in a highly differentiating manner. What may be termed a socialist system of values (social justice, security, solidarity) Gomulka regards *a contrario* as non-conducive to growth and thus

not likely to acquire a high measure of acceptance ... as long as there is a strong social demand to improve material standards of living and as long as the technological means to meet this demand are present. ... While capitalism and state-dominated socialism are both natural sociocultural systems for relatively poor people faced with large possibilities of improving their standard of living rapidly, 'true' socialism may gain a greater measure of acceptance in the period after the growth explosion brought about by the industrial revolution has come to an end.

There may exist a long-term link between economic progress and democracy, however, not of the 'Brus kind' (democracy as a *sui generis* factor of production), but the other way around: 'As economic development proceeds, the intelligentsia rise in numbers, the shortage of material goods abates, the demand for non-material goods rises, and the need for democracy may well tend to increase.'[3] In this respect there is a difference between Gomulka and authors like Karl de Schweinitz, Jr (1964) who deny any regular interconnections between democracy and economic progress.

The article summarised above raises several basic issues that go beyond our immediate interests here; some of them, however, touch upon the very heart of the matter. Foremost among the latter is the question of the relative roles of technological and systemic factors in economic development. Gomulka cannot be accused of neglecting systemic factors in general, particularly when semantic questions are brushed aside (as, for instance, whether the degree of exposure to the pressure of domestic and international competition should be labeled 'economic' or 'non-economic'). However, in his essay, (1) the 'x-efficiency' factor, compared with technology, is relegated to minor importance, and (2) not the political aspects of the economic system are considered relevant but those that bring it closer to capitalism as 'the natural social system of the historical epoch of the industrial revolution'. Is this so obvious for the East European case?

Available evidence—if we can speak of the term—hardly supports Gomulka's contention that the gap between those economies on the technological frontier and those falling short of it exerts a determinant effect on the growth of the technologically more backward economies. The rate of growth of national income per head in the USSR since 1950 shows an almost continuous decline, and even if we assume fulfilment of the 1976–80 plan, it will be less than half of the rate for the 1956–60 period. During this time, and particularly in the later stages, direct and indirect transfers of technology from the West to the USSR substantially increased without, however, resulting in a lessening of the technological gap. A very cautious study edited by the Birmingham team of Amann *et al.* (1977) presents, after meticulously warning the reader of a great number of methodological and substantive limitations, the following conclusion: 'In most of the technologies we have studied there is no evidence of a substantial diminution of the technological gap between the USSR and the West in the past 15–20 years, either at the prototype/commercial stages or in the diffusion of advanced technology' (p. 66). A highly interesting observation is made by David Holloway in the chapter on military technology, usually regarded as 'taken out' of the system:

Although the focus of this chapter was relatively narrow, it emerges quite clearly that the defence sector is part and parcel of the Soviet system as a whole. Soviet history has left its mark on the Soviet military—technological effort: the development of the defence sector cannot be explained without reference to the industrialization drive, to the purges, the war and post-war stability. (ibid., p. 489)

Diffusion of technology is not a simple transfer of equipment and know-how; it obviously includes adaptation, which means not merely putting an imported or imitated production-line on stream but also (or mainly) generating a secondary technical advance by spreading its influence and developing indigenous technology on top of the newly-acquired base. Diffusion in this sense requires some minimal level of education and of technological and organisational potential in the country in question: given this premise, it must depend on the way the economic system functions as well. In the East European case the system seems to have acted as a powerful brake both on the generation and the diffusion of technological innovations. This is one of the reasons why the otherwise apparently sound idea of massive injections of western technology bought on credit to be paid back from the output of the newly-created industrial base ran into such serious difficulties, notably in Romania in the second half of the 1960s and in Poland in the 1970s.

However, to give full credit to systemic influence is by no means tantamount to accepting the role of democracy as a 'production factor' under socialism; other systemic factors, beginning with such a fundamental one as the public ownership of the means of production, may be decisive in preventing the 'culture of growth' from reaching its necessary level. This is true; but if systemic factors are duly acknowledged, there is equally no ground for dismissing one of them offhand by simple extrapolation of findings obtained from an entirely different sample. The scope of the Adelman–Morris study was limited to the Third World; before its results can be applied to the present and near future of the East European countries, several points call for examination:

(a) The stage of economic development: when factors are available for extensive growth, the main task (and hence in some sense also the main macro criterion of the achievement of economic efficiency) is to mobilise vast unutilised resources, primarily labour, and to allocate them to rather easily specifiable key development sectors. I have never shared the theory of 'everything right in its time', which summarily suggests the complete suitability of an authoritarian growth-committed regime for a take-off stage. Nevertheless, it seems reasonable to expect a need for more sophisticated methods of resource allocation as an economy becomes more complex; such an economy is bound to rely increasingly on the ability to raise the productivity of labour and capital, to widen the variety of both producer and consumer goods, to meet more stringent quality requirements—in other words, to progress continuously. This is by and large the stage in which Eastern Europe finds itself since the beginning of the 1960s, and any discussion of the relationship between economic efficiency and the political system must take this into account.

(b) The degree to which 'the economic affairs of the society belong to the public sphere' (Schumpeter, 1976): the greater this degree, the greater will be what may be called 'the politicisation of economic management'. This phenomenon is widely felt nowadays in the western world (deplored by some, welcomed or accepted as inevitable by others) and obviously prevails under East European socialism. No one would deny the significance of the quality of management for economic efficiency; with the strongly politicised system of management in Eastern Europe, this entails appropriate recognition of the economic consequences of the political set-up.

(c) The relative weight of the political system as an economic bottleneck: as usual, this depends on the extent of the shortage (or the abundance) of particular elements identified as influencing economic performance. Weakness of the democratic form of government may not qualify as a constraint on economic development in Italy or in India (other constraints may make themselves felt long before this particular one). In Eastern Europe, where the classical social impediments to economic development seem to have been removed, the political factor—lack of any form of political pluralism—may become at some stage *the* economic bottleneck (taking into account what has been said under point (b) above).

Lack of political pluralism seems to be the major cause of blockage of information flows in Eastern Europe, and hence the major cause of misallocation of resources on a long-term macro scale. Here, and not so much in the absence of the market which in my view cannot nowadays be relied upon to make long-run allocative decisions, I see the main source of *arbitrariness* of economic decisions—shown in the disregard for constraints and the neglect of alternative courses of action. The absence of direct risk in terms of political penalties for failure that might function as a substitute for personal financial responsibility also plays a role here. When the mechanism of the 'negative selection of cadres' and the alienation of the people from the state (both discussed at some length in Brus, 1975) are also taken into consideration, the autocratic syndrome goes a long way toward explaining not only the imprecisions but also the lack of elementary coordination in the construction and implementation of the plans. The ensuing 'planned chaos', and particularly the investment cycles peculiar to this form of socialism, seem to be firmly rooted in the political system. Poland in the 1970s provides an exceptionally strong case in point; but the experience of other East European countries in various periods tends to indicate that differences are in degree rather than in kind (see Čobeljič and Stojanovič, 1969; Goldmann and Kouba, 1969). As for a more general aspect of comparative analysis within Eastern Europe, I do not think that the search for direct correlation between the 'level of liberalisation' (however measured) and the level of economic performance in individual countries should yield meaningful results. For various reasons the relative *economic potentials* differ, and one has to judge performance against this background; from such a point of view the GDR and Czechoslovakia—the most often cited examples—hardly undermine my thesis.

Nevertheless, let me emphasise again that this rejoinder to Gomulka's challenge does not in itself prove much in a positive sense. It may well be that the entire problem is beyond the domain of proof properly understood: too many intangibles, no possibility of applying anything even remotely resembling the *ceteris paribus* clause. What I tried to do was to show that a summary view of democracy as having little relevance for economic efficiency under socialism has yet to be demonstrated.

2. DEMOCRATISATION OF SOCIALISM—THE INSIDERS' VIEW

The difficulty of finding hard evidence that democracy is positively correlated with economic efficiency could, at least in part, be overcome by extensive field studies in the course of which not only new data but also appropriate new methodologies might be discovered. Unfortunately, the very nature of the political system in Eastern Europe prevents an objective analysis of this kind, although there are social scientists in the West who regard public opinion polls or even election results in Eastern Europe as valid tools for examining some basic political questions (instances of such use, along with methodological considerations, can be found in Brown and Gray, 1977). As for East European literature, paradoxically enough the proposition about the relevance of democracy for economic efficiency is accepted on both sides of the fence, by the official and dissident literature alike. 'Only' the interpretation differs diametrically: the official view links economic achievements with *existing* democracy of a 'participatory character' (as opposed to the 'competitive character' of bourgeois democracy) based on an allegedly solid social foundation of unity of essential interests of (almost) the entire population: the dissident view frequently traces most of the gross inefficiencies in the economy to lack of pluralism in the political system. During periods of profound liberalisation —such as in Poland and Hungary in 1956, or even more so in Czechoslovakia in 1968–the dissident view came strongly into the open, presenting several versions of the basic proposition stated above. One of a number of debates concerned the role of economic reform—whether it should be regarded as an independent or as a dependent variable of the democratisation process. The emphasis on the former, sometimes without even a mention of the political consequences to be expected from economic decentralisation and from giving a wider scope to the market mechanism, became more pronounced in the relatively permissive periods in the USSR, where political problems of the economy, even in these 'grey' periods, could only be raised behind the protective curtain of apparently pure economic concerns, frequently dressed in very technical language. (An interesting picture of this aspect of Soviet economics is given in Lewin, 1974.) The emphasis on the latter (i.e. the primacy of the democratisation process to achieve economic reform) is stronger in samizdat literature (e.g. the Sakharov–Turchin–Medvedev memorandum of 1970) and generally in the more recent period; this reflects perhaps the experience mentioned above, namely the negligible political effects of a strictly economic reform. (This should not, however, be taken as a general change of attitude toward 'marketisation', still conceived by some reformers—like O. Šik and R. Selucký of Czechoslovakia—as an indispensable element of and basic condition for democratisation).

In the last few years the question of the interrelation between the political system and economic efficiency has been debated most intensely by Polish dissidents. Twice in a period of six years (1970 and 1976), Poland was the scene of violent explosions caused by a combination of economic and political factors. Even the official soul-searching after the bloody repression of the 1970 strikes pointed to the neglect of the 'principles of socialist democracy' (by the already toppled rulers—of course, nothing of this sort can ever be said publicly about the existing regime). The new team promised to introduce substantial changes into the methods of government, including the use of uninhibited expert advice, the resort to various forms of consultation before taking important decisions, and the revitalisation of local self-government. In actual fact, however, the political system continued to operate along the old familiar lines, and the economy failed to show clear signs of sustained improvement on the '*x*-efficiency' side. Material concessions granted after the 1970 events under constant pressure of large segments of the industrial workforce were made possible mainly by drawing on outside sources. When in June 1976 an attempt was made to check the deepening disequilibrium by a drastic increase in food prices, the normal channels of political communication between the authority and the population proved as effectively blocked as before; however, the government's rapid retreat prevented violence on the 1970 scale.

There is no need to elaborate here on the general arguments put forward in the Polish dissident literature (circulated inside the country and in many cases republished in the West, particularly by the Paris *Kultura* and the London *Aneks*) in favour of the proposition that the totalitarian political system should be held responsible to a major extent for Poland's economic inefficiences; these fall by and large under the three headings introduced in the last part of section 1 of this paper. Two points seem, however, to deserve special emphasis. The first concerns the failure to develop in any significant measure a rank-and-file participation and control even at the local level. By itself this type of popular activity would not necessarily conflict with the interests of the national ruling élite, notably in the post-Stalin era when many areas of life ceased to be regarded as politically sensitive and requiring strict control for the overall stability and expansion of the regime. However, the very logic of the system makes each component of the hierarchical organisation (party, state administration, economy, trade unions, etc.) responsible to and dependent on the superior level; this in turn frustrates attempts at local independent initiative even when it is sincerely desired by the top echelons. The second point calls attention to the disastrous long-term deterioration of the moral values in the society at large: deprived of any sense of participation in decisions affecting most aspects of social and economic life and aware of the enormous cleavage between reality and the incessantly preached ideology, the population becomes increasingly intent on pursuing private material goals at any price; this breeds widespread cynicism, indifference and negative attitudes to work and public property, corruption and black-marketeering—particularly acute in conditions of endemic shortages. A rather curious additional factor has often been mentioned recently: the desperate efforts by the government to lay hands on any source of convertible foreign exchange have led, in Poland as well as in the GDR and, to a lesser extent, in other countries, to the circulation of western money as a sort of parallel and privileged currency, with significant demoralising effects.

How much weight should one give to the prevailing dissident view of the existence of a clear link between totalitarianism and economic inefficiency in Eastern Europe? If we bear in mind the intangibles involved, any sort of 'eye-witness testimony' should be taken seriously. I do not think that the occasionally voiced suspicions of a sociologically determined bias—dissident literature supposedly reflecting the vested interests of the intellectuals who suffer directly from restrictions on cultural freedom and may feel thwarted in their political ambitions—should invalidate this testimony. After all, the gist of the argument looks plausible and is consistent with deductions from observed phenomena. What is more, the general tenor of the dissident literature, even in countries with a relatively strong opposition that scored some practical successes (as in Poland after 1976), hardly exaggerates the prospects of and the pressures for political change. In a document issued by a group calling itself 'The Polish Independence Alliance' and pointedly entitled 'The balance of our weaknesses' (*Kultura*, 1977), we come across the following paragraph that seems worth quoting in full:

We have become used to thinking that the political and economic system in which we live is unchangeable. This makes us angry, sometimes to the point of despair, but at the same time provides us with a guarantee of external and internal security. Our system plagues us with perennial queues in front of shops and with regular butter, meat, fuel, electricity crises; it squashes any zeal for independent initiative; but it avoids general economic depression and the disasters of unemployment and bankruptcies that accompany them. By banning the free interaction of political forces it deprives us of the freedom to decide our own destinies; but it provides us with quietude—a bit deathlike, but not without its cozy aspects. And most of all it takes away any sense of responsibility by assigning everyone to a predetermined place.

This picture seems to be realistic enough. It also helps to understand the factors that push toward some sort of accommodation within the framework of the existing political and economic system. Even leaving aside the difficulty repeatedly emphasised here of proving the net positive effects of democratisation on economic efficiency, the attraction of this type of accommodation is enormous in view of the remote prospects of radical political transformation in the present international environment.

3. 'KADARISM'—AN ALTERNATIVE?

It is from this point of view that *Hungary* is attracting so much
attention recently, both by outside observers and by the East Euro-
peans themselves. Over the last two decades Hungary has displayed
a far greater degree of internal stability than perhaps any other East
European country, including the USSR. By this I mean not only the
absence of violent upheavals in party leadership accompanied by
sweeping purges in the higher echelons of state and economic
hierarchy—let alone crises of Czechoslovak or Polish dimensions—
but also many fewer signs, if any, of open dissatisfaction of the
population at large with policy measures even as irritating as large
price increases of essential consumer goods. (A case in point was
the 30 per cent increase in meat prices a few days after the Polish
débâcle of June 1976.)

All this can hardly be ascribed to a change in the fundamentals
of the political system, which has retained its totalitarian essence,
or remained 'monocentric' to use Ossowki's terminology (1962), or
'monoarchic' as a counterpart of Lindblom's 'polyarchy' (1977):
complete domination of the 'leading party' apparatus (Hungary
does not even have 'other parties' which nominally exist in some
East European countries); a Soviet-approved ruling élite independent of the electoral process, and subject to renewal by co-optation
at the top and by effectively controlled appointments to all positions of authority; a ban on any autonomous political activity and
unlicensed forms of association (save, in a limited sense, the
Church); the monopolisation of the mass media, if not through
universal preventive censorship, then through control of personnel.

However, even such a fundamental framework does not rule out
variations in methods and degree of control; the post-Stalin era as
a whole has shown that quite convincingly for all countries of
Eastern Europe. The distinctive feature of Hungary has perhaps
been not so much the loosening of tensions in all instances and at
all times (some other countries at some periods in some respects
have gone further than Hungary), but that that has been accomplished consistently, without major retreats since 1958 (when large-
scale executions were reported around the time of the condem-
nation to death of Imre Nagy), and on a relatively broad front. The
famous slogan launched by János Kadar, 'who is not against us, is
for us', indicated quite clearly the basic approach used: the widening of what I call the 'political indifference zone', concentrating active interference only (or mainly) on matters of direct relevance to
the foundation of authority. Among other things, this opened the

way to wider use of genuine expertise on the part of the decision-makers. In many respects this approach proved unexpectedly more effective as a control mechanism than the crude one it replaced, because it induced individuals and groups previously in a position of not having anything to lose to compromise. Now they did have something to lose: passports, the opportunity to publish or to influence some course of action important both professionally and socially, and—most commonly and simply—living standards that were gradually rising above bare essentials.

With respect to the latter, the 'socialist enlightened absolutism' of the Kadarist-type became particularly sensitive and attentive to the population's wants. Hungarian economic policy, especially since the mid-1960s, has been clearly focused not on spectacular growth rates but on balanced development with concomitant increases in real income of the population, again rather without spectacular jumps in statistical indices but with the purchasing power of the population relatively well covered by the supply of consumer goods on the market. This required, among other things, a pragmatic agricultural policy. The 1959/60 collectivisation drive might have been considered as out of tune with these exigencies; however, apart from strong Soviet pressure on the then still very weak Kadar regime, the relative scarcity of labour probably made Hungarian collectivisation more attractive macroeconomically than in a country such as Poland. In any event, the methods of collectivisation, and particularly the economic system established both within the cooperatives (including individual plots) and in the relationships between the cooperatives and the state, differed considerably from the Soviet model, and in some respects from other East European countries as well. Hungarian agricultural policy has not been completely free from ideological rigidities. The 1975/76 attempt to double the fiscal burden on individual plots is a case in point. But on the whole it has been relatively less affected by mistakes than in other socialist countries, and such mistakes as have been committed have been more rapidly repaired.

The best known feature of 'Kadarism' is *the reform of the functioning of the economy,* the only case throughout Soviet-type Eastern Europe of a consistent reform implemented as a comprehensive package on a single date (1 January 1968) after careful preparation. That it has basically been kept in operation to this day, some drawbacks notwithstanding, points to a unique record of endurance. The Hungarian 'New Economic Mechanism' (NEM) impressed many western analysts so much that they put it into the same category as the Yugoslav system, which they regarded as differing only in its scope and 'depth'. This seems to me incorrect. The Yugoslav concept, linked to the idea of local self-management as a fundamental aspect of socialism, assigns the priority role to the market; its central planning has become mainly 'indicative', chiefly performing special redistributive functions (e.g. for its underdeveloped regions); it is hardly accidental that a solid 400-page report on Yugoslavia by a World Bank team (Yugoslavia, 1975) did not mention the word 'planning' even once. The Hungarian system, on the other hand, is clearly intended to maintain the principle of effective central planning and to make it more efficient by changing the methods of plan construction and plan implementation: only the chief macroeconomic decisions (the 'fundamental' ones, in János Kornai's terminology) are to be taken directly at the centre; while other, 'standard' decisions are devolved onto lower echelons of economic organisation which have been freed of obligatory targets and physical allocation orders. These lower levels are in principle guided indirectly through a set of controlled market parameters and corresponding incentive schemes. This may be called a 'centrally planned economy with a regulated market mechanism' (Brus, 1972). Note also that the institution of workers' self-management is absent in Hungarian enterprises despite their enhanced autonomy. It is hardly necessary to go into detail here of the operation of the Hungarian NEM. What needs to be emphasised is the influence of the changes within the state sector on other sectors: cooperatives became more genuinely independent and market-oriented, and private enterprises found the new conditions of dealing with the state sector more conducive to their activities. Thus the economic reform strengthened the peculiar coexistence between autonomous activities and the state-run economy taken by some Hungarian scholars as the basic feature of 'Kadarism' (Kovacs, 1978; this article was written under a pen-name in Hungary).

The Hungarian economic reform has not brought about political changes of a more profound nature. It was in line with the intentions of the party leadership to keep the reform strictly in the economic sphere, especially in view of the Czechoslovak experience of 1968 where aspirations for change in the economic and in the political systems were conjoined. The idea seems to have been to raise the level of efficiency by means of an exclusively economic reform. In a sense it can be said that the economic reform was a substitute for political change.

In order to link up the Hungarian case with our general problem, at least two points need examination: (a) What made the Hungarian pattern possible, and were the factors involved unique or 'transferable' to other countries?; (b) What can be said about the impact of 'Kadarism' on economic performance, and what are the longer-term prospects in this regard?

(a) As for the first point, I should like to refer here to a paper by two Hungarian scholars working in the West (Kemeny and Kende, 1978); they describe current Hungarian realities as being the result of a 'triple compromise':

(i) a compromise between Soviet and Hungarian leaderships: acceptance by the latter of Soviet control of military, foreign, and security affairs, as well as of the basic principles of the political system and by the former of a wider autonomy (compared with the pre-1956 position) in internal policies, within this framework;

(ii) a compromise between the Hungarian leadership and the population: acceptance of (or better, resignation to) the party monopoly of authority with all the ensuing internal and external political consequences, in exchange for a non-return to the Stalinist policies, with special emphasis on relative autonomy *vis-à-vis* the USSR, some degree of personal security, improvement in material conditions, freedom of movement and cultural liberalisation. I have heard a Hungarian scholar referring to all this as a source of 'negative legitimacy' for the regime.

(iii) a compromise between the leadership and apparatus of the party and the state: preservation of the basic positions of the apparatus and assurances against their erosion in the future, in exchange for acquiescence in more pragmatic policies and greater autonomy in economic and cultural life, especially for managers and creative élites.

One can hardly understand this subtle fabric without full appreciation of the shock-wave engendered by the 1956 revolution; the personality of Kadar might have played a part as well. Nevertheless, if we see 'Kadarism' as a model—i.e. without some specifically Hungarian features—there is nothing in it that prevents transplantation. Perhaps slow and in a zigzag fashion, a movement toward an 'enlightened absolutism' of a 'Kadarist' type seems to be at least a possibility for other East European countries as well.

(b) We now turn to the second point, 'Kadarism''s impact on

economic performance. As already indicated, the medium-term economic record of Hungary (of the last decade or so) has been rather favourable but by no means spectacular as far as aggregate indices are concerned when compared with other East European countries. They show regular progress, particularly in the sphere of consumer goods, resulting in an improved balance between demand and supply, 'Econometric work on the consumption goods market in Hungary suggests that households were able to spend their incomes and were not forced to save more than they desired' (Portes, 1977, p. 779). One should also bear in mind that external circumstances after 1973 were particularly unkind to Hungary, which suffered a far greater loss in 'terms of trade' than any other East European country; on the other hand, its very slow population growth made it easier to avoid an excessive investment pressure (as compared to Poland). Hungary's indebtedness to the West increased substantially over the period 1971–75, though relatively less so than Poland's, GDR's or Bulgaria's.

Can this record, on the whole more satisfactory to consumers, be attributed to 'Kadarism' as described above? It would be very risky to make generalisations about attitudes to work under conditions of this type of political compromise, the more so as the government did not introduce institutional forms of shop-floor participation in management. However, all observers of the Hungarian scene emphasise the atmosphere of social peace; no reports of work stoppages have reached the West for some time. As for the economic reform, the prevailing (but not unanimous) view is that it made a substantial positive contribution to economic performance, particularly by increasing flexibility and making it possible to adjust the structure and quality of output to internal and external demand. This view seems to me rather well founded in the general terms of the three composite sources of inefficiency listed in section 1: (i) the quality of personnel selection is likely to improve under the pressure of more stringent economic exigencies; (ii) informational inadequacy is likely to be somewhat reduced by removing plan fulfilment as the main indicator of performance and by the smaller amount of information needed at the centre, which may thus be better placed to tackle major developmental problems; (iii) the alienation aspect—least affected, given that the economic reform has not been used to promote self-management—may stand a slim chance of improvement in so far as the incentive system provides a better and more palpable link between individual and social objectives. In addition a feedback may be found between the market-broadening effects of the economic reform (both within and outside the socialist sector) and the allaying of tensions between the population and the political authority, which may now cease to be in charge of (and hence be held responsible for) every detail in economic life. This point comes close—with a reverse sign—to the very apt observations by Lindblom (1977, p. 353) that 'as ... decisions move from market to government, there is more to fight about in politics and a greater burden, consequently, on whatever political devices there are to keep the peace.'

Now, what are the prospects that 'Kadarism' will provide the foundations for sustained economic development in the long run? A number of factors pointing in different directions must be considered before even a most tentative answer can be given. On the one hand, (i) for all East European countries except Hungary, 'Kadarism' is still a more or less distant prospect, the attainment of which would mean a step forward in achieving the premises for economic efficiency; (ii) there is obviously room for improvement within the existing 'Kadarist' framework: 'learning by doing'; fuller use of the opportunities contained in the reformed economic system; and institutional developments shunned as too risky under Hungarian conditions that are not incompatible in principle with the system (such as workers' participation in the management of enterprises, which is likely to make a contribution to 'x-efficiency'; autonomous local communal initiative and activity).

On the other hand, the limitations to 'Kadarism' are significant, due first of all to the economic role of the state. This role, clearly maintained in the concept of 'a centrally planned economy with a regulated market mechanism', should not be dismissed, in my view, as an expression of a group political interest vested in centralisation; it stems from underlying trends in the changing nature of modern economic problems. I can understand and even sympathise with the Yugoslav interpretation of the withering away of the state theory according to which 'depolitisation of the economy' will bring a solution to the present ills, but I cannot accept it as realistic. Whatever the strains noted above, the political element in the economic mechanism will have to reign supreme, if not always in the form of direct decision-making, then certainly in formulating the general framework and parameters of choice. This means that the release of presently blocked information flows and the more open criteria of personnel selection, obviously relevant for economic efficiency, cannot forever be kept out of the political sphere *sensu stricto*. The attitude of the population to *the state* will also retain its great economic relevance. To expect that this can be taken care of *exclusively* by material incentives seems doubtful both for practical and general reasons. As Schumpeter (1976, pp. 423–4) says, 'no social system can work which is based exclusively upon a network of free contracts between (legally) equal contracting parties and in which everyone is supposed to be guided by nothing except his own (short-run) utilitarian interest.' This view seems in the longer run to gain validity for any industrial system but especially so for a socialist one because of the type of ideology used to justify its claim for legitimacy. With the growing time-lags between outlays and effects, increasing ecological needs and the exigencies of redistribution on an international scale (Third World), the difficulties of translating greater current efficiency into immediate consumer gains increase as well, to the detriment of the prospect of a political bond between the state and the population built solely on material incentives.

Popular control of the state machinery is, of course, not the only possible way to induce people to look at their activities as part of a common whole. Recourse to nationalism is another, and judged from a distinctive trend in ideological change in Eastern Europe (in the USSR since the 1930s), it is used more intensely all the time. However, it does not help with the information and personnel selection problems; hardly provides a basis for a *sustained* integration in the economic sphere; in the concrete situation existing in Eastern Europe it is enormously conflict-loaded.

The conclusion seems to be that 'Kadarism' as it now stands can hardly satisfy the conditions for increasing economic efficiency in the long run, despite the unexhausted dynamic potential inherent in its own framework and the substantial progress it might mean for the 'pre-Kadarist' East European countries. In order to satisfy these conditions 'Kadarism' would have to evolve from 'socialist enlightened absolutism' toward democratic socialism. Thus, 'Kadarism' adds a new dimension to our problem not so much with regard to the basic hypothesis (of interdependence between economic efficiency and democratisation under socialism) as with regard to the ways in which the political conditions of economic efficiency could be met; not in the 1968 Czechoslovak way (rightly called by Skilling, 1977, 'the interrupted revolution') but by a slow process of gradual transformation of the substance of the existing institutional framework.

NOTE

[1]The first draft of this paper was presented to the Conference on 'Power, Participation, Rationality' held at the Rockefeller Centre, Bellagio, Italy in September 1978, and was supported by a travel grant from the Ford Foundation. At various stages problems raised in the paper have been discussed in seminars at the Birmingham and Glasgow Centres for Russian and East European Studies, as well as at the London School of Economics. The author has had many friendly discussions with Stanislaw Gomulka. All comments and suggestions received are gratefully acknowledged. The paper is dedicated to Edward Lipinski, the doyen and spiritual leader of Polish political economy.

REFERENCES

Adelman, I. and Morris, C. T., *Society, Politics and Economic Development: A Quantitative Approach,* Baltimore: Johns Hopkins Press, 1967.

Amann, R., Cooper, J. and Davies, R. W. (eds), *The Technological Level of Soviet Industry,* New Haven, Conn. and London: Yale University Press, 1977.

Brown, A. H. and Gray, J. (eds). *Political Culture & Political Change in Communist States,* New York: Holmes & Meier, 1977.

Brus, W., *The Market in a Socialist Economy,* 1961; English translation, London: Routledge & Kegan Paul, 1972.

Brus, W., *Socialist Ownership and Political Systems,* London: Routledge & Kegan Paul, 1975.

Cobeljič. N. and Stojanovič, R. *The Theory of Investment Cycles in a Socialist Economy,* White Plains, N.Y.: Internat, Arts & Sciences Press, 1969.

De Schweinitz, K. Jr, *Industrialization and Democracy,* New York: The Free Press of Glencoe, 1964.

Goldmann, J. and Kouba, K., *Economic Growth in Czechoslovakia,* White Plains, N. Y.: International Arts & Sciences Press, 1969.

Gomulka, S., 'Economic Factors in the Democratization of Socialism and the Socialization of Capitalism', *Journal of Comparative Economics,* **1**, 4:389–406, December 1977 (Chapter 1, this volume).

Kemeny, I. and Kende, P., 'Le compromis hongrois', *Commentaire,* **2**: 1978.

Kovacs, J., 'Le compromis social de la Hongrie post-revolutionaire', in *1956 Varsovic-Budapest, La Deuxième Révolution d'Octobre,* textes réunis par Pierre Kende et Krzysztof Pomian. Paris: Editions du Seuil, 1978.

Lewin, M., *Political Undercurrents in Soviet Economic Debates.,* Princeton, N.J.: Princeton University Press, 1974.

Lindblom, C. E., *Politics and Markets. The World's Political-Economic Systems,* New York: Basic Books, 1977.

Ossowski, S., *Osobliwości Nauk Spolecznych* (Singularities of the Social Sciences), Warszawa: PWN, 1962.

Polskie Porozumienie Niepodległościowe (Polish Independence Alliance), 'Rachunek naszych słabości' ('The Balance of Our Weaknesses'), *Kultura,* no. 11, pp. 3–12, November 1977.

Portes, R., 'Hungary', in *East European Economies post-Helsinki,* Compendium of Papers, Joint Economic Committee, US Congress, Washington D. C.: US Government Printing Office, 1977.

Schumpeter, J. A., *Capitalism, Socialism and Democracy,* 5th edn, London: Allen & Unwin, 1976.

Skilling, H. G., *Czechoslovakia's Interrupted Revolution,* Princeton, N.J.: Princeton University Press, 1976.

Yugoslavia: Development with Decentralization, Report of a Mission sent to Yugoslavia by the World Bank, Baltimore and London: Johns Hopkins University Press, 1975.

3 The Incompatibility of Socialism and Rapid Innovation*

1. INTRODUCTION

One important aspect of the Marxian theory of economic development and social change is the strong emphasis given to economic efficiency and productivity levels as key factors that decide, in the course of history, the outcome of the competition between different forms of organisation of economic activity. [1] This idea rests on seeing societies as constantly searching for ways of achieving the highest standard of living. Systemic changes, whether evolutionary or revolutionary, are an outcome of that search. False or true, the idea has been and, despite present economic difficulties, probably continues to be, highly influential in shaping the ideological make-up of the political leaders and professional economists in the Soviet Union, China and other centrally planned economies (CPEs).

Economic efficiency is measured in terms of the actual output taken as a proportion of the maximum (potential) output, given the quantities and qualities of the resources. The starting point for the USSR in 1917 was one of technological inferiority and, therefore, the productivity levels were initially low. Thus, to prove the superiority of the Soviet economic system, it has been and is essential for the USSR to achieve an internationally superior rate of innovation [2] for some time, at least until the gap in output per man-hour could be closed.

*An earlier version of this chapter appeared under the same title in *Millennium: Journal of International Studies*, vol. 13, no. 1, 1984; and, in French translation, in *Revue d'Etudes Comparatives Est-Ouest*, vol. 15, no. 3 1984. I wish to thank Mark Schaffer, the Editor of the first journal, for many useful discussions and comments, as well as for the invitation to write this paper in the first place. I am also grateful to Philip Hanson and Alan Smith for their helpful criticisms.

To this end, the USSR has given an extraordinary emphasis to technical education, research and development (R & D) and industrial technological innovation. The Soviet R & D sector has been expanding since 1928 at so high a rate that, according to a study by Nolting and Feshbach (1979), the number of Soviet R & D scientists and engineers in 1978 was 'nearly 60 per cent greater than the US'.[3] The non-personnel expenditure on R & D is now probably of comparable size in both countries. This remarkable (quantitative if not yet qualitative) progress has been accomplished despite the unusually high human and material losses that the Soviet economy had sustained in the war years 1914–23 and 1941–45, as well as those from the massive government terror, especially in the 1930s. The USSR was also successful in building up, in a short period of time, a vast education sector which now supplies about twice as many technicians, engineers and scientists as the US sector.

The pace of industrialisation has been slower than in Japan, but of comparable speed or faster than that experienced in Western Europe. The result is that, in 1976, 'in rouble prices, Soviet GNP was 50 cent of US GNP; in dollar prices, the USSR produced final goods and services equal to 74 per cent of the US national product.'[4] The geometric mean of the two size comparisons increased from 40 per cent in 1955 to 60 per cent in 1976;[5] it was probably not more than 25 per cent in 1928. The outputs of the two key industrial sectors, one producing machinery and equipment for investment purposes and the other defence goods, are also thought to have outpaced the corresponding outputs of the US industries.[6] Productivity performance has not been poor either. In Soviet industry, the trend rate of growth of output per man-hour, in the years 1928–75, was about 5.5 per cent according to Soviet data[7] and some 4 per cent according to western estimates.[8] This is lower than the equivalent growth rate for Japan, but comparable to that for Western Europe and markedly higher than the rates in the United States and Great Britain in the same period.

On the other hand, a large body of microeconomic evidence has been accumulated in Eastern Europe and the USSR which indicates a high degree of resource misallocation both in conventional production and R & D, a large but rather slow and often wasteful amount of investment activity, and a generally high resistance to innovation, especially in existing enterprises. Despite its large size, equal to at least one-quarter of the size of world R & D, the contribution of Soviet and East European R & D activity to the world flow of new inventions is negligible. In the 1970s, member countries of the Council of Mutual Economic Assistance (CMEA) were importing about ten times more licences in terms of dollars paid than they exported, the exports representing merely 1 per cent of the estimated total of world exports.[9] The analogous ratio for Western Europe in recent years has been approximately 2, and for the US about 0.2.[10] Similarly insignificant is the Soviet and East European share of the western world market for manufactured products, the countries continuing to exchange mainly raw materials and standard intermediate goods for western imports.[11] Another indicator of poor efficiency is the apparently high use of primary and intermediate inputs per unit of final demand outputs. An aggregate indicator of this phenomenon is that the consumption of energy per unit of GNP in the CMEA is about twice what it is in the West. Moreover, following the 1973 price rise, this unit consumption has been falling in the West, but rising still further in the CMEA as a region.

Somewhat paradoxically, in the past this high micro inefficiency has not prevented the USSR and other CPEs from achieving a respectable growth performance. However, since about 1975 the rates of output and productivity growth have fallen markedly in the USSR and most other CPEs. The fall which occurred in the small European CPEs can be attributed largely to the forced reduction of western imports, following the failure of the import-led growth strategy of the 1970s sufficiently to stimulate exports to the West. The reasons underlying the Soviet growth slowdown are less self-evident. Are they similar to those which have caused the productivity slowdown in the developed capitalist economies? Or has the traditional method of running the Soviet economy exhausted its growth potential? If so, is there a feasible economic reform that can be effective in improving the Soviet and East European economic positions *vis-à-vis* the West?

These are some of the questions which I shall address in this chapter. I shall first discuss the innovational characteristics that appear distinctive for CPEs. I then take up the same topic in relation to Hungary under the New Economic Mechanism. This is followed by a discussion of the influence of West–East technology transfer on the East's economic growth. In the next section, broad relationships between innovation, competition and socialism are suggested. The paper ends with a section on the Soviet growth strategy, the present slowdown and the prospects for economic reform.

2. R & D AND INNOVATIVE ACTIVITY IN CENTRALLY PLANNED ECONOMIES: FIVE MAJOR CHARACTERISTICS

The subject of R & D and innovative activity in the USSR and Eastern Europe—its organisation, size and performance—has been studied particularly intensively since the late 1960s. Among the most systematic and substantial western writings in this field are those by Zaleski *et al.* [12] and Cooper [13] on the organisation of R & D and science policy, and Berliner [14] on innovative activity itself. A concise and incisive survey of this by now extensive literature, western and Soviet, has been made recently by Philip Hanson. [15] In what follows I shall, therefore, be very selective in the choice of institutional and policy detail, emphasising instead what appear to be the major organising principles, or distinctive characteristics, of innovative activity under central planning. At the same time, a number of empirical findings will be called upon to provide grounds for the interpretative analysis and theoretical generalisations in this and the following section.

Two Polish empirical studies: The first three characteristics

The two separate Polish studies differ considerably in method and scope, yet their empirical findings share a number of important characteristics that are likely to be common to all CPEs. One is the work by Poznański, which represents an in-depth investigative study of 86 innovations in seven industries in the 1970s. [16] The other study, by Kubielas, reports the results of an extensive inquiry of some 7600 innovations that were implemented by 55 large industrial firms in four manufacturing industries in the year 1973–78. [17]

Both samples exhibit a number of features that would also be familiar to investigators of western innovation processes. For example, about 20 per cent of the innovations turned out to be technical failures; about 80 to 90 per cent of the total were small innovations, of which about half were really minor in-house improvements; only 2 per cent are classified as 'major structural innovations'. In Poznański's sample, as many as 80 per cent of the innovations were of domestic origin. However, about three-quarters of these represented direct adaptation of (or were said to have been directly inspired by) foreign technology. Similarly, as in market-based economies, most of the innovations were initiated locally by the innovating firms or by the R & D staff. Only in about 5 per cent of the cases was the role of the decision-makers from above the firm decisive; these were the really important innovations.

The two studies also provide evidence on the basis of which I shall suggest three characteristics of innovation which appear to be specific only to centrally planned, Soviet-type economies. One such characteristic is that *innovating firms are motivated primarily by the need to overcome supply difficulties*. The need to adapt to new demand conditions, especially in export markets, has also been found to be important, but enterprises are resource- rather than demand-constrained and, as a rule, take little initiative in exploiting new technological opportunities for the purpose of creating new demands, at home or abroad, something that happens often in market-oriented economies. The enterprise's innovation strategy would thus appear to be primarily defensive rather than offensive, with the resource-constrained rather than demand-oriented nature of the economy emerging as a key underlying factor.

The second characteristic is that *not product but process innovations appear to dominate* (about 60 per cent in both samples). When faced with supply difficulties, firms would use the same tools and equipment but investigate the use of somewhat different intermediate inputs (ingredients) to produce essentially the same product. Consequently, many of the new process innovations reflect the widespread phenomenon of forced substitution, and as such represent technological necessity rather than actual improvement. This interpretation would appear to be consistent with the finding that, in the judgement of firms themselves, 30 per cent of the innovations in Kubielas's large sample were known to represent technological regress and that, in most cases, no serious cost-benefit analysis was undertaken.

The third systematic characteristic is that *financial incentive for undertaking an innovation is weak, and although industrial R & D personnel have considerable freedom in their work, the decision-making freedom and the resources available to enterprises for implementing inventions are severely limited*.

The average bonus for an invention is small, amounting to the average monthly salary, and is related to the expected, not actual, cost savings by the producer; it would be given even if the invention is not implemented at all. Inventors are expected to be motivated primarily by professional ambition rather than financial benefit or promotion prospects. In large enterprises the management and workforce would have a great number of different 'bonus titles', but few or no separate titles for implementing the innovative part of the directive plan. The enterprises in the sample were aware that some of the innovations they implemented had a positive influence on value-added and profits, but these categories were much less important than gross output in determining the sum of wages and bonuses per employee.

Other empirical studies: Two further characteristics

The fourth characteristic is that *enterprises in CPEs tend to be large in scale and to trade off choice and quality for quantity.*

Market-oriented economies are characterised by the presence of large risk capital, the purpose of which is to sustain a high rate of birth of enterprises set up to exploit promising domestic or foreign inventions. The innovation/investment decision is thus diffused and decentralised, and these numerous small-scale enterprises are often used as a testing ground for new inventions. The market is thus used as a screening device for the purpose of channelling resources from old to new industries in a rational way.

In centrally planned economies, the original stimulus to innovate comes from the (domestic or foreign) inventor. This is inevitable in any economy. However, screening of almost all innovation possibilities which involve significant investment expenditures is centralised, and risk-taking is almost fully nationalised. The limited screening capacity of the centre would call for the construction of new firms that are limited in number and large in scale. Such a bias for large size has indeed been confirmed by studies of size distributions of firms in the two types of economies. If scale economies are present, as they often are in the manufacturing sector, then suppressing choice and emphasising scale is also an effective method of raising output levels. It appears that Soviet decision-makers have used this method extensively, and not only in consumer goods industries. For example, summarising his survey of a major industry, James Grant notes:

The Soviet machine tool industry, developing independently of western assistance, has become the world's largest producer of machine tools. However, emphasis has been on large-scale production of relatively simple-to-produce, general-purpose machine tools at the expense of special-purpose and complex types.[18]

But the preference for vertically-linked large organisations and the inevitable presence of many organisational barriers (plans, directives, committees) leads to certain costs. These arise because of high economic inertia in the form of limited output and innovative flexibility of individual firms, something which Balcerowicz calls the 'limited elasticity of the organisation structure',[19] and which western economists would associate with a monopolistic market structure.

In any case, the emphasis on large-scale production, with the ensuing limited choice, poor quality and high inertia, would appear so strong among all CPEs that it deserves classification as a major characteristic of innovative activity under central planning.

The fifth characteristic is that *in CPEs the time-lag between domestic inventing and innovating is high and that the subsequent spread of inventions tends to be slow.*

In terms of the two measures of innovative responsiveness—the average time-lag between (domestic) inventing and innovating and the speed with which an innovation (domestic or foreign) subsequently spreads through an economy—the CPEs appear to lag behind the major western economies. A comparative study by Martens and Young (1979) finds that for a fairly large sample 'the US and West Germany implemented over 50 per cent of their [domestic] inventions in little more than one year, whereas the Soviets needed slightly more than three years to achieve this percentage of implementation.'[20]

The rate of diffusion of new steelmaking technology has also been markedly slower in the USSR than in the West. The first oxygen converters were introduced in the USSR, the US, West Germany and Japan in the period 1954–57; by 1974, oxygen steel as a proportion of total steel output was 23 per cent in the USSR, compared with 56 per cent in the US, 69 per cent in West Germany and 81 per cent in Japan.[21] It is worth noting that the steelmaking industry is a relatively modern and high-priority Soviet industry, and that diffusion was slower despite a faster rate of capacity expansion than in the US, suggesting that the example may well be a good indicator of generally slower rates of diffusion throughout Soviet industry.

Still, the rate of innovation depends also on the size of the flow of the inventions that are being implemented, whatever their implementation time-lags may be. In principle, enough R & D and investment could thus compensate for slow implementation. The extra resources needed represent a cost of systemic origin. However, should the longer time leads and lower diffusion rates continue indefinitely, they would contribute to keeping the Soviet and other centrally planned economies permanently below the technological level of the West, a subject to which we shall return in section 4.

3. THE HUNGARIAN NEW ECONOMIC MECHANISM AND THE FIVE INNOVATION CHARACTERISTICS

The small East European countries appear to share with the USSR the main weaknesses of its innovative activity, without enjoying some of its strengths, such as a large R & D sector, the possibility of exploiting economies of scale, and presumably considerable competitive pressures in military-related research and innovation. These small countries are not without advantages of their own, however, the main being that they trade relatively more with the developed West. In particular, the share of machinery imports in total machinery investment in Eastern Europe, at about 10–30 per cent, is roughly five times greater than the share of imports in Soviet investment.[22] The presumably much larger technological transfer from the West compensates to some extent for their much smaller (original and imitative) R & D activity. The greater exposure to western markets for manufactured goods has also produced some competitive pressures of its own. In order to withstand these pressures, the East European governments have been forced to think seriously about introducing systemic changes that would give greater managerial and financial autonomy to the exporting firms. In the case of two countries, Hungary and Poland, major changes of this kind have actually been undertaken. The Polish reform of 1981–82, while still fluid, is unlikely to be more radical than the Hungarian New Economic Mechanism, introduced in January 1968.

Under this system, prices are much more flexible and rational, enterprises nominally have no centrally-imposed output targets and input quotas, and the role of the profitability principle in the firms' own choices is significantly larger. Since plan fulfilment is no longer the main criterion of management evaluation, the negative economic consequences of the practice of bargaining for low output targets and high input quotas are almost absent. Yet most of the major investment and price decisions and key managerial appointments continue to be made centrally, and they are used, apparently to great effect, for the purposes of influencing the production, market and innovation decisions of enterprises, especially large enterprises. As the Hungarian forint is not freely exchangeable into foreign currencies, domestic markets remain well sheltered from foreign competition. Since the economy is small, these markets tend to be dominated by one or a few firms. The absence of bankruptcies is a further indication that financial constraints continue to remain rather soft and market competition low, although in both these areas there has probably been a marked improvement compared to the pre-reform years. The national plans continue to be ambitious, producing a high degree of tautness in the economy. Consequently, resource constraints are often binding more than is socially desirable, micro imbalances are present, and forced substitution is widespread.

The reformed Hungarian economy also retains some of the essential innovation characteristics of the other centrally planned economies. From among the five characteristics I have discussed above, the first (supply difficulties a primary stimulus of innovation), the third (limited resource capability of enterprises in implementing inventions), and the fifth (high time-lag between innovating and inventing, and slow diffusion) appear to be valid for Hungary too. They place the Hungarian economy closer to the other CPEs than to market-based Western Europe. Yet a somewhat greater degree of decision-making flexibility and much greater export of manufactured goods to competitive western markets do induce firms to put greater stress on quality and product innovation. Consequently, the second and fifth characteristics are less in evidence. The case-study of the Hungarian motor industry by Bauer and Soos[23] provides a good deal of evidence in support of the points made above. In particular, it brings into sharp focus the relation between innovation and foreign trade. The firms of the CMEA countries which provide components for the Hungarian motor industry are found largely to ignore innovative requests from their Hungarian customer because, it is suggested, the Hungarians have practically no choice of suppliers within the CMEA. On the other hand, the local R & D input is insignificant compared with that of the Western European motor industry, and hence little attempt is made to enter the dollar market. The import of suitable licences is a possibility but, it is suggested, this would bring in large imports of components from the West without necessarily resulting in high dollar exports.

4. THE INFLUENCE OF WEST–EAST TECHNOLOGY TRANSFER

Over the last two decades or so a significant number of studies have attempted to estimate net gains to a recipient—whether firm, industry or country—that come from the international transfer of technology. The literature pertaining to the USSR and Eastern Europe has been recently surveyed in OECD-initiated studies by George Holliday,[24] and Alec Nove and myself.[25] It is transparent that the subject of technology transfer is a very complex one, and our knowledge of it is not yet satisfactory. The description of the various channels of technology transfer and the evaluation of their relative significance and total net effect shows remarkable variation among different case-studies. Despite this variety, resisting generalisation, the literature does offer a few helpful facts, estimates and interpretations. They may be summarised as follows.

The well-known S-shaped diffusion curves for the cumulative spread of individual innovations within industries or among households—curves indicating that the diffusion process is slowest at the start and towards the end—have their aggregate equivalent in the world economy in the form of a hat-shaped growth path of the type indicated in Figure 3.1. For any particular country, the innovation rate tends to be highest at medium levels of develop-

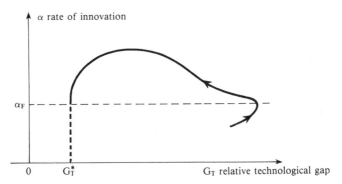

Figure 3.1: The Growth path of a latecomer in the course of technological catching-up, in terms of the innovation rate and the relative technological gap.

Note: α_F denotes the rate of innovation, assumed constant over time, in the technologically most advanced area, such as the US for most of the twentieth century. The relative technological gap increases whenever $\alpha < \alpha_F$ and declines otherwise.

ment, when the country in question still has much to learn from the outside world and, at the same time, has already developed the means—a high level of education, an R & D sector, an investment goods sector, an export capability—of transferring directly or being otherwise capable of absorbing outside knowledge. The magnitude by which the actual rate of innovation may exceed the equilibrium rate (the distance between α and α_F in Figure 3.1) is country-specific, depending critically on the volume of resources being allocated to capital accumulation and technological change and on the efficiency with which these resources are utilised. A country which has a highly inefficient economic system may still enjoy a high innovation rate provided that G_T is greater than G_T^* and that the country is prepared to compensate for that inefficiency with larger quantities of labour and investment resources. In particular, although the rate of diffusion of a given new product or process may be low, a high growth rate of investment effort would ensure that the volume of all newly-introduced products and processes increases rapidly, with the consequence that the resulting overall innovation rate may also be high. This is the reason why in an economy such as that of the Soviet Union, low static efficiency need not be inconsistent with high dynamic efficiency, the paradox to which I alluded in the Introduction.

Eventually, a state of international growth equilibrium is reached in which the innovation rate is the same in all countries, but the aggregate relative technological (and labour productivity) gaps are also country-specific, probably depending above all on countries' systemic and cultural characteristics—things which usually change slowly. In Figure 3.1, G_T^* denotes such an equilibrium relative technological gap. When the actual relative gap is near the equilibrium one, a continuing large transfer of technology would be usually indispensable to keep it here, and yet the innovation rate would be, by past standards, low and, given systemic and cultural factors, not very responsive to any further increase in the flow of technology. In other words, the average return on accumulated investments in technology transfer capability is high but, in the neighbourhood of G_T^*, the marginal return is low.

An aspect of the Soviet strategy of growth has been a limited use of the foreign trade as an instrument of transferring western technology. With the notable exception of the years 1928–32, when trade was used on a large scale across industries, and the years 1945–51, when forced acquisition of German technology was significant, it was largely the Soviet R & D sector that had been given the task of imitating or adopting western technology or, based on world-shared science, of inventing independent technology. (There are, to be sure, a few sectoral exceptions where capital imports have been crucial, such as chemicals and the motor car industry.[26]) The purpose of the extraordinary emphasis on technical education, R & D and industrial innovation to which I referred in the Introduction, has been in part to serve this end. The strategy has so far been largely successful despite a high degree of allocative inefficiency and resistance to innovation in existing enterprises, as the innovation rate has benefited from the Soviet economy starting out, in 1928, on the high segment of the hat-shaped curve.

However, the Soviet method of compensating for allocative inefficiency and innovation resistance with larger conventional and innovation inputs would cease to be feasible as a way of sustaining a high innovation rate once the initial reserves of these inputs have been exhausted and, consequently, when the output and investment growth rates have declined substantially. Especially important is the growth rate of industrial output. In the years 1928–55 (war years excepting), that rate was unusually high due to an extraordinary investment effort in industry at the expense of other sectors, and to a rapid absorption by that sector of a large fraction of the underemployed labour reserve. In the years 1955–75 the growth rate of industrial capital stock continued to be high. It is only since the 1970s that the growing investment claims of the non-industrial sectors, the growth-limiting influence of the underdeveloped productive and social infrastructure, and the exhaustion of the labour reserve, have forced a substantial fall in industrial employment and capital stock. The expansion of Soviet R & D has also slowed down substantially. A slowdown in the growth rate of labour productivity has followed, and this indicates that the USSR may have entered the phase when the Soviet economy is near the international growth equilibrium, characterised by both the technological gap G_T^* and the innovation rate α_F in Figure 3.1. If so, in the absence of substantial efficiency-enhancing institutional changes, the Soviet Union's relative (technological, productivity, and standard of living) position *vis-à-vis* the developed West would in the future continue to remain approximately the same as it is at present.

As a proportion of total machinery investments, imports of western machinery are known to amount to (depending on year and exchange rate assumed) some 3–8 per cent in the USSR and some 10–30 per cent for the East European countries.[27] The latter countries have developed considerable R & D capability, but there seems to be little international cooperation and much duplication of effort and, in any case, their total inventive and imitative capability is much weaker than that of the Soviet Union.[28]

5. RELATIONSHIPS BETWEEN INNOVATION, COMPETITION AND SOCIALISM

After reviewing the reality of innovation under Soviet-type socialism, with some occasional comparison with market capitalism, I now turn to considering a number of generalisations that are in part implied by that reality and in part are intended to interpret it. Three propositions are suggested, each followed by a brief comment.

First proposition
Rapid innovation is incompatible with idealised (Marxian) socialism; such innovation not only sustains high inequality and competition by constantly supplying many new products for a few, but it also requires high inequality and competition as incentives.

That rapid innovation produces inequality is obvious, but that it requires competition is much less so. It was Schumpeter who warned us that in a highly competitive economy, where firms are many and therefore small, there may be too much R & D effort, but too little innovation.[29] The point is that in such an economy duplication of R & D effort would be very extensive, and hence total R & D effort large. But the small size of operations of each firm would prevent taking advantage of economies of scale, and since as a consequence both the incentive to innovate and the inventive effort by each firm would be small, so too would the economy-wide innovation rate. Moreover, the presence of risk would hinder the assimilation of potentially useful inventions which require large capital expenditure. Thus, Schumpeter suggested, there operates a trade-off between static efficiency (meaning the best use of existing technology) and dynamic efficiency. A recent theoretical model of innovation and market structure by Dasgupta and Stiglitz[30] does exhibit this Schumpeterian property.

The interesting implication of this argument, also confirmed by the Dasgupta–Stiglitz model, is that the innovation rate would be highest in a socially managed, competition-free economy. This implication was often used by socialist writers to argue that the planned social economy provides basic preconditions much more favourable to innovation than those afforded by the capitalist economy. However, this argument appears to be contradicted by the evidence we have about the innovation rates under different economic systems and, in Eastern Europe, is now rarely used and even openly questioned.

It is certainly true that industrial inventive and innovative activity often require substantial set-up costs. Consequently, rapid innovation does appear incompatible with perfect competition. But the Schumpeterian theory must not be stretched so far as to miss the vital point that in a competitive economy the incentive for a firm to innovate is, above all, *survival*, rather than the gain of windfall profits. Such opportunity costs—the costs which would arise if the firm did not innovate—are the driving force behind the innovation effort that originates from within the firm, the point which Schumpeter himself stressed. However, that force would be declining as competition declines; it would be small under monopoly and virtually absent under socialism. It follows that to secure a maximum rate of innovation, the degree of competition must be intermediate, neither high nor low.[31]

Second proposition
As long as the scope for innovation (in an economy, in the world as a whole) remains high and, at the same time, the satisfaction of material needs is perceived by most to be (strongly) inadequate, the innovation-conducive forms of organisation of economic activity will continue to be in demand, despite the (income and status) inequalities and competitive pressures such forms may entail.

This conjecture is an empirical generalisation of how today's societies, both in the East and in the West, appear to respond to the choice of an economic system, when they have any say in that choice.[32]

Third proposition
Since material needs are likely to remain virtually unlimited forever, it follows from propositions 1 and 2 that for idealised socialism to come about at all, it is necessary, though it may not be sufficient, that the innovation and growth explosion of the past two centuries runs its course.

Substantial innovation slowdown may or may not occur in the future, but if it does, for instance for reasons which I spell out elsewhere,[33] then the rate of improvement in per capita consumption would also drop substantially. In such circumstances, there would clearly be less incentive for the bulk of the population to accept arrangements which imply a privileged position for the inventive and innovative social groups. The inherent inequality among people in terms of wealth-creating abilities may then be of lesser or even little consequence, as even the most able would not be particularly more productive. Moreover, when innovation is slow, the pace of allocative adjustments needed to conduct business efficiently could also be slow and, therefore, the inflexibility of non-competitive or mildly competitive economic systems would be less costly than it is at present.

As is well known, both Marx and Schumpeter argued that capitalism would give way to socialism, and it is interesting that their different arguments also rest on particular assumptions concerning the characteristics of innovations. These assumptions have so far proved to be wrong (Marx) or doubtful (Schumpeter). Innovations have indeed been largely labour-saving but, contrary to Marx's expectations, have not caused the increasing and eventually massive unemployment which was supposed to lead to the overthrow of the capitalist system. For Schumpeter, the capitalist economic system was one in which the individual initiative of the entrepreneur, rather than the collective efforts of organisations, was central. However, the innovation economies of scale argument apparently led Schumpeter to believe that small firms would be at a disadvantage compared with large firms, and so the latter would eventually dominate. Firms would be increasingly so large and complex that they would have to be run by hierarchical organisations. A bureaucratised economic system would emerge, 'an order of things which it will be merely a matter of taste and terminology to call Socialism or not.'[34] Such a system would be less competitive and could in due course become less innovative than the initial capitalist system. Thus for Schumpeter the direction of causality runs from entrepreneurial capitalism to increasing concentration of production and bureaucratisation of management (which at some stage he would be prepared to call socialism), and only then to possible innovation slowdown. So far the nature of the innovation process would appear to have been different, however, since the innovation activity and economic significance of small-scale firms continue to be large. Moreover, both advances in information technology (making market information more readily available) and the opening of national borders for trade have tended to sustain a high degree of competition, especially for internationally traded goods, despite the emergence of super-large firms. Our argument, on the other hand, is that the major causality runs from slowdown in R & D growth to innovation slowdown and to systemic changes in the direction of idealised socialism. Furthermore, such a development would be largely a matter of social or political choice made possible in part by the satisfaction of economic preconditions (of high output and slow change).

6. THE SOVIET GROWTH STRATEGY AND THE RECENT SLOWDOWN

The present Soviet economic system shares some of the features of what Marx called crude or primitive communism.[35] The emphasis in such a system is on rapid economic growth rather than the strict application of socialist ideas. The growth strategy of the Soviet planners has been to activate quickly two major growth reserves: underemployed domestic labour and underemployed world-best technology. The strategy is not particularly Soviet—it is in fact common to all developing, industrialising countries—but its implementation does bear the imprint of the peculiar Soviet system. In particular the system has been instrumental in the past in rapidly raising not only the rate of capital accumulation and the rate of labour participation, but also the expansion rate of the educational and R & D sectors. The strategy has been largely successful until recently, despite the systemic characteristics that make the Soviet economy rather inefficient and resistant to innovation.

However, as noted in section 4, the state of the Soviet economy may now be one of international growth equilibrium, in the sense that in the absence of substantial efficiency-enhancing institutional changes, its position relative to the developed West would continue to remain approximately the same. Such an equilibrium state would thus imply freezing the present Soviet inferiority in technology and consumption per head indefinitely. The suggestion that this is an inevitable consequence of the present economic system would likely be challenged by the Soviet leadership. But should the evidence in its support continue to accumulate, the pressure to initiate a substantial economic reform would probably continue to build up as well. In any case, such a reform in the USSR is unlikely to be adopted in the near future.

The experience of the Soviet and East European countries in the 1970s has exposed vividly the weaknesses and limits of the strategy of import-led growth. The prevailing western view—that at this quite advanced stage of Soviet and East European development, such a strategy cannot be effective in further closing the technological gap between the East and the West without substantial exposure of the eastern economies to market competition and financial discipline—has apparently been vindicated by this experience. It is interesting that after what happened in the 1970s, many East European economists, especially Polish and Hungarian ones, would now probably agree with this western view. It may be noted that the imports of machinery and expertise from the West have fallen substantially in the 1980s, in order to arrest the rise in a sizeable dollar debt. It seems that disillusionment—a feeling that increased western technology imports alone cannot pull their economies up—might also have been a contributing factor.[36]

The responses of the communist élites, in terms of economic reforms and foreign trade policy, may differ significantly between those of the USSR and those of the East European countries. The USSR does not need to import western machinery on a large scale to take good advantage—although admittedly with some delay—of western innovative activity. The pressure there to decentralise is therefore weaker than, say, in Poland or Hungary, where domestic R & D activity is too insignificant to be an effective instrument of international technology transfer and where, consequently, larger export capability must instead be developed in order to sustain larger imports of technology embodied in machinery. By the same argument, reform designed to enhance economic efficiency and trade competitiveness would become less pressing for Eastern Europe if an embargo on technology exports to this region is imposed. Should such an embargo hold successfully, Eastern Europe might consider moving towards still closer technological integration with the USSR, even though any attempt of this kind may be unpopular in Eastern Europe—and perhaps not very attractive for the USSR either. In any case, Eastern Europe is probably the weak spot of the Soviet bloc and is likely to suffer more than the USSR from any determined policy of the West to reduce substantially the West–East technology flow. (These matters are discussed further in Chapter 13, section 3.)

7. SUMMARY

The propositions and the arguments of this paper fall into two categories. One concerns the grand relationships which are suggested to operate worldwide between innovation dynamics and the type of economic system. At that high level of abstraction our primary aim was to provide an interpretation of the paradox of increasing interest in CPEs in returning to market-based systems, even though these systems are known to entail strong material rather than moral incentives, competition rather than cooperation and high income, wealth and status inequalities. The other category deals with the CPEs of the present day. At that lower level of abstraction our main purpose was to interpret another paradox, namely that there is a high resistance to innovation in those economies and yet high innovation rates have been achieved until recently. Our hat-shape relationship explains at once this paradox and the recent innovation slowdown. By linking the type of economic system with the size of the equilibrium technological gap, it also helps to interpret the first paradox.

NOTES

1. Elliot, J. E., 'Marx and Contemporary Models of Socialist Economy', *History of Political Economy*, vol. 8, no. 2, 1976, pp. 151–84.
2. For the purposes of this article, 'invention' and 'innovation' have usually their standard economic meanings—an 'innovation' is the first application by a firm or enterprise of an 'invention'. However, the rate of innovation, or the rate of technological change, is also meant to include the effects of innovation spread, or diffusion.
3. Nolting, L. E. and Feshbach, M., 'R & D Employment in the USSR—Definitions, Statistics, and Comparison', in United States, Congress, Joint Economic Committee, *Soviet Economy in a Time of Change*, 'Washington, D.C.: US Government Printing Office, 1979, p. 747.
4. Edwards, I. Hughes, M. and Noren, J., 'US and USSR: Comparisons of GNP', in *Soviet Economy in a Time of Change*, p. 377.
5. ibid., p. 370. These percentages should be reduced by a fifth for per capita comparisons.
6. ibid., p. 378, Table 1.
7. Gomulka, S., 'Slowdown in Soviet Industrial Growth 1947–1975 Reconsidered', *European Economic Review*, vol. 10, no. 1, 1977, pp. 37–50 (Chapter 8, this volume).
8. Bergson, A., *Productivity and the Social System: the USSR and the West*, Cambridge, MA: Harvard University Press, 1978.
9. Zaleski, E. and Wienert, H., *Technology Transfer between East and West*, Paris: OECD, 1980, p. 116, Table 29, n. 8.
10. Freeman, C. and Young, A. J., *The Research and Development Effort in Western Europe, North American and the Soviet Union*, Paris: OECD, 1965, p. 74, Table 6.

11. Zaleski and Wienert, *op. cit.*, p. 75, Table 7.
12. Zaleski, E. *et al.*, *Science Policy in the USSR*, Paris: OECD, 1969.
13. Cooper, J., 'Research, Development and Innovation in the Soviet Union', in Fallenbuchl, Z. M. (ed.), *Economic Development in the Soviet Union and Eastern Europe*, vol. 1, New York: Praeger, 1975, pp. 139–96; Cooper, I., 'Innovation for Innovation in Soviet Industry', Discussion Paper of the Centre for Russian and East European Studies, University of Birmingham (1979).
14. Berliner, J., *The Innovation Decision in Soviet Industry*, Cambridge, MA: MIT Press, 1976. See also Levine, H. S., 'On the Nature and Location of Entrepreneurial Activity in Centrally Planned Economics: The Soviet Case', in Ronen. J. (ed.), *Entrepreneurship*, Lexington, MA: Lexington Books, 1983 and McAuley, A., 'Central Planning, Market Socialism and Rapid Innovation', in Schaffer, M. (ed.), *Technology Transfer and East–West Relations*, London: Croom Helm, 1985. The latter paper is in part a response to the present paper, but one which significantly develops and strengthens our case.
15. Hanson, P., *Trade and Technology in Soviet-Western Relations*, London: Macmillan, 1981.
16. Poznański, K., 'A Study of Technical Innovation in Polish Industry', *Research Policy*, vol. 9, no. 3, 1980.
17. Kubielas, S., 'Mechanism of Technological Progress Under the Economic/Financial System in Polish Industry', unpublished manuscript in Polish, 1980.
18. Grant, J., 'Soviet Machine Tools: Lagging Technology and Rising Imports', in *Soviet Economy.*, *op. cit.*, p. 555.
19. Balcerowicz, L., 'Organizational Structure of the National Economy and Technological Innovations', *Acta Oeconomica*, vol. 24, nos. 1–2, 1980, pp. 151–67.
20. Martens, J. A. and Young, J. P., 'Soviet Implementation of Domestic Inventions: First Results', in *Soviet Economy...*, *op. cit.*, pp. 505–6.
21. Cooper, J., 'Iron and Steel', in Amann, R., Cooper, J. and Davies, R. W. (eds), *The Technological Level of Soviet Industry*, London: Yale University Press, 1977, p. 96, Table 3.11, p. 98, Table 3.12.
22. Hanson, P., 'The End of Import-Led Growth? Some Observations on Soviet, Polish and Hungarian Experience in the 1970s', *Journal of Comparative Economics*, vol. 6, no. 2, 1982, p. 136, Table 3.
23. Bauer, J. and Soos, K. A., 'Inter-Firm Relations and Technological Change in Eastern Europe: The Case of the Hungarian Motor Industry', *Acta Oeconomica*, vol. 23, nos. 3–4, 1979, pp. 285–303.
24. Holliday, G. D., 'Transfer of Technology from West to East: A Survey of Sectoral Case Studies', in *East–West Technology Transfer*, Paris: OECD, 1984.
25. Gomulka, S. and Nove, A., 'Econometric Evaluation of the Contribution of West–East Technology Transfer to the East's Economic Growth', in *East–West Technology Transfer, op. cit.*
26. Hanson, P., *Trade and Technology in Soviet-Western Relations, op. cit.* pp. 154–5.
27. Gomulka, S. and Sylwestrowicz, J. D., 'Import-led Growth: Theory and Estimation,' in Altman, F-L., Kyn, O. and Wagener, H-J., (eds),

On the Measurement of Factor Productivities, Gottingen: Vandenhoeck and Ruprecht, 1976. Gomulka, S., 'Growth and the Import of Technology: Poland 1971–1980', *Cambridge Journal of Economics*, vol. 2, no. 1, 1978 (Chapter 10, this volume).

28. Gomulka, S., 'Growth and the Import of Technology', *op. cit.*
29. Schumpeter, J. A. *Capitalism, Socialism and Democracy*, London: Allen & Unwin, 1976.
30. Dasgupta, P. and Stiglitz, J., 'Industrial Structure and the Nature of Inventive Activity', *Economic Journal*, vol. 90, no. 358, 1980, pp. 266–90.
31. For a recent survey of the empirical literature on this point, see Kamien M. I. and Schwartz, N. L., *Market Structure and Innovation*, Cambridge: Cambridge University Press, 1982, Chapter 3.
32. This is discussed further in Gomulka, S., 'Economic Factors in the Democratization of Socialism and the Socialization of Capitalism', *Journal of Comparative Economics*, vol. 1, no. 4, 1977, pp. 389–406 (Chapter 1, this volume).
33. Gomulka, S., *Inventive Activity, Diffusion, and the Stages of Economic Growth*, Aarhus, Denmark: Aarhus University, 1971; Gomulka, 'Economic Factors in the Democratization of Socialism', *op. cit.*
34. Schumpeter, J. A., 'The Instability of Capitalism', *Economic Journal*, vol. 38, no. 151, 1928, p. 386.
35. According to Elliot's interpretation of Marx, 'Crude or primitive communism is the form which communism takes when it emerges in a preindustrialized, underdeveloped economy...The institutions of crude communism are merely primitive versions of capitalism. Ownership of capital is vested in the community as a "universal capitalist" instead of a private property owning capitalist class. ... Lacking control over production and investment, workers are both alienated—from their output, the work process, their own human nature to control and direct the forces of nature, and from other men—and exploited, and focus upon satisfactions from consumption rather than creative work.' Elliot, J. E., 'Marx and Contemporary Models of Socialist Economy', *op. cit.* p. 156.
36. This observation is due to Peter Wiles of the London School of Economics.

4 Innovation Activity in the Yugoslav Economy*

1. INTRODUCTION

When starting its post-war reconstruction in 1945 Yugoslavia was one of the least developed countries of Europe. Industrialisation and modernisation in such a country is, under any economic system, bound to rely on the import of technology and machinery from abroad, and on learning from foreigners the art of putting these imports to good use. Having said that, one may still be surprised by the extent to which this general principle has apparently been followed up by the Yugoslavs in the years 1945–85. The evidence which we are going to present suggests that the Yugoslav's own inventive activity continues to be almost non-existent, and that the country's R & D sector—which has grown rapidly and is now quite sizeable—serves the country primarily as an instrument for transferring and assimilating foreign-made technology. In this paper we shall also consider how that transfer and assimilation are influenced by the Yugoslav economic system. In that respect some tentative comparisons will be made both with western and centrally-planned economies.

2. R & D AND INNOVATION ACTIVITY IN YUGOSLAVIA

From Table 4.1 it may be seen that in terms of the size of the

*The institutional affiliations of the authors are, S. Gomulka, the London School of Economics and S. Ostojic, Institut za EkonomikuIndustrije, Belgrade. The paper was written partly in Philadelphia where the first author was Visiting Professor at the University of Pennsylvania in 1984–85. We wish to acknowledge the helpful assistance of the British Council and its Yugoslav counterpart by financing the first author's visit to Belgrade in Summer 1984. We are also indebted to Branko Stamenkovic, Djordje Vrcelj and Caslav Ocic for helpful research advice and assistance, and to Leonore Taga of the University of Pennsylvania for helpful comments.

R & D sector relative to the size of its economy, Yugoslavia was, by the end of the 1970s, in the middle position between the developed countries and the developing ones. Yugoslav R & D activity, at about 0.5 per cent of the world R & D sector, is of course very small. One might have thought, however, that the flow of the home inventive output would be commensurate with that size. This clearly has not been the case. Pooling all the developed OECD and CMEA countries together, in 1978 the Yugoslav share of the total was 0.6 per cent for R & D personnel, but 0.25 per cent for domestic patent applications by residents, and only 0.06 per cent for foreign patent applications by residents (Slama, 1983, Table 8). In terms of the number of patent applications per person of the R & D personnel, taking inventive productivity of the combined R & D sector of the OECD countries as 100, the Yugoslav productivity was 26 in terms of domestic patent applications by residents and only 5 in terms of foreign patent applications by residents (derived from Slama's Table 8, *op. cit.*). It is also interesting that the corresponding productivity indicators for the CMEA countries were 50 and 3; that is, they were similar to those for Yugoslavia.

Patent applications at home (abroad) need not be a good indicator of a country's total (really original) inventive activity. To the extent that they are such an indicator, the productivity data above suggest that the R & D sector in Yugoslavia serves a very different purpose than does the R & D sector of the OECD countries,

Table 4.1: *R & D activity in Yugoslavia, in developing countries and in the developed world, 1978*

	Yugoslavia	*Developing countries*	*Developed countries*
Population[*]	0.8	62.2	37.0
R & D personnel[*]	0.6	6.1	93.3
R & D expenditure[*]	0.5	2.5	97.0
R & D personnel per 1 ml. population	530	100	2580
R & D expenditure as % of GNP	1.3	0.32	2.3

Source: Science and ..., 1982, p. 49.
Note: According to the source above, the Yugoslav R & D personnel represents only 0.4 per cent of the world's total. This share is given as 0.9 per cent by Vrcelj and Brkanović (1983, p. 103) and as 0.6 per cent by Slama (1983, Table 8). We adopt the last figure.
[*]All countries except China, Mongolia, N. Korea and Vietnam; world total = 100.

namely one of assisting the Yugoslav economy to assimilate the (old and new) technology of the OECD countries. This assimilation may, but need not, involve the import of machinery and licences— usually the most conspicuous form of technology transfer. Instead, it may have the form of copying foreign products or processes in full or in part, being stimulated by foreign solutions, adapting these solutions to local production possibilities and consumer tastes, adopting the inventions of whole institutions, such as banks, large shopping centres or education systems, as well as adopting management methods.

This interpretation of Slama's data appears to be strengthened by the statistics on inventions actually patented. According to the data supplied to us by the Yugoslav Federal Bureau of Patents (FBP), in the years 1971–83 only 7.5 per cent of domestic patent applications were actually approved and the inventions involved patented. In the same period the FBP approved 25 per cent of the applications by foreigners. The corresponding figures for the period 1981–83 are 6.4 per cent and 40.3 per cent, domestic patents numbering a mere 275, or 92 per annum. With the output of some 4 patents annually per 1 million of the population, Yugoslavia has been and, in the early 1980s continues to be, very much at the bottom of the European list (Ocic, 1984, p. 111).

The interview with the officials of the FBP and the Belgrade Chamber of Commerce helped us to identify a number of detailed features of the Yugoslav inventive activity that shed further light on its actual role. These are as follows:

(i) The vast majority of reported inventions are minor improvements of known products and methods of production, relating mainly to product design, parts of products and packaging methods;

(ii) About 80 per cent of domestic patents are awarded to individual inventors (usually self-employed or retired), only 20 per cent originate from organised activity of the R & D institutions. (In the West the institutional R & D accounts for about 80 per cent of the total: Vrcelj, 1975, p.96.);

(iii) Implementation of domestic inventions is almost always financed by firms' own funds, banks rarely (if ever) participating in such projects. This practice is partly due to the projects usually being small, but apparently it also reflects the banks' judgement about the inventive capability of the domestic R & D sector;

(iv) The main reasons for inventing and innovating are similar to those in any market-based economy: meeting changing market demands or creating new demands, reducing costs, import substitution, the improvement of working conditions;

(v) Individual inventors are under heavy social pressure not to demand the financial and status recognition commensurate with the economic significance of their inventions.[1] This reduces both the actual inventive output and the reported output. The reason for the latter is that in some cases individual inventors, R & D institutions and firms find it not worth while to protect their inventions by patent, especially since the patenting process itself is administratively cumbersome and costly. Nevertheless, the actual inventive output is not thought to be very much higher than the patent statistics indicate.

(iv) Individual inventors, but not managers, appear to be the main interest group within enterprises promoting local inventive activity and the implementation of their inventions (Ostojic and Medenica, 1984).[2]

Now we turn to consider briefly the extent and forms of the technology transfer to Yugoslavia. The following data, reported by Ocic (1984, p. 112), give the size of two such forms: *Joint ventures,* years 1968–79. The number of these was 206. The value of the projects involved was $400 million, clearly a modest sum, of which foreign partners were to supply 25 per cent; and *industrial cooperation agreements* other than joint ventures, 1968–78. The number of these was 639, of which 80 per cent were in the metal and electric engineering industries. These agreements usually involve the purchase of licences (in the period 1945–79 some 790 were bought) as well as marketing, after-sales service and R & D cooperation.

These data, even though not particularly useful in evaluating the quantitative significance of the two channels for total technology transfers, do indicate the proportionately greater use of the two channels by Yugoslavia than, in the same period, Hungary, GDR and Poland (the CMEA countries most heavily engaged in importing western technology). More useful is the fact that western machinery imports represented, in the years 1953–78, some 50 per cent of all the Yugoslav machinery investment. The labour productivity growth that would have been generated by such imports is, according to the model of Chapter 10, equal to

$$0.5 \frac{I}{K} \left(\frac{y^F}{y^Y} - 1 \right)$$

where I/K is the ratio of gross investment to the stock of fixed assets and y^F/y^Y is the ratio of labour productivity on new machines of foreign origin to that on new machines made in Yugoslavia. To generate the labour productivity growth that has been actually observed in Yugoslav industry in the years 1953–78, some 5 per cent per annum, the ratio y^F/y^Y would have to be about 2, which it might well have been. This illustrative calculation is thus consistent with the earlier evidence suggesting that, in post-war Yugoslavia, the overt technology transfer from the West has been by far *the* dominant source of innovation and, therefore, also of productivity and consumption growth.

Despite the obvious and huge benefits which Yugoslavia must have derived from the transfer of foreign technology, the high foreign debt that was accumulated in the years 1980–84 and the balance of payments problems have recently led many Yugoslav experts to ask whether the time has not come to reduce the expensive, embodied component of the total technology flow, expanding instead the domestic R & D sector with a view to increasing the less expensive, disembodied component of the technology flow. Yugoslavia's dependence on foreign technology has to remain nearly total. This is unavoidable. However, a more developed and efficient R & D activity at home may render the import of less sophisticated foreign technology (and machinery that goes with it) unnecessary. It may also enable a wider use of the well-tried methods of imitation and adaptation, with the same aim of lifting the balance of trade constraint to growth.[3]

3. SYSTEMIC FACTORS IN THE YUGOSLAV INNOVATION ACTIVITY

In Chapters 1, 2 and 3 it has been noted that in centrally-planned economies (CPEs) there operate powerful systemic factors which tend to reduce the economic interest of enterprises (managers and workers) in introducing the demand-creating or cost-reducing innovations. Some of these factors are the same as those which produce excessive demands for most goods, others have to do with the extent to which the related principles of little competition and highly soft budget constraints are adhered to. The question we must face is: Where does Yugoslavia fit in that context?

Since in Yugoslavia national planning is heavily decentralised and largely of the indicative type, the factors of the first category do not operate. However, the Yugoslav economy is socialist in many respects and, as such, it does have a number of features which, as we shall explain below, give rise to factors of the second category. The economy is also essentially market-based. To the extent that enterprises compete among themselves for customers, they are subjected to the discipline of the market place. However, the pressure of market competition is often lessened by the strong political regionalism. The institutions of the six republics and two autonomous provinces at the regional level, and the several hundred communes at the local level act frequently to protect 'their' own firms in two ways: (i) by making it difficult for other Yugoslav firms to sell in the markets under their control, and (ii) by exerting political pressure on regional banks to grant low interest credits, and on the Federal Pricing Board to increase some or all of the prices of the locally-produced goods which are administratively controlled. Because most Yugoslav banks are cooperatives in which the labour-managed firms are both major borrowers and share-holders, lending to these firms tends to be based on 'soft' principles. These banks are effectively an instrument of the firms for using the resources of the private savers (the household sector and the private producer sector) to subsidise the socialised sector. Although not easily visible, political influence on actual lending practices is also strong. There appears to be two major reasons for this: (i) almost all Yugoslav banks are organised regionally, within the boundaries of individual communes and republics, and (ii) most top managerial appointments of any kind are substantially influenced by local political authorities. These two institutional features may be expected to increase further the scope for softening the firms' budget constraint (Schrenk et al., 1979, pp. 140–147). Consequently bankruptcies are, by western standards, rather rare, and budget constraints are highly soft (Tyson, 1980, p. 49). In the period 1976–81 the total number of the organisational changes (called *likvidacija*) which include bankruptices as well as closing downs for reasons other than financial, was 834. According to Ocic (1984, p. 15) and Ostojic (1984, p. 92), the dominant mechanisms for dealing with faltering firms are either forced merger with a profitable firm (1784 mergers of all kinds were recorded in the years 1976–81) or forced acquisition (1292 recorded in the same period), thus very much the same mechanisms which the authorities use in CPEs.

An empirical study by Prasnikar (1983), based on a sample of 147 Yugoslav industrial firms, gives an insight into the market

structure, product diversification and product innovation. Some of
his results are collected in Table 4.2. It may be seen that 92.8 per
cent of the sampled firms had at least two competitors, and 37.5 per
cent had more than ten competitors. However, as we already noted,
the high and apparently increasing regionalism of the republics and
the autonomous provinces tends to reduce the economy-wide competition. The inter-republic trade flows, as a proportion of total
trade volume, decreased from 27.7 per cent in 1970 to 21.7 per cent
in 1980. These data imply that the level of product mobility between Yugoslav republics is now lower than that between Western
European countries (Ocic, 1984, pp. 62,74). The inter-republic
mobility of capital is also low. Pooling of funds on joint projects
by different firms—a major innovation of the Law of Associated
Labour (1976)—is in practice limited to individual republics, a fact
usually attributed to heavy regional political influence (L. Tyson,
1980, p. 47 and S. Ostojic, 1984, p. 142). On the other hand, in

Table 4.2: The market structure, product diversification and product innovation in Yugoslav industry, 1975–79

	Distribution					*Statistics*
	Market structure					
Number of competitors	0 or 1	2–10	11–50	51–100	101–	$\bar{x} = 2.76$
Percentage distribution of sampled firms	7.8	54.7	28.5	3.9	5.1	S.D. = 1.12
	Product diversification					
Percentage share of dominant product in total sales	0–20	21–40	41–60	61–80	81–100	$\bar{x} = 3.09$
Percentage distribution of sampled firms	19.1	17.6	15.3	32.1	16.0	S.D. = 1.10
	Product innovation					
New products, 1975– as percentage of all	0	1–10	11–20	21–30	31–100	$\bar{x} = 2.84$
Percentage distribution of sampled firms	16.5	32	20	12	18	S.D. = 1.36
Products abandoned, 1975–79, as percentage of all	0	1–10	11–20	21–30	31–100	$\bar{x} = 2.28$
Percentage distribution of sampled firms	34	35	13	8	8	S.D. = 1.24

Source: Prasnikar (1983), p. 52.
Note: $\bar{x}$ is the group or column, from among the five listed above, to which the
'average' firm belongs. S.D. is the standard deviation of $\bar{x}$, as implied by the
distribution of the sampled firms among these groups.

some important industries the strong regionalistic sentiments have led to parallel technological cooperation agreements with Western firms, and perhaps too much competition.[4] The latter has had such negative effects as limited ability to make use of scale economies in conventional production and innovation, or to compete internationally. Prasnikar's data also imply that in about half of the sampled firms product innovation may be regarded as zero or near to it.

The second important systemic factor is the labour-management system. The question is: what is the influence of that factor on innovation, in particular, what is the extent to which it induces workers and discourages managers to behave in an entrepreneurial manner? This important topic has been discussed recently by Abram Bergson (1983, pp. 209–216), and we must refer the reader to his interesting analysis. The tentative conclusion which Bergson draws, one with which we go along, is that the self-managed Yugoslav firm was, before the 1974–76 reform, unlikely to be 'as entrepreneurial as the typical Western private enterprise firm' (p. 212); and 'that, overall, risk taking and innovation are probably being adversely affected' by that last major reform (p. 215). From among many factors underlying this conclusion the following two are possibly crucial: (i) limited ability of the market to eliminate poor performers, that is, Schumpeter's creative destruction factor continues to be weak, and (ii) limited motivation, occasionally also limited ability, of the managers to impose rapidly the technological and organisational changes which imply redistribution of skills, income or status within their firms.[5] Despite a sequence of market-oriented reforms, the competitive market pressure is still rather weak and the economy is yet highly politicized, the institutional features which continue to bias the attitudes and efforts of Yugoslav managers and their firms from improving internal efficiency towards gaining resources from the outside, the extent of bias being too elusive to measure.

4. CONCLUDING REMARKS

Despite strong systemic obstacles, the climate for innovation in Yugoslavia may well be better than it is in CPEs. Of course, comparisons of the two types of economies are very difficult, partly because, in CPEs, the system as such and, within it, the huge hierarchical bureaucracy—communist party organizations included

—act on many occasions to promote innovation and, on many other occasions, to promote the *status quo* and inefficiency. In Chapter 3 of this book an attempt has been made to describe the net effect. However, the distinctive features of the Yugoslav economy are a relatively high price flexibility and the absence of directive plans. Consequently, shortages both of producer and consumer goods are not much in evidence. As a further consequence, the resource allocation flexibility is probably, and the inter-firm competition certainly, higher in Yugoslavia than they are in CPEs. These two features and their implications for innovation place Yugoslavia somewhere between the typical CPE and the typical western economy, perhaps somewhat closer to the latter than the former.

NOTES

1. Prasnikar (1983, p. 83) reports that, in his interviews, workers' opinion on the incentives to innovate was divided as follows (in terms of the strength of the stimulating effect): none—23.9 per cent, little—20.4 per cent, some—20 per cent, significant—20.3 per cent, strong—15.3 per cent.
2. According to this study of the innovations that were implemented by 15 Belgrade enterprises in 1979–84, managers take no or little interest in having home-produced inventions actually implemented. The reasons for this disinterest are not clear, especially as managers are known to be the primary force in assimilating foreign technology.
3. Following the very extensive and critical inquiry into these and related matters by Kraigher's Commission (1983), there is now a growing awareness also within the Federal Government of the need for a national technology development strategy and a more active governmental role in promoting domestic invention and strengthening the whole R & D sector.
4. A detailed analysis of 'parallelism' in manufacturing industries is given in *Science* ... (1982), pp. 288–298. The industries singled out are chemicals, where 63 firms produce basically the same products without any technological cooperation among them; pharmaceutical products, where 14 leading firms cooperate closely with foreign technology suppliers in a parallel manner; and automobiles and tractors where the production is said to be too fragmented to be efficient.
5. Vanek (1970) provides the elements of a counterargument. He notes that 'In the same sense as the top five per cent in a large Western corporation are production-minded—that is, follow and are concerned about the performance of their organisation, the entire working collective of the labour-managed (L-M) firm will tend to be production-minded' (p. 266). Consequently, 'The L-M firm will be in a better

position to accommodate and adjust to some negative effects which the innovation may have—by retraining, postponement of or phasing in the new techniques, temporary overemployment, or other means. ... In contrast to featherbedding (under capitalism), the L-M firm may tolerate over-employment in the short-run while doing away with it in the long-run through attrition, retraining, or in other ways' (p. 255). This argument overlooks that, at the economy level, innovation is a continuous process which constantly produces Vanek's short-run situations of high over-employment, thus preventing his long-run solution to arrive. Only when the rate of innovation is low or, better still, zero, would the gentle ways of adjustment to change be consistent with low over-employment, the point already made in Chapter 3. However, Vanek need not be wrong when he insists that the responses to innovation of the L-M firm 'will be closer to a social optimum than the solution in other than L-M firms' (p. 265). More questionable is Vanek's view that entire working collectives of L-M firms tend to be production-minded. For a different, in our judgement more realistic, view see Neuberger and James (1973: 269–271).

REFERENCES

Bergson, A., 'Entrepreneurship under Labour Participation: The Yugoslav Case', in J. Ronen (ed.), *Entrepreneurship,* Lexington Books, 1983.

Federal Commission for Economic Stabilisation (Kraigher's Commission), *Osnove za strategiju techoloskog razvoja,* vol. 3, Belgrade, 1983.

Neuberger, E. and E. James., 'The Yugoslav Self-managed firm: A systemic approach', in M. Bornstein (ed.), *Plan and Market,* Yale University Press, 1973.

Ocic, C. (original in Serbo-Croate), *Regional Aspects of Integration and Disintegration Processes in Yugoslav Economy,* Institute of Economic Science, Belgrade, 1984.

Ostojic, S. (in Serbo-Croate), *Labour-managed Corporations*, Poslovna Politika, Belgrade, 1984.

Ostojic, S. and Lj. Medenica (in Serbo-Croate), 'Analysis of the innovation process in Belgrade industry', Institut of Industrial Economics and Belgrade Chamber of Commerce, November 1984.

Prasnikar, J. (in Serbo-Croate), *Theory and Practice of the Yugoslav Organization of Associated Labour,* RCEF, Economics Department, Ljubljana University, 1983.

Science and Technological Development in Yugoslavia until the Year 2000 (in Serbo-Croate), Institute of Economic Research, Ljubljana, and Institut of Industrial Economics, Belgrade, 1982.

Slama, J., 'Gravity model and its estimations for international flows of engineering products, chemicals and patent applications', *Acta Oeconomica,* vol. 30(2): 241–253 (1983).

Schrenk, M. et al., *Yugoslavia: Self-management Socialism and the Challenges of Development,* The World Bank, 1979.

Tyson, L. D., *The Yugoslav Economic System and Its Performance in the 1970s.* Berkeley: University of California Press, 1980.

Vanek, J., *The General Theory of Labour-Managed Economies,* Ithaca, NY: Cornell University Press, 1970.

Vrcelj, Dj. (in Serbo-Croate), *Some Aspects of Industrial Innovation,* Institut of Industrial Economics, Belgrade, 1975.

Vrcelj, Dj. and Lj. Brkanovic (in Serbo-Croate), 'Present state and problems of technological development in Yugoslovia', paper presented at: II Yugoslav Conference on the Strategy of Technological Development, Split, December 1983.

5 Kornai's Soft Budget Constraint and the Shortage Phenomenon: A Criticism and Restatement*

1. INTRODUCTION

It is a textbook proposition that if, in a capitalist market economy, some or all prices are fixed or remain otherwise upward-inflexible, a state of market disequilibrium may obtain in which some or all inputs and consumer goods would be in shortage (in surplus, if the prices are downward-inflexible). In several recent writings, especially in the *Economics of Shortage,* János Kornai appears to maintain that such an explanation of the shortage phenomenon does not hold in socialist economies, whether market-based (prices fairly flexible) or centrally-planned (prices nearly fixed). The conclusions of his analysis may be articulated as follows:[1]

(i) An essential aspect of any socialist economy is that firms face a budget (or financial) constraint that is much 'softer' than it usually is under capitalism;

(ii) This softness of the budget constraint causes socialist economies to be resource-constrained, in contrast to capitalist, hard-budget economies, which are demand-constrained. This softness is, consequently, also the reason why, in centrally-planned economies (CPEs), shortages are widespread and

*This paper was written when the author was Visiting Professor at the Department of Economics, University of Pennsylvania. Its ideas were presented earlier at seminars at the London School of Economics and the University of Oxford. The paper benefited much from detailed critical comments from Włodzimierz Brus of Wolfson College, Oxford, Philip Hanson of the University of Birmingham, UK, Cezary Józefiak of Łódź University, Poland, János Kornai of Harvard University, Kazimierz Laski of Linz University, Austria, Herbert Levine of the University of Pennsylvania and Peter Wiles of the London School of Economics.

persistent, and why they would be so even if prices were flexible;

(iii)   To the extent that respecting socialist principles necessitates high budget softness, shortages are a distinct characteristic of any socialist economy, similarly as unemployment is for any capitalist economy.

As in Kornai's analysis, the initial premiss of this paper is also the view that firms' and state authorities' budgets, both in real and money terms, tend to be much softer under socialism than they are under capitalism. It will be argued, however, that when prices are sufficiently flexible this greater softness need not result in shortages. The argument rests in part on the distinction between budget softness and budget flexibility (p. 79 below); it leads us to suggest that (ii) and (iii) above should be modified as follows:

(ii)*   The size and incidence of shortage is related not to the degree of budget softness, but to the excess of budget flexibility over price flexibility.[2] In CPEs, the price flexibility is limited, and to the extent the principle of detailed physical planning implies high, even infinite, budget flexibility, the elimination of serious shortages of some intermediate and investment goods may be impossible, irrespective of the degree of firms' budget softness. However, households' budget flexibility is low and consumer shortages are caused primarily by the high inflexibility of the consumer goods prices, the latter in turn caused by reasons of politics, ideology and limited capacity of the price-setting offices.

(iii)* Budget constraints are softer when and where tolerated economic inefficiency is greater, and it is relatively high efficiency losses, not chronic shortages, that are probably an unavoidable characteristic of the economic systems which are influenced particularly strongly by socialist principles.

I should stress that I find much of Kornai's analysis theoretically stimulating, in touch with the reality of CPEs and, I believe, also closely related to the prevailing view of western analysts of these economies. However, his analysis seems to me to play down seriously the potential role of the price mechanism and overplay the role of the budget softness in explaining the shortage phenomenon, especially in consumer markets. The primary purpose of this paper is to seek to identify the proper role of the price mechanism, budget softness and budget flexibility in CPEs as well as under socialism in general, with reference to that particular phenomenon.

My criticism is directed in particular at Kornai's general view that 'in a socialist economy, although it does matter whether prices are flexible or not, the distinction is of secondary importance' (1980 p. 343). We shall dispute the validity of this proposition even in the case of CPEs. To make our point sharper still, we shall also consider a socialist economy in which prices are highly upward-flexible. We shall call the economy 'Leyland-type', to indicate that it consists only of firms which are state-owned or cooperatives, which may be heavily subsidised and inefficient, yet which are self-managed and guided largely by markets; firms such as Leyland, UK's major cars and trucks producer, used to be in the 1970s. The Yugoslav economy is a close relative of what we have in mind, especially when price controls remain minimal.

We start developing our case in the following two sections with a discussion and interpretation of Kornai's key concept: budget softness.

2. HARD, ALMOST HARD AND SOFT BUDGET CONSTRAINTS: KORNAI'S DEFINITIONS

Kornai (1980, pp. 302–3) lists five conditions, each said to be necessary, and all taken together sufficient, to guarantee 'perfect hardness' of a firm's budget constraint. These are as follows:

H1. The firm is a price-taker for both its inputs and outputs;
H2. the firm cannot influence the tax rules; these rules base taxes on observable and measurable criteria; no individual exemption can be given concerning the volume of tax or the dates of collection;
H3. the firm cannot receive any free state or other grants to cover current expenses or as contributions to finance investment;
H4. no credits from other firms or banks can be obtained: all transactions are made in cash;
H5. no external finance for investment purposes is possible.

The budget constraint is said to be almost hard if H2 and H3 fully stand, but some or all of the remaining three conditions are somewhat relaxed: price-making takes place within narrow limits, credits can be obtained on 'orthodox' principles, and external finance for investment purposes can be obtained on hard conditions. Perfect softness is the state of affairs when the budget does not restrict the firm at all. We move towards that end of the softness spectrum by relaxing one or more of the five conditions H1 to H5 significantly. Consequently, the budget constraint is said to be simply soft if either the firm is a price-maker, the tax system is soft, or as a result of bargaining with the patronising bureaucratic institutions the firm can get free grants and subsidised credits.

The meaning Kornai gives to the term 'soft budget constraint' is therefore such that it would be difficult to find a firm under any economic system to which the term does not apply. Kornai himself notes that, in the capitalist economies,

the normal degree of hardness of the constraint seems to have shifted: *the trend is in the direction of softening.* Perfect hardness in its absolute purity may never have existed, even though the capitalist system came close to this abstract extreme point ... in the 19th century. Bankruptcy was real bankruptcy; the firm that failed was not helped out by anyone but crushed ruthlessly by more successful competitors. ... The economy is becoming highly concentrated; huge corporations being founded. They are no longer price-takers but price-makers. This is one of the basic factors from the point of view of softening the budget constraint. A large capitalist corporation is able to react to input price changes not by adapting its input-output combination, but by adjusting output price to actual costs plus the expected mark-up. By its price-making power it can almost 'automatically' guarantee its survival, its self-perpetuation. (1980, pp. 311–12)

However, Kornai maintains that in the contemporary capitalist economies there are spheres

in which it could be said that the budget constraint is still 'almost hard', and other spheres where it is 'not very hard' or 'rather soft'—although nowhere under capitalist conditions has the budget constraint reached full softness, with an automatic guarantee of the firm's survival. (1981, p. 313)

Since budget softness is so universal a phenomenon while shortages are not, the latter cannot be simply an effect of the former. Kornai clearly implies that the key variable is not budget softness as such but its degree, shortages appearing only or mainly when that degree is sufficiently high. The problem that arises immediately is that his descriptive definitions are not precise enough to provide a convenient measure of that degree. The purpose of the next section is, first, to suggest such a measure and, secondly, to make the distinction—important in the later part of the paper—between budget softness and budget flexibility.

3. SOFTNESS, FLEXIBILITY AND INEFFECTIVENESS OF THE BUDGET CONSTRAINT

We have seen that in describing the soft budget constraint Kornai refers to all kinds of situations in which a firm can obtain an income through the exercise of economic power in the market place, bargaining power in government and other offices, or simply as a consequence of the paternalistic relationship between state institutions and the firm. This income would be additional to what the firm would have earned, given its outputs and inputs, if it fully met Kornai's conditions H1 to H5. These conditions appear to imply that firm budgets would be perfectly hard only under perfect competition. If so, what would be a suitable conceptual measure of that additional income?

In its actual circumstances the firm produces different types and quantities of outputs and uses up different inputs than it would produce and use if it were perfectly competitive. Applying competitive equilibrium prices the revenue of the imaginary, perfectly competitive firm would be just sufficient to cover its costs. At the same competitive equilibrium prices the revenue of the actual firm, given its actual inputs and outputs, would usually be *in*sufficient to cover costs, the actual firm's activity resulting thus in a competitive cost-over-run. It seems to me to be in the spirit of Kornai's analysis to regard that cost-over-run, taken as a proportion of the total competitive costs of producing its actual outputs, as a measure of the *degree* of the firm's budget softness. By this definition the degree of budget softness is nothing else than the unit resource loss that is tolerated by markets and/or planners, taking the unit resource cost that would obtain under a perfectly competitive market structure as the standard against which to compare the performance of firms. The budget softness as such, rather than its degree, is correspondingly the total resource loss that a firm incurs in the course of its economic activity within the budget period. We shall call this resource loss, or efficiency slack, the budget *r-softness* if it is evaluated at a given set of competitive prices, and the budget *m-softness* if evaluated at actual prices, the letter *r* standing for real and *m* for monetary or nominal.[3] From these definitions it follows that the degree of budget softness can be measured to the extent that competitive prices can be calculated or are observed. In practice this must mean that the degree may be measured only approximately. One possible practical course to take would be to evaluate, at the prices actually observed, the maximum input savings that a firm can make and still produce the actual outputs. Another course would be to estimate, given observed both prices and inputs, the maximum value of additional outputs that a firm can still produce. To make such estimates would be, presumably, one of the main tasks of the firm's supervisors.

To the extent that the perfectly competitive ideal is in the real world unobserved, budget constraints are r-soft for all firms under any economic system. However, they may be expected to be r-softer in CPEs than in economies under market socialism, and under welfare or monopoly capitalism than under 'competitive capitalism': r-softness as such is therefore not a systemic characteristic, but its degree probably is.[4]

In market-based economies that degree is determined in part by a particular market structure in which a firm happens to operate. In CPEs firm managers negotiate the output targets and the allocation of resources to meet these targets with the controlling centre. As long as prices are fixed and the financial plan is a mirror reflection of the physical plan, the monetary value of the resources to be bought would be the firm's anticipated expenditure, which may be regarded as the firm's initial budget. Managers in CPEs, in view of incentives which penalise for under-fulfilment of output plans but tolerate high unit costs, might like to have output targets near zero and inputs virtually infinite. In practice, however, each manager would be competing with other managers for the same limited resources and be subjected to immense administrative pressure from the centre to accept highly taut output targets. Moreover, firms would be visited by inspectors from a variety of controlling and supervising agencies whose job would be to satisfy themselves that production reserves—including labour reserves—are not in excess of levels deemed as needed to cover emergencies. If these production reserves are too low, the manager risks under-fulfilment of his firm's output target. If they are too high, he risks being reported for flagrant inefficiency. In either case he may be fired or demoted. Between these two extremes there lies a point of economic efficiency which, given the particular circumstances of his own and his firm, the manager in question would judge as optimal. That optimum point would reflect the manager's subjective perception of the effectiveness of the controlling bureaucracy, that is, his best judgement about the maximum inefficiency he can still get away with. Therefore at that point the manager acts as if the marginal budget softness in real terms ends. Hence here the marginal budget effectively becomes hard.

Now we turn to consider the distinction between budget softness and budget flexibility. In economic theory the term flexibility is well established in relation to prices; it means the speed at which the price of a good changes in response to a unit excess in demand for that good. By analogy, the *budget flexibility* of a firm is the speed at which the firm's total income, including subsidies and the effect of increasing the prices of its outputs, changes in response to a change in the value of its inputs. The difference between budget softness and budget flexibility is thus that between competitive cost-over-runs and the speed of changes in actual income. In a small period of time, a zero budget flexibility may be consistent with the firm's budget continuing to be highly soft. If the adjustment of incomes, subsidies and grants included, to cover increased costs is instantaneous, the budget flexibility is infinite, and would be so irrespective of the degree of the initial budget softness.

Now we are ready to consider the relation, in reference to a budget constraint, between being soft and being binding. A budget constraint—any constraint—is not binding when its lifting does not induce the firm to change its initial decisions. This is the situation when these initial decisions represent either an internal optimum, in which case none of the constraints is binding, or a constrained optimum in which a factor (factors) other than the one in question, budget in our case, is (are) binding. An internal optimum occurs when the firm, in order to meet particular output targets, has access to more resources of any kind, financial and physical, than the firm's manager thinks it would be wise to use, on the grounds mentioned on the opposite page in relation to his optimal budget r-softness. Such situations are likely to be rare, but may plausibly occur in firms or institutions doing the top priority tasks for military, political or security authorities. The monetary budget constraint would not be binding either when the firm has the finance to spend but, because of ill-balanced plans or other reasons, cannot obtain some or all of the physical resources it needs or wants. In this case, the budget's r-softness may be forced to be below the desired optimum. Finally, there are situations of the third kind, in which the budget constraint would be effective. This happens when the firm's financial resources are lower than what its manager's own optimum (his maximum r-softness) would require and, at the same time any physical resources can be obtained in open markets or through the planning machinery. Cases of this category may be infrequent; they may occur if the firm in question needs inputs that happen to be surplus at the economy level.

Whether binding or not, the budget constraint of a socialist firm operating in a CPE is, as Kornai argues and empirical evidence suggests, highly soft in both real and monetary terms. (Kornai does not distinguish between r-softness and m-softness.) A high degree of r-softness results largely from two reasons. First, imposed financial plans and local controls by the central bureaucracy have proved to be disciplining firms not particularly effectively. Secondly, overtly inefficient managers may be fired, but firms which are inherently uneconomic would be usually allowed to continue their operations, although sometimes they may be closed down gradually or, more often, converted to produce other things. In CPEs, the very notions of 'economic' and 'uneconomic' are suspect anyway. Planners are well aware that since prices are highly distorted, firms which on paper are profitable, may in fact be more inefficient than the firms showing financial losses.

4. INVESTMENT BUDGET FLEXIBILITY AND SHORTAGES IN CPEs

Kornai's case for tracing shortages to soft budgets seems strongest when he considers the investment activity in CPEs, in particular the part which is centrally financed. This activity is based on the practice of dual planning, in physical terms and in financial terms, and on the principle of subordinating the latter to the former, rather than the other way around as in market-based economies. The investment plan in physical terms is a list of projects to be implemented and the rate of progress to be achieved within a given period. Planners strive to make sure that the plan is feasible; that is, consistent with the expected supply of all the necessary inputs. The list once approved at an appropriate level becomes a shopping list for these inputs. Investment credit, however, may not be predetermined on some independent criteria, such as the availability of profits or savings, but, up to a point, is created automatically, in volume equal to the value of these inputs. This is thus the case of intended investments creating their own savings, of money being 'passive', in the western sense. Moreover, there may be a standing order to the banking authorities to amend these savings (or credits) instantly, in line with possible changes in the investment costs of the approved projects.

Shortages of investment inputs would not arise in this case only if planners happened to set investment demands at or below the levels which it is feasible to supply. However, as Kornai emphasises, in CPEs the hunger for new capacity is so high that investment demands, as expressed by approved investment plans, tend to exceed actual supplies almost all the time.

But is it correct to infer from this description that the root cause of the ensuing shortages of investment inputs is the softness of the investment budget? Note what would happen if prices of the shortage inputs were flexible. These prices would be rising at a rate reflecting the assumed price flexibility. As long as that rate is finite, excess demands could not be eliminated by virtue of the investment credits being adjusted instantly to cover fully any price increases. This is thus a very special and, indeed, extreme case in which investment budgets are infinitely flexible, indicating the possibility of no financial limit at all in implementing the approved plan. This extreme case, however, should not be taken as the only or typical possibility under central planning, even less so as characteristic for all economies under socialism. It is evident that the flexibility of investment budgets is a variable that can be controlled by a suitable policy or institutional choice. In the following section, to make this point more sharply, we shall consider a case on the other end of the socialist spectrum, one in which prices are much more flexible than budgets, even though the latter are highly soft.

5. PRICE FLEXIBILITY VERSUS BUDGET FLEXIBILITY, AND THE SHORTAGE PHENOMENON

In this section we consider first a Leyland-type economy in which all investment activity is decentralised. Investment projects originate from enterprises and remain under the control of enterprise managements. At the centre there may still be an investment fund the purpose of which is to part-finance enterprises' investment activity. Enterprises compete for credits from that fund, the size of which is decided on economic and political grounds to be briefly discussed in the next section. These credits may be interest-free or even outright gifts. However, in contrast to the practice in CPEs, the financial budget of the government is not merely a mirror reflection of the approved investment plans in physical terms, neither at the planning phase nor in the course of plans' implementation. Adjustments of the central investment fund may be made, but they would not follow automatically and precisely changes in the volume or costs of the investment projects in the financing of which the government participates. Prices of investment inputs are upward-flexible. Given these circumstances, under what conditions would the shortages of these inputs be rare or absent?

Suppose that initially the total investment finance (of the government and enterprises) in this Leyland-type economy exceeds the market value of the investment supplies and, as a result, shortages of (some or all) investment goods have arisen. If prices are infinitely (upward) flexible, the purchasing power of that investment finance would be reduced instantly to the level of actual supplies. The only exception to this outcome is the extreme case in which investment finance is adjusted to compensate fully for price increases, and with speed that is also infinite. The result would be, in this case, an instant hyperinflation. In the cases which are more relevant empirically, the flexibility both of input prices and investment finance is considerable, but not unbounded. In particular, any changes of the investment finance would have to be debated and approved by the parliament or the Politburo (the government finance) and by workers' councils (firms' finance). This takes time, making credit flexibility limited or the softness of the investment budget constraint bounded. In such cases the initial shortages may or may not vanish, depending on what is more flexible, budgets or prices. To give an example of a situation when the shortages could vanish, suppose that, whatever the initial excess demand, it takes one month after the budget day (which we assume to be the same for all firms and the government) for prices to increase to their market-clearing levels, but in order to give time for discussion of alternative projects, budgets are decided only once a year. In this example prices are, therefore, more flexible than is the total investment budget. Shortages of investment inputs may arise, but only during the first month after the (annual) budget day. It may be seen that what matters, in this *or any other economy,* is not the (monetary) budget softness as such, but whether the upward flexibility of prices can be higher than the upward budget flexibility.

In CPEs, price flexibility is often (not always) so limited that this condition is not met.

Kornai's case for tracing shortages to soft budgets seems to me to be particularly weak with reference to consumer markets. Yet we would hardly discuss the 'shortage economy' if the shortages of consumer goods were absent. Kornai is, of course, aware of the damping effect of price rises on consumer demands. He nevertheless maintains that price rises, while effective in reducing demands for consumer goods, are not effective enough to eliminate their chronic shortages under socialism. His argument begins as follows:

Obviously, if a product the demand for which is insatiable is distributed free of charge, a shortage arises. ... In chapter 16 we made clear that the total money income reaching the households is firmly controlled by the economic leadership. The total demand is thus given in nominal terms. ... Why, then, do shortages appear again and again in this sphere? Is the explanation not simply that prices of the shortage commodities have been set too low? Or, if prices are taken as given, does not the trouble arise because the relation between the total household purchasing power and the total supply of consumer goods has been planned incorrectly? It would be tempting to give simple answers to these seemingly simple questions. (1980 p. 476)

The major reason for Kornai's resistance to saying yes to these questions is the possible 'siphoning-off effect' of sectors other than the household one. As he explains,

The household sector competes for the product with other sectors, but this is competition on unequal terms. The household has a hard budget constraint, and the firm has a soft one. ... [Consequently], an increase in the level of consumer prices will reduce the intensity of shortage only if (and this is one of the necessary conditions) the amount siphoned off by these sectors is restrained administratively. [However, in some] areas it is particularly difficult to enforce such restrictions if what producers siphon off is not a final output but a direct input in the production of such an output. This would happen if, for example, industry draws labor away from the retail sector, which worsens the service offered to households. (1980 p. 487)

Thus also in consumer markets the root cause of the shortage phenomena is, according to Kornai, the soft budget constraint of firms, supposedly giving rise to their 'almost insatiable' demands for resources. Our example of the Leyland economy and our references to Yugoslavia were intended to counter, or at least to qualify, that proposition. In the context of CPEs, Kornai's analysis appears to assume, implicitly, that firms' budgets in real terms can be so soft that these economies may, in certain circumstances, be nearly unproductive; that is, almost incapable of producing any net outputs for the consumer. His explicit discussion rests on the so-called 'shortage preserving' supply response (1980, sections 19.3–19.6, 21.4 and 21.9). The major point of this discussion is that while the household demand for a consumer good typically falls in response to a rise in the good's price, its shortage need not fall, the reason being that the planners may reduce the good's production or increase its net export in response to the price-induced fall in demand. Such responses of planners cannot be excluded. However, for Kornai's argument really to bite the implied reallocation of resources should be not just within the consumption sector of the economy—some supplies being reduced in order to increase the supplies of other consumer goods—but at the expense of that sector in order to benefit the sector producing intermediate and investment inputs. Such intersectoral reallocations would be necessary only if input/output coefficients become higher when shortage is reduced. Kornai apparently thinks that, in response to signals of reduced consumer shortages, planners would be disciplining firms less strictly, tolerating greater inefficiency (or higher budgets' r-softness). For this behaviour to occur, the population must be presumed to suffer from what may be called the 'shop window illusion', whereby a mere improvement in the availability of consumer goods would lessen the social pressure on planners to supply more of the consumer goods. By the same argument, widespread shortages would induce the population to maintain that pressure, and in turn induce planners to keep the r-softness under control.

This argument, which I think must underlie Kornai's, is theoretically attractive, but its significance depends ultimately on how relevant it is empirically. Judging from the experience of market-based economies, it would seem that workers evaluate the performance of governments by their own consumption rather than by what they see in shop windows. If this were the case also in CPEs, the link between the average degree of r-softness and the incidence of shortage would be weak or nonexistent, planners continuing—in their own self interest—to keep the former comfortably below its critical, non-productiveness level also when consumer prices are highly flexible.

In practice the authorities are reluctant to raise some important prices sufficiently high for reasons of politics or ideology. In the case of several basic consumer goods, such as bread, milk and meat products, central authorities may keep prices low either in order to support low income groups or for fear of political troubles in response to any significant rise in these prices. Polish experience of the 1970s and early 1980s is particularly instructive in the latter respect. In other cases political considerations are of a quite different kind. For example the prices of cars are kept low so that, it seems, officials and others who would be given special ration tickets can afford to buy the cars. These are thus the cases where allocating goods through rationing is thought to be politically less damaging than through setting different prices for different consumer categories. In many, perhaps most, cases prices of consumer goods remain the same for long periods simply due to limited processing capacity of the price offices. Moreover, these price offices have to guess what the market-clearing levels are, and these guesses can easily be wrong. The overall effect of these political, ideological and administrative reasons is very low price flexibility. At the same time the demands may change rapidly, especially for goods with high income elasticities. Widespread and persistent disequilibria in individual consumer markets must, in such circumstances, be the outcome.

The siphoning-off effect is of some significance in periods of accelerated industrialisation, when firms producing investment and intermediate goods may obtain inputs at the expense of the consumer industry. The disruptions of consumer supplies by this effect are usually gradual rather than abrupt, and therefore a flexible price system should again be able to equilibrate individual consumer markets most of the time, provided of course that consumer prices can be more upward-flexible than aggregate household incomes.[5]

However, eliminating shortages of intermediate and investment goods would, in CPEs, be vastly more difficult. In the case of consumer goods the task is relatively easy as long as the planners are not interested in securing a particular distribution of goods among households. If what they care for is only the control over the total money incomes and its distribution among households, the job of physical allocations may be left to prices. However, any central plan is written in physical terms and if it by mistake or design implies excess demand for some intermediate or investment goods, as it often does, then clearly their prices are immaterial. Kornai's analysis in this case fully applies. But even in this case it should be noted that central planners take particular interest only in a limited number of goods and investment projects. These are called respectively, centrally-planned commodities and priority investment projects. A large part of the economy is in effect decentralised, firms receiving only aggregate monetary targets for a substantial proportion of their total sales and themselves contracting supplies of many inputs directly from other firms. Should prices of such 'non-listed' commodities be upward-flexible, a CPE would in effect become a mixed economy, partly command-type and partly Leyland-type. Provided the budget flexibility in the latter part is lower than the price flexibility, the incidence of shortage would be largely limited to the part that remains of the command-type. The economic reforms in Hungary and Poland have taken the two countries' economies precisely in that direction.

6. LIMITED SOFTNESS OF THE GOVERNMENT BUDGET

In section 2 we argued that it is the degree of economic competition that largely determines the degree of softness of firms' budgets in real terms, the r-softness. We shall end this paper by suggesting that at the government level the correspondingly crucial role may be played by the degree of 'political competition'.

The concept of budget softness must have the same meaning whatever is the economic unit the budget of which we happen to consider: a member of a household, the household itself, a firm or the state. It must always mean the ability of the unit concerned to *co-determine* its own budget by influencing the terms of contract(s) between it and its income source(s). The greater that budget-making ability is, the softer is also the budget constraint and the higher the degree of the budget softness. The means that may be deployed to the end of influencing income may of course vary greatly, from persuasion to the application of power: economic, political or (the threat of) physical coercion. The point about governments, whether local or national, is that they may impose budgets which are different, in terms of size and composition, than they would be if chosen under 'perfect democracy', a state of affairs when nobody, acting individually or in collusion with others, can influence effectively budget decisions. Just as perfectly competitive firms have no effective influence over their budget-forming terms—those which adopt prices or production methods that are distinctly of their own choice would be instantly eliminated—also the people forming governments would, under the imaginary perfect democracy, lose power the moment they fail to follow precisely the majority wishes of their electorates. In as much as they, under actual institutional arrangements, need not follow these wishes precisely, they have some freedom of independent action. The actual government budgets thus reflect partly the government's own separate preferences. The proportion of these budgets which is spent on projects reflecting these preferences is then the degree of government budgets' softness. (It may be noted that with this definition of softness, the size of budgets and whether they are balanced or not are in themselves immaterial. However, government budgets in CPEs, remaining as they are under one-party rule, may be expected to be softer than those under parliamentary democracy.)

Be that as it may, the point is that the softness of government budgets must be limited under any political system. The budget in real terms is, of course, limited ultimately by the economy's real outputs, and before that by political implications of excessively depressed consumption levels. The softness of the budget in money terms is limited by the political implications of excessively high inflation rates, open, disguised and repressed. Since at all times all governments would be striving to make immediate use of any margin of freedom they may judge themselves to have, their budget constraints may be expected to be binding most of the time. These limitations at the government level would in turn impose limits on the extent of government-financed softness, both in money and real terms, at the level of firms.

7. CONCLUDING REMARKS

In this paper we have sought to modify Kornai's analysis of the shortage phenomenon. One point and two modifications are suggested. The point is that firms' budget softness in real terms, even if generally higher under socialism than capitalism, is always limited enough for any economies still to remain very much productive. One modification is that, in the theory of the shortage phenomenon, the key operational variable is not the degree of budget softness, provided it is not too high as to make the economy unproductive, but a quite different concept of the degree of budget flexibility. Our example of the Leyland-type economy and references to Yugoslavia were intended to make this proposition evident. In these and any other economy the degree of budget softness is, instead, linked with inefficiency, both static and dynamic. The other modification is that while the household does have a hard budget constraint and the firm has a soft one, sufficiently high prices for consumer goods would nevertheless be able to abolish any consumer goods' shortages.

An important topic which has been alluded to but not discussed in this paper is Kornai's suggestion that there may operate a trade-off between the rate of unemployment and the degree of goods shortages. This topic is related to a number of issues, one of which is the validity of equating 'shortage economy' with 'resource-constrained economy'. To indicate a potential problem, it may be noted that an abstract, perfectly competitive economy is free of shortage (as well as of unemployment), and yet it is resource-constrained (as well as demand-constrained). Actual market-based economies are from time to time also resource-constrained, but the distance to full employment is, in those economies, related to the inflation rate (the Phillips curve) rather than to the incidence of shortage (Kornai's suggestion), especially if the upward price flexibility is high. However, these are matters which may be better left for separate treatment.

NOTES

1. For a good survey and an appraisal of Kornai's ideas the reader may consult a review article by Hare (1982) and a note by Marrese and Mitchell (1984). A useful survey of the disequilibrium literature, both western and eastern, is provided by Kemme and Winiecki (1984).
2. This statement needs a qualification. As indicated in proposition (iii)[*] of the Introduction, we shall associate the degree of budget softness in real terms with the excess of resource use, per unit of output, over that which would have been under perfect competition. Given the primary resources of labour, capital and land, the supplies of net outputs—meaning consumer, investment and export goods—would therefore be declining as the degree of budget softness in real terms increases. Indeed, at some critical level of the degree these supplies would fall to zero. The qualification is, therefore, that the representative firm's budget softness in real terms remains below that critical level. We shall return to this point in section 5 of the paper.
3. Portes (1983) gives implicitly an interpretation of Kornai's 'soft' budget constraint which may seem similar, but is in fact quite different from ours. He writes: 'The priority of output among the objectives of planners, enterprise managers, and party secretaries means that the bank will often have to concede finance for above-plan payments, either directly or by extending general credit to enterprises whose costs exceed plans and which consequently find themselves with liquidity problems [Kornai's 'soft' budget constraint]. Bank managers are understandably reluctant to bankrupt state enterprises, and in any case this would probably be useless. So violators of cost targets are 'financed when they overshoot' (Wiles 1977, p. 372). Even Stalin never used the monetary control technique of shooting the bankers when they overfinance, which doubtless would have been quite effective' (p. 157). However, from Kornai's analysis it is quite clear that firms' budgets may be soft even when, given prices, their cost targets are fully respected. This point is important; it rests on the view that, being the outcomes of bargaining with the planners or manipulating the markets, the cost targets

themselves are usually soft nearly as much as the actual costs. In CPEs the phenomenon of 'planned losses' is indeed widespread. Kornai is therefore quite right in insisting, if only implicitly, on the use of competitive costs as the standard for calculating cost over-runs.

4. In the context of CPEs the various manifestations of poor economic efficiency have been well documented by the East European economists. Western sources which discuss the evidence and offer its interpretation run into hundreds. Some of the most recent ones, especially with reference to innovation, are listed and discussed in McAuley (1984) and Smith (1983), Chapter 4.

5. It is interesting that Kornai pays little attention to the operation of free markets for consumer goods in CPEs. Many of these markets are officially approved, perhaps most of the others are illegal but tolerated. In these markets nearly anything can be obtained. Of course, the free market prices tend to be higher than the official prices, the difference being the market evaluation of the inconvenience of waiting and searching. Planners themselves have always seemed to be well aware that, given the way prices are set, little can be done to eliminate shortages of some consumer goods and surpluses of others. Consequently, forced substitution has been and probably continues to be large-scale. However, maintaining macroeconomic equilibrium—that is, a rough equality of the value of consumer supplies and the money incomes households wish to spend on consumer goods—does not appear to be evidently impossible. The data on aggregate households savings (e.g. those collected by Rudcenko, 1979), show households' savings ratios in all CPEs to have been usually below those observed in market-based economies, and therefore would seem to support that view (in the years 1978–83 Poland and probably Romania would be exceptions to this rule, but also for rather exceptional reasons). Kornai's criticism of the macroeconomic equilibrium thesis, defended particularly strongly by Portes (1977, 1983) and Portes and Winter (1978), is really definitional; it rests on his view that in calculating the excess aggregate demand we should ignore the value of the goods consumers did not really wish to buy at the prevailing prices and incomes, but have bought merely as substitutes for the goods in shortage. Again, the difference between the two types of aggregate excess demand, one which aggregates over both shortages and surpluses and the other which aggregates only over shortages, is price-related: most of it would be probably eliminated by a suitable change of *relative* prices.

REFERENCES

Hare, P. G., 'Economics of Shortage and Non-Price Control', *Journal of Comparative Economics,* 6, 1982, pp. 406–25.

Kemme, D. M. and Winiecki, J., 'Disequilibrium in Centrally Planned Economies', University of North Carolina at Greensvoro, Working Papers in Economics, mimeo.

Kornai, J., 'Resource-Constrained versus Demand-Constrained System', *Econometrica,* 47, 1979, pp. 801–19.

Kornai, J., *Economics of Shortage,* Amsterdam: North-Holland, 1980.

Kornai, J., *Growth, Shortage and Efficiency,* Oxford: Basil Blackwell, 1982.

Marrese, M. and Mitchell, J. L., 'Kornai's Resource-Constrained Economy: A Survey and an Appraisal', *Journal of Comparative Economics,* 8, 1984, pp. 74–84.

McAuley, A., 'The Incompatibility of Central Planning and Rapid Innovation', University of Essex, 1984.

Portes, R., 'The Control of Inflation: Lessons from East European Experience', *Economica,* 44, 1977, pp. 109–30.

Portes, R., 'Central Planning and Monetarism: Fellow Travelers?' in *Marxism, Central Planning and the Soviet Economy in Honor of Alexander Erlich,* ed. Padma Desai, pp. 149–65, Cambridge: MIT Press, 1983.

Portes, R. and Winter, D., 'The Demand for Money and for Consumption Goods in Centrally Planned Economies', *Review of Economics and Statistics,* 60, 1978, pp. 8–18.

Rudcenko, S., 'Household Money Income, Expenditure and Monetary Assets in Czechoslovakia, GDR, Hungary and Poland, 1956–1975', *Jahrbuch der Wirtschaft Osteuropas,* 8, 1979, pp. 431–50.

Smith, A., *The Planned Economies of Eastern Europe,* London: Croom Helm, 1983.

Wiles, P., *The Political Economy of Communism,* Oxford: Basil Blackwell, 1962.

Wiles, P., *Economic Institutions Compared,* Oxford: Basil Blackwell, 1977.

Part B

INDUSTRIALISATION, GROWTH, AND
GROWTH SLOWDOWN

6 Industrialisation and the Rate of Growth: Eastern Europe 1955-75*

1. THE HYPOTHESIS OF MANUFACTURING AS THE ENGINE OF GROWTH: THE ARGUMENTS

The countries that abound in natural resources, be it good quality soil or low-cost oil, may become wealthy without recourse to developing their own manufacturing activity. Yet even a resource-rich country would need some manufacturing products for setting up productive farms or for generating demand for its oil. At a global level, therefore, the establishment of a sizeable manufacturing sector is widely seen as a necessary precondition for making possible rapid, sustained discovery and application of useful new products and new cost-saving methods of making old products. This type of innovation activity has almost always been the primary source of per capita economic growth, especially in the long run.

The region of Eastern Europe is neither very rich nor particularly poor in natural resources. In the early 1950s, Eastern European nations, especially Bulgaria, Romania, Yugoslavia and Poland, were predominantly agricultural. The overall size and sectoral allocation of investment in the seven countries of Eastern Europe (the four mentioned above, plus Czechoslovakia, East Germany and Hungary) were, except for Yugoslavia, centrally planned. The central planners placed unusually strong emphasis on fast industrialisation, for they saw it as the 'engine of growth', as the

*This paper arose out of an SSRC-financed project on Economic Growth in Eastern Europe 1946–1975: The Causes of Variation over Time and between Countries. The author wishes to thank Anthony Thirlwall for inviting him to write the paper and for many useful comments. He is also grateful to Paul Davidson for his substantive editorial contribution. Reprinted with permission from Stanislaw Gomulka, *Journal of Post Keynesian Economics*, Spring 1983, vol. V, no. 3, pp. 388–96.

only way to social advance and modernisation. The arguments for regarding the manufacturing sector as the 'engine of growth' may be divided into two categories, of which one emphasises the supply side and the other the demand side.

On the supply side, industrial activity may stimulate the economy's overall production capacity in three ways: (i) It may activate the resources that remain idle, especially the labour surplus in agriculture and the unemployed or underemployed in the city sector. Moreover the level of labour productivity to be achieved at a given capital/output ratio in manufacturing is often higher than that prevailing in other sectors at the same capital/output ratio. In this case a change in the sectoral composition of employment in favour of manufacturing would increase the overall level of labour (as well as joint input) productivity. (ii) By supplying itself and other sectors with new or improved products at a faster rate, it may, via technological progress, raise the rates of productivity change of the resources that are actually employed. (iii) The size and quality of the manufacturing activity influence the country's exports and, hence, gains that accrue from international trade.

The growth-stimulating role of the supply side factors may be additionally reinforced by changes in the composition of total demand. These changes take place in response to the arrival of new goods, lower relative prices of old goods when they are produced more economically, and to increases in income per head. All three factors are both closely linked with the innovative activity of the manufacturing sector and, in countries such as those of Eastern Europe at least, have tended to induce changes in the composition of demand in favour of that sector.

2. TESTS AND INTERPRETATIONS

In the tests below the total output is represented by net material national product. This includes the output (net value-added) of three major sectors: agriculture, industry (manufacturing, gas and electricity, and mining), and material services (mainly construction, transport, communication, and trade). The growth rates of output, employment, capital stock and labour productivity for the three sectors and their aggregates are given in Table 6.1 for the seven East European countries for three sub-periods between 1961 and 1975.

A number of features of this data sample are worth noting. Total employment has been fairly stable in all countries, except for Poland, where it has been rising. In all the nations the composition of employment has been changing consistently, with the agricultural share declining. In each of the nations the growth rates of employment in industry and in the sector of material services have been about the same. The rate of productivity growth in agriculture has been higher in periods in which the outflow of labour was greater, indicating the presence of labour surplus in that sector.[1]

The respective estimates of the Kaldor and Verdoorn relations are as follows (standard errors in parentheses):

$$g_Y^T = 2.6 + 0.42\ g_Y^{IND} \qquad R^2 = 0.51 \tag{1}$$
$$\ (0.8)\ \ (0.09)$$

$$g_P^{IND} = 3.1 + 0.33\ g_Y^{IND} \qquad R^2 = 0.37 \tag{2}$$
$$\phantom{g_P^{IND} = 3.1}\ (0.9)\ \ (0.09)$$

where g stands for the growth rate of the variable indicated by the subscript (Y is output, P is labour productivity) in the sector indicated by the superscript (T stands for total economy, IND is industry). Although the fits are not particularly good, the two empirical relations indicate that industrial output growth in Eastern Europe has been positively related to both industrial labour productivity growth and the overall growth of the economy.

Is it safe to interpret these relationships as causal? Since total output includes industrial output, is equation (1) not spurious? Moreover, as I indicated in the preceding section, there are grounds to think of equation (2) as reflecting two relationships, one in which causality runs from g_P to g_Y and another in which it runs in the opposite direction. Is there a way of finding out which, if any, of these (causal) relationships has in fact dominated?

Some light on the significance of (1) is thrown by the following relations:

$$g_Y^{AGR} = -0.4 + 0.21\ g_Y^{IND} \qquad R^2 = 0.18 \tag{3}$$
$$\phantom{g_Y^{AGR} = -0.4}\ (0.9)\ \ (0.10)$$

$$g_Y^{MS} = 5.4 + 0.15\ g_Y^{IND} \qquad R^2 = 0.04 \tag{4}$$
$$\phantom{g_Y^{MS} = 5.4}\ (1.4)\ \ (0.16)$$

$$g_P^{AGR} = 0.5 + 0.39\ g_Y^{IND} \qquad R^2 = 0.23 \tag{5}$$
$$\phantom{g_P^{AGR} = 0.5}\ (1.4)\ \ (0.15)$$

Table 6.1: Economic growth in Eastern Europe: basic facts (growth rates are average annual, in per cent)

Country	Period	Industry (IND)				Agriculture (AGR)				Material services (MS)				Total (material) economy (T)			
		g_Y^{IND}	g_K^{IND}	g_L^{IND}	g_P^{IND}	g_Y^{AGR}	g_K^{AGR}	g_L^{AGR}	g_P^{AGR}	g_Y^{MS}	g_K^{MS}	g_L^{MS}	g_P^{MS}	g_Y^{T}	g_K^{T}	g_L^{T}	g_P^{T}
East Germany	1961–65	4.6	6.4	−0.2	4.8	1.8	6.5	−2.1	3.9	3.8	4.5	−1.9	5.7	3.6	5.9	−0.3	3.9
	1966–70	5.7	5.0	0.0	5.7	−0.8	5.6	−3.3	2.4	5.6	3.8	0.6	5.0	5.1	4.8	0.0	5.1
	1971–75	5.7	6.1	1.9	3.8	1.5	4.9	−2.1	3.6	5.2	4.9	1.0	4.3	5.2	5.7	0.1	5.1
Czechoslovakia	1956–60	8.5	4.4	3.3	5.2	0.0	5.0	−5.1	5.1	3.6	3.1	2.1	1.6	5.1	4.0	0.0	5.1
	1961–70	3.5	4.6	1.7	1.8	−2.1	4.7	−2.0	−0.1	4.5	3.6	1.5	2.9	4.2	4.3	0.9	3.3
	1971–75	5.9	5.4	0.0	5.9	1.9	5.6	−2.6	4.5	6.3	4.9	2.6	3.7	5.6	5.2	0.9	4.7
Yugoslavia	1961–65	9.8	9.2	4.1	5.6	3.1	4.7	−1.2	4.4	8.4	7.3	4.1	4.2	6.6	7.4	0.6	6.0
	1966–70	6.1	7.5	−0.2	6.4	3.5	4.1	−1.2	4.7	7.6	7.8	1.2	6.4	6.0	6.7	0.0	6.1
	1971–75	7.4	8.0	3.8	3.6	2.3	3.6	−2.1	4.4	5.2	7.3	4.5	0.8	5.8	6.9	0.7	5.1
Hungary	1961–65	6.9	7.1	1.9	5.0	0.0	3.6	−5.0	5.0	4.3	3.6	1.7	2.6	4.0	4.9	−0.4	4.4
	1966–70	7.0	6.8	2.1	4.9	1.2	5.7	−1.0	2.2	9.5	4.2	2.9	6.6	6.6	5.6	1.5	5.1
	1971–75	7.4	7.8	−0.4	7.8	1.5	7.8	−2.6	4.1	6.1	6.2	1.6	4.6	6.1	6.9	0.0	6.1

Poland	1956–60	7.4	7.2	1.7	5.7	3.0	1.2	0.0	3.0	8.2	3.1	1.2	7.1	5.0	4.0	1.1	3.8
	1961–65	9.5	6.6	3.6	5.9	1.4	2.3	0.2	1.2	4.8	4.7	2.3	2.5	6.0	4.5	1.4	4.6
	1966–70	7.7	7.6	2.6	5.1	1.0	3.9	0.2	0.8	7.6	5.4	2.6	4.9	4.6	6.0	1.8	2.8
	1971–75	9.5	9.2	1.7	7.8	0.0	4.7	0.2	−0.2	11.8	7.3	3.5	8.3	9.4	7.5	2.0	7.5
Bulgaria	1956–60	18.5	10.5	10.1	7.1	3.8	5.4	−5.8	9.5	5.0	3.2	5.2	1.8	8.7	6.3	−1.4	10.1
	1961–65	8.6	13.9	3.6	5.0	1.8	10.2	−4.1	5.9	7.6	5.4	5.4	2.2	6.1	10.0	−0.4	6.5
	1966–70	11.8	12.7	3.1	8.6	−0.8	7.0	−3.8	2.9	9.7	8.4	3.5	6.3	8.3	10.2	0.5	7.8
	1971–75	9.0	9.3	0.2	8.8	1.5	6.4	−4.0	5.5	9.0	8.9	1.0	8.1	7.8	8.6	0.2	7.6
Romania	1956–60	10.7	7.9	3.0	7.8	0.0	2.7	0.4	−0.4	3.1	3.3	1.2	2.0	4.2	4.9	0.0	4.2
	1961–68	12.8	9.5	5.9	7.0	3.5	4.0	−2.8	6.3	7.4	5.8	6.0	1.4	7.6	6.8	−0.1	7.7
	1966–70	12.1	12.1	4.1	7.9	2.3	6.1	−2.3	4.6	5.6	7.7	3.3	2.2	7.9	9.5	0.1	7.8
	1971–75	12.4	12.1	6.1	6.3	3.3	8.8	−4.5	7.8	9.4	8.8	3.1	6.3	10.7	10.6	0.2	10.5

Source: Calculated from data reported by Rudolf Nötel (1980). The original sources are all official.

Notes: g_Y is the growth of output, g_L is the growth of labour, g_K is the growth of capital, g_P is the growth of labour productivity.

$$g_P^{MS} = 6.1 + 0.23\ g_Y^{IND} \qquad R^2 = 0.09 \qquad (6)$$
$$\phantom{g_P^{MS} =}(1.4)\ (0.16)$$

$$g_P^{AGR} - 2.4 + 0.23\ g_P^{IND} \qquad R^2 = 0.02 \qquad (7)$$
$$\phantom{g_P^{AGR} -}(1.9)\ (0.31)$$

$$g_P^{MS} = 1.9 + 0.38\ g_P^{IND} \qquad R^2 = 0.07 \qquad (8)$$
$$\phantom{g_P^{MS} =}(1.8)\ (0.29)$$

where *AGR* is the symbol for agriculture and *MS* for material services sector. It may be observed that g_Y^{IND} has had a noticeable positive influence on g_P^{AGR}, but practically no influence on g_P^{MS}. The productivity growth rates in agriculture and material services are also seen to be independent of g_P^{IND}. How are we to interpret these results?

One should not be particularly surprised by the weak dependence of g_Y^{AGR} from g_Y^{IND}. In countries and periods of fast industrialisation industrial supplies for agriculture were rising slowly. The concern for agriculture has been considerably greater in more industrialised countries of the group, such as the GDR and Czechoslovakia. But these countries have also reached a degree of maturity, and therefore the growth rates of their industrial employment and output were relatively low. It therefore follows that g_Y^{IND} is probably a poor proxy for the growth rate of industrial supplies to agriculture.

Equations (1) to (3) together indicate that it was the variation in the rate of expansion of the manufacturing sector alone, rather than the influence of its output upon the growth of other sectors, that differentiated the overall growth performance of the Eastern European nations. This variation in industrial output growth was in turn due, above all, to wide variation in industrial employment growth; the major source of industrial employment growth was the activation of agricultural labour surplus.

Another factor differentiating the rate of growth of industrial output among these nations was the rate of growth of industrial labour productivity as shown by equation (2). There are three alternative interpretations of this equation. One is that the rate of innovation was constant over time and the same across countries, and therefore (2) reflects (static and/or dynamic) economies of scale in industry. Another interpretation would be that the innovation rate varies among countries and over time. In particular, the rate was higher in the less industrialised countries, such as Bulgaria and Romania, which through imitation, licensing and machinery imports, had been gaining from international technological diffusion more than the technologically more advanced countries, such as the GDR and Czechoslovakia. The former countries happened to be also those which had a labour surplus in agriculture. Therefore, once the investment rate was raised sufficiently, they were able to increase both the industrial labour force and labour productivity faster than the latter countries. This gave rise to the significance of equation (2). A third interpretation would be simply a superimposition of the economies of scale hypothesis (first interpretation) and what may be called the Gerschenkron hypothesis (second interpretation).

The data in Table 6.1 are instructive. They show g_P^{MS} to be very low in Romania in the years 1956–70 and in Bulgaria in the years 1956–65. But the growth rate has increased sharply more recently. Industry was initially very much the priority sector, itself using up most of its output. Therefore one must expect the time-lags in spreading qualitative improvements from industry to other sectors to be long, certainly longer than the five-year time unit which we have adapted.[2]

3. VARIATION IN PRODUCTIVITY GROWTH: ECONOMIES OF SCALE VERSUS DIFFUSIONAL EFFECT

It has been widely noted that the relationship of the Verdoorn type, of which equation (2) is an example, would arise in the presence of economies of scale. In this case the causality would run from g_Y to g_P rather than the other way around, as would be the case if the diffusional effect was the dominant factor varying g_P. In Gomulka (1982) I tested the explanatory power of these two effects for the industrial sector. The main result of this test appears helpful in judging the plausibility of the two interpretations of equation (2) that are spelled out in section 2. In this 1982 study, the Soviet Union replaced Yugoslavia, and the other six East European countries for which the test was conducted were the same as in this paper. The time coverage was the same.

Suppose that $Y = K^{a_1} L^{a_2} e^{\lambda t}$. The sum $a_1 + a_2$ is the scale elasticity. It follows that:

$$g_P = a_1 g_k + s g_L + \lambda, \tag{11}$$

where $s = a_1 + a_2 - 1$, the returns to scale coefficient, and $k = K/L$.

By substituting $g_v + g_Y$ for g_K, where $v = K/Y$, and $g_Y - g_P$ for g_L, we also get that

$$g_P = \frac{s}{a_2} g_Y + \frac{a_1}{a_2} g_v + \frac{1}{a_2} \lambda. \tag{12}$$

If both the capital/output ratio and the (Hicks) rate of technological progress are constant, equation (12) collapses into the Verdoorn relationship, such as (2). Since in centrally-planned economies industrial output is constrained by the supply of inputs rather than by demand for outputs, equation (11) rather than (12) may be thought to be more appropriate for estimating the scale coefficient. As we wish to relate the explanatory power of the two alternative interpretations of equation (2) that are discussed above, equation (11) must be amended to allow for the possibility that international diffusion of technology influences the rate of technological change. In the period 1950–75 machinery imports by each of the seven countries originated mainly in the other six countries of the group, East Germany and Czechoslovakia being the primary sources. The seven undertook also to exchange freely or at a token price the inventive output of their R & D sectors. In the light of this practice I have altered the specification of (11) to read:

$$g_P = a_1 g_k + s g_L + \gamma x + \lambda, \tag{13}$$

where x stands for the relative (labour) productivity gap between any specific country and the productivity leader among the seven at a given time. I expected γ, the technological gap coefficient, to be positive.

Equation (13) was estimated to give the following result:

$$g_P = 0.24 g_k + 0.11 g_L + 1.4x + 3.6, \qquad \bar{R}^2 = 0.366. \tag{14}$$
$$\quad (0.12) \quad (0.15) \quad (0.5) \quad (0.95)$$

The scale coefficient is positive, indicating the presence of increasing returns to scale, but its standard error is large. When the coefficient is restricted to be zero, there was little loss in the error sum of squares, and $\bar{R}^2$ was in fact higher. When γ was restricted to be zero, the results were:

$$g_P = 0.31 g_k + 0.33 g_L + 3.7 \qquad \bar{R}^2 = 0.180. \tag{15}$$
$$\quad (0.13) \quad (0.15) \quad (1.1)$$

Specification (15), if regarded as a sub-model of (14), fails to pass the F-ratio significance test, the probability that $\gamma = 0$ being less than 5 per cent. Although this significance test is not decisive, since it assumes that equation (14) is the true specification which it may not be, the gap variable in that equation does appear to command a significantly greater explanatory power than the scale variable.[3]

4. CONCLUSION

The key role assigned to the industrial sector has been, in the post-war period, a critical element of the economic strategy that was adopted in the seven centrally-planned economies of Eastern Europe studied in this paper. The first major finding of the paper is that it was the variation in the rate of expansion of the industrial sector alone, rather than the influence of its output (or output growth) upon the growth of other sectors, that had differentiated the overall output growth rate among the seven countries in the years 1955–75. The industrial sector has been expanding particularly fast in the least developed countries of the region: Bulgaria, Romania, Yugoslavia and Poland. In these countries industrial employment and labour productivity were both increasing rapidly. Evidence presented in the paper suggests—and this is the second finding worth noting—that this was due to the industrial sector being able to activate two major growth reserves, the agricultural labour surplus of their own countries and the accumulated technology of their more advanced neighbours. It was also found that productivity growth neither in the material services sector nor in the agricultural sector was positively related to industrial productivity growth.

NOTES

1. The relevant relationship has been as follows (standard errors in parentheses)

$$g_P^{AGR} = 1.3 - 1.04g_L^{AGR} \qquad R^2 = 0.60.$$
$$\phantom{g_P^{AGR} = } (0.5) \ (0.18)$$

2. In the second interpretation I have, more or less, equated the rate of innovation with the rate of growth of labour productivity, thus ignoring any productivity effect of changes in the capital : labour ratio. This point may be met if we were able to calculate the joint input productivity residuals and substitute these for the growth rates of labour productivity in equations (7) and (8). Alas, the estimation of such residuals is fraught with well-known difficulties. But to illustrate the implications of this substitution to some extent, let us assume that the

underlying production function is of the Cobb–Douglas type and that returns to scale are constant. I have calculated such productivity residuals. I assume furthermore that capital elasticity is common in all three sectors, equal to 0.2, 0.3 and 0.4. In all three cases the regression results were qualitatively quite similar to those indicated by equations (7) and (8). For example, when 0.3 is taken for the capital elasticity, the results are

$$\lambda^{AGR} = 0.1 + 0.32\lambda^{IND} \qquad \bar{R}^2 = 0.06 \qquad (9)$$
$$\qquad\quad (1.2) \ (0.27)$$

$$\lambda^{MS} = \ 3.1 + 0.3\lambda^{IND} \qquad \bar{R}^2 = 0.001 \qquad (10)$$
$$\qquad\quad (1.3) \ (0.28)$$

where $\lambda = g_Y = 0.3g_K - 0.7g_L$. The effort to upgrade the quality of the capital and labour inputs has clearly not gone to all the three sectors at the same time.

3. For the data in Table 6.1 of this paper g_L^{IND} has no explanatory power to account for variations in g_P^{IND}, the relationship being as follows:

$$g_P^{IND} = 5.8 + 0.05g_L^{IND}, \text{ and } R^2 = 0.005.$$
$$\quad (0.5) \ (0.15)$$

REFERENCES

Alton, T. P., 'Production and Resource Allocation in Eastern Europe: Performance, Problems, and Prospects', in *East European Economic Assessment*, Joint Economic Committee, Congress of the United States, July 1981.

Cornwall, J., *Modern Capitalism, Its Growth and Transformation*, Oxford: Martin Robertson, 1977.

Eversley, J., Gomulka, S. and Kowalski, W, *The LSE Bank of Industrial Data for Eastern Europe,* 1980.

Gomulka, S. 'Britain's Slow Industrial Growth: Increasing Inefficiency versus Low Rate of Technological Change', In Beckerman, W. (ed.), *Slow Growth in Britain: Causes and Consequences*, Oxford, 1979.

Gomulka, S., 'Kaldor's Stylized Facts, Dynamic Economies of Scale and Diffusional Effect in Productivity Growth', mimeo, 1982.

McCombie, J. S. L., 'What Still Remains of Kaldor's Law?' *Economic Journal*, March 1981.

Nötel, R., 'Capital, Labour and Net Material Product 1950–1975', *Papers in East European Economics*, no. 59, St Anthony's College, Oxford, 1980.

Stafford, G. B., *The End of Economic Growth? Growth and Decline in the UK since 1945*, Oxford: Martin Robertson, 1981.

7 Soviet Post-war Industrial Growth, Capital–Labour Substitution, and Technical Changes: A Re-examination*

Over the recent years a broad consensus has been reached that whatever the origin of the data, Soviet or western, the Soviet Union has experienced a major retardation in the post-war growth of its industrial output without a slowdown of the same magnitude in the growth of inputs. In the debate on the causes of slowdown several alternative interpretations have been offered. They could be classified into two groups, which are homogeneous enough to be regarded as simply two alternative interpretations. One interpretation, which I shall call the standard explanation (Balassa, Bergson, Brubaker, Kaplan, Moorsteen and Powell, Noren, and others),

*An earlier draft of this chapter was presented to the Banff 1974 International Conference, September 1974, and to Professor Bergson's seminar at Harvard University. Extensive numerical experiments, which proved very helpful in the formulation of the final model were done by Jerzy Sylwestrowicz of the London School of Economics aided by Joanna Gomulka from the Numerical Optimisation Centre (NOC) at Hatfield Polytechnic. The computer programs used at NOC have been developed by Michael Riggs and John J. McKeown. I am also indebted to Padma Desai for providing me with her man-hours estimates for 1966–71, as well as with her unpublished estimates of Soviet industrial data at the branch level. For suggestions, comments and criticism, my thanks are due to Abram Bergson, Stanley Cohen, Philip Hanson, Raymond Hutchings, Oldrych Kyn, Judith Thornton, Martin Weitzman, Peter Wiles and Alfred Zauberman. I am also indebted to Raymond Hutchings for his invitation to write this paper for the Banff Conference and to Zbigniew Fallenbuchl for editing it.

Reprinted with permission from Fallenbuchl, Z. (ed.), *Economic Development in the Soviet Union*, vol. 2, *Sectoral Analysis*, © 1976 Praeger Publishers with the omission of Tables 2–5 and Figures 3, 4, 5, 8 and 9, and the inclusion of some minor revisions by the author.

assumes that capital's (imputed) share in output was essentially constant over time and stresses the notion that except for the period 1954–58 the growth rate of technical progress, or the so-called productivity residual, was gradually declining.[1] In contrast, the other explanation (Weitzman, Desai, and others) suggests that the Soviet growth record is adequately accounted for by the productivity residual constant over time and the elasticity of capital–labour substitution significantly less than one, the combination implying a sharp decline in the (imputed) capital share.[2]

Within the standard approach the following are thought to be the primary reasons for decreased growth in the productivity residual: (i) diminishing decline in the average age of capital goods during the 1950s,[3] (ii) decline in organisational efficiency, especially in the post-1958 period, because of increased complexity of resource allocation,[4] (iii) post-war recovery from wartime disruption in the period 1947–55,[5] (iv) change in the structure of production more favourable to growth in the 1950s,[6] (v) decline in the rate of increase in the educational attainment of the labour force,[7] (vi) increased difficulty to allocate resources efficiently within almost unchanged institutional arrangements.[8]

However, with one exception the standard approach has largely failed to offer any quantitative estimate of the above listed potentially contributing factors.[9] Consequently, it has failed to identify the relative importance of these factors and thereby the exact causes of growth retardation. Being a qualitative statement rather than a quantitative one, the standard explanation is also not very helpful in making judgements concerning future Soviet industrial growth performance.

In contrast, Weitzman's study offered not only an alternative explanation, but also a more rigorous approach. His emphasis on low elasticity of substitution as the most likely factor contributing to slowdown generated a wide interest in estimating various CES (constant elasticity of substitution) and VES (variable elasticity of substitution) production functions for the Soviet industry as a whole, as well as for its individual industrial branches. Although the results vary widely in terms of the estimated parameters, they largely tend to support Weitzman's major hypothesis that in Soviet industry of the post-1950 period the productivity residual was stable over time and that the (imputed) capital share was instead sharply declining.

Yet, I shall argue in this study that Weitzman's hypothesis may be incorrect. As a first step, attention will be drawn to certain peculiar properties of the labour productivity data. In view of these properties, a case will be made that the technical progress terms in the production functions estimated so far may have been (mis)specified in a manner that crucially affected the estimation results as well as the implied interpretations. This point applies especially to the Weitzman-type interpretation. Third, a new economic interpretation of slowdown will be developed. It will be based on a new specification of the technical progress terms. This specification attempts to capture the growth effects of several phenomena that were so far either assumed to be unimportant (Weitzman, Desai) or only verbally mentioned as potentially relevant (the standard approach). Two such phenomena are claimed in this study to have been of major importance: (a) the post-war recovery trend in technical progress, to be referred throughout as the post-war recovery factor (PRF), and (b) a 20 per cent reduction in the annual number of working hours per man in the period 1956–61. The growth effects of these two phenomena are estimated and their prominent role in the post-war industrial growth scenario discussed. Also estimated are growth effects of changes in the branch composition of production, in the age composition of fixed capital, and in the 'sub-vintage composition' of investments. All these three growth effects are found to be comparatively much less significant than (a) and (b).

The major claims of this study are as follows: (i) When the growth effects (a) and (b) are taken into account, then the Soviet industrial growth record is explained well by a CES production function with technical progress of predominately labour-saving type; (ii) the rate of technical progress is suggested to have been a sum of three components. Two of these components, associated with phenomena (a) and (b) respectively, were variable over time and transitory. They were superimposed on a third, constant term, which is associated with a long-run trend in technical progress; (iii) the error sum of squares is found to be almost insensitive to variations in the (assumed constant over time) value of the elasticity of substitution.

Finding (ii)—in particular the fact that the assumption of constant long-run term in the residual is found consistent with data—seems to be in variance with the notion of long-run downward trend in Soviet economic efficiency, although the latter might well have been low all along. On the other hand, findings (i) and (iii) are at variance with Weitzman's hypothesis that serious difficulties in substituting capital for labour have been the main cause of the Soviet growth slowdown. Moreover, finding (i) combined with a moderate increase in the Soviet industrial capital/output ratio implies the (imputed) capital share to be almost constant over time, irrespective of the value of the capital–labour elasticity of substitution. This result supports the basic assumption of the traditional school. All the findings imply—and this is the central hypothesis of this study—that instead of either low magnitude of the elasticity of substitution or a decline in economic efficiency, and apart from the effect of some decline in the growth rate of labour and capital, the variable components of technical progress associated with phenomena (a) and (b) may have alone been responsible for slowdown in the output growth, at least until 1973.

Concluding this introduction, it should be emphasised that, of course, this study is not an attempt to set forth definitive conclusions about the factors underlying the retardation in growth. The margin of error that still remains present, weak theoretical underpinnings of the aggregate production function and unavoidable pitfalls of the estimation techniques, cannot simply allow for this. Therefore other interpretations, and in particular interpretations of the Weitzman-type, cannot now, and indeed may never, be ruled out as possible alternatives.

1. PRESENTATION OF BASIC DATA AND THEIR PRELIMINARY INTERPRETATION

The basic facts of Soviet industrial growth are given in Table 7.1 (see Data Appendix). [10] However, it will prove useful to present these facts also in the form of several diagrams. The purpose of this presentation is to see whether a search for a correct specification of the production function can be helped by revealing the time trends that have underlined the growth of Soviet industry in the period 1928–73.

In Figure 7.1, a decline in the growth rate of output is seen to be fairly systematic, though much more evident in the years 1948–52. The growth rate of labour (in man-hours) is somewhat irregular, with a downward trend relatively weak. The growth rate of labour productivity was in the years 1947–51 extremely high, despite the fact that the capital/output ratio was at that time falling. One inevitably thinks that we see here, in the years 1947–51 at least, an imprint of the extraordinary opportunities for rapid growth operating during the post-war reconstruction period.

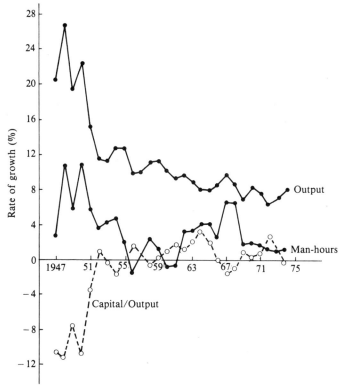

Figure 7.1: Basic facts of Soviet post-war industrial growth: annual percentage growth rates of output, labour in terms of man-hours, and capital output ratio.
Source: Data Appendix, Table 7.1.

Figure 7.2 reveals an interesting regularity in the growth rate of output per man-hour. It is seen that rather than a slowdown in this rate there was in fact a jumpdown in 1962 from a high level of about 10 per cent prevailing until 1961, to a level of about 5 per cent prevailing since 1962. A slowdown may however be detected in the growth rate of output per worker. The years of rapid growth of output per man-hour are seen more clearly in Figure 7.3. Two observations can be made: (i) the years 1947–61 are exceptional for both the pre-war and the post-war growth experience; (ii) they follow a six-year period (1941–46) of negative growth of output per man-hour. Also, there appear to be two distinct sub-periods of the 1947–61 period, 1957–53 and 1954–61. Just from inspection of Figure 7.3 one may be tempted to associate the effect of the PRF

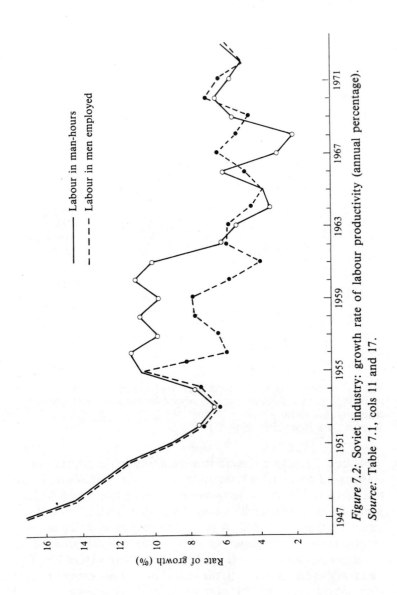

Figure 7.2: Soviet industry: growth rate of labour productivity (annual percentage).
Source: Table 7.1, cols 11 and 17.

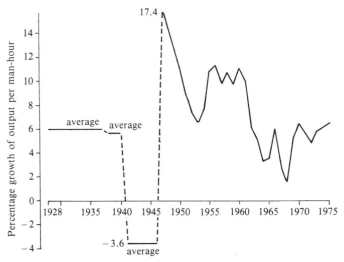

Figure 7.3: Soviet industry, 1928–75: Changes in the growth rate of labour productivity (labour in man-years).
Source: 1928–66, Gomulka (1976, Fig. 1.3); 1967–75, Table 8.1.

only with the first of the two sub-periods. One thus has to look for a separate explanation of the high growth record in the years 1954–61.

Let us now turn to Figure 7.4. The level of labour productivity, the index of working hours, and the capital/output ratio are all given on the logarithmic scale. The growth rate of these variables is thus given by the slope of the respective curves. The period 1947–73 may now be seen to fall into four separate sub-periods: (a) 1947–55, (b) 1965–61, (c) 1962–68, and (d) 1969–73. In 1946 the level of output was equal to about 0.74 of the 1944 level. In that year the level of output per man-hour was also at the bottom, being just about 0.85 of the 1944 level and about 0.8 of the 1940 level, the latter being despite the fact that the 1946 capital/output ratio was at the level of about 1.25 of the 1940 capital/output ratio. Clearly two powerful phenomena were then operating: war destruction and the post-war major reduction in the production of arms. A switch from war to peace economy needed time, resulting in the fall of both output and labour productivity in 1946. But from 1947 the labour productivity was increasing rapidly, though with a gradually declining rate of growth as the distance to the long-run trend was diminishing. In period (b) there was, however, a significant increase in this growth rate. This is the same period of six

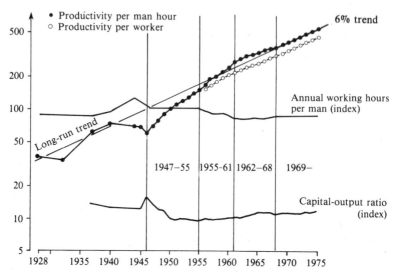

Figure 7.4: Basic facts of Soviet industrial growth, 1928–75.
Source: 1928–66, Gomulka (1976, Fig. 1.4); 1967–75, Table 8.1.

years when the annual number of working hours per man was being reduced at the average annual rate of about 3.6 per cent. My reading of Figure 7.4 is that the policy in period (b) was to keep the old tempo of gains in the productivity per man rather than per man-hour. An increased labour efficiency was needed for this policy to succeed. Several measures to this end must have been taken and the policy was apparently successful.[11] From this preliminary interpretation it would appear that (b) was a period when the economic efficiency was, over time, increasingly above its 1955 level. The extra pressure applied to keep the labour productivity high would then be expected to end by the end of 1961 when the reduction in working hours per man was completed. A sudden relaxation of tension in the following years should then result in at least partial, if not full, return of the overall efficiency to its 'equilibrium' level. (c) would thus be a transitory period when the reduction in the number of annual working hours per man finally showed up in a decreased growth rate of labour productivity in terms of both per man and per man-hour.

From the above broad interpretation of data it would follow, first, that periods (b) and (c) are interlinked in the sense that period (c) absorbed a delayed effect of what happened in period (b). This created a characteristic gap between above 'normal' performance in the years 1956–61 and below 'normal' performance in the following several years. Second, only from about 1970 the growth rate of labour productivity has been moving in the proximity of its long-run trend path of about 6.0 per cent gain per annum.

Finally, let us turn to the trends in investments and capital. Since 1950 there has been a moderate decline both in the share of the industrial investments in the total state investments and in the ratio of the industrial gross investments to the industrial value-added. But because the growth rate of the industrial value-added declined quite rapidly, we have a definite downward trend in the growth rate of (gross) industrial investments. The latter was more or less the same as the growth rate of the total GNP, which was somewhat less than the growth rate of industrial output. Thus, the growth rate of capital must imitate, though clearly with some delay, the growth rate of output. My preliminary interpretation of these data is, therefore, that the reason for the decreased growth rate of investment and (recently) capital is the slowdown in output, not the other way around.[12] Of course, a slowdown in the growth of capital stock is likely to contribute to a further slowdown in output; these two variables are closely interlinked. But my working hypothesis is, first, that the chain of events along a path down the hill toward a long-run growth equilibrium was set by an external factor, namely by an extraordinary starting point on this path in 1947. And second, that after 1955 this movement toward the equilibrium was seriously disturbed by another external factor, namely by the 20 per cent reduction in the work year introduced in the years 1956–61.

2. PRELIMINARY TEST WITH A PRODUCTION FUNCTION: PERIOD 1951–73

Our preliminary interpretation of the data still has many loose ends, and the aim of the rest of this paper is to make this interpretation more precise. The first priority will be given to finding a good specification of the production function. Somewhat arbitrarily, I want this specification to satisfy the following three requirements: (1) to have high explanatory power in terms of the error sum of squares, with the essential parameters statistically significant; (2) to imply that the asymptotic growth rate of labour productivity is at a reasonable level, say in the range of 4 to 6 per cent; and (3) to take an account of both the post-war opportunities for rapid growth and the growth effect on the productivity per man-hour of the 20 per cent reduction in working hours in the years

1956–61. A CES production function estimated by Weitzman satisfies (1), but it implies that the growth rate of labour productivity will continue to decline until it reaches a 2 per cent level, which I regard as too low. Moreover, his interpretation assumes (3) to have been unimportant for the post-1950 years.

Our tests cover data for the years 1951–73. These are Weitzman's data for the period 1951–68[13] extended by Soviet official data for the years 1969–73 (see Table 7.1, columns 4, 8 and 10). To reduce the influence of multicollinearity, a CES production function to be estimated is expressed directly in terms of growth rates, rather than in terms of levels or loglevels:

$$g_{Y,t} = \pi_t(g_{K,t} + \lambda_1) + (1 - \pi_t)(g_{L^*,t} + \lambda_{2,t}) \tag{1}$$

where $\pi_t \equiv \delta\gamma^{-\varrho}e^{-\lambda_1\varrho t}v_t^{-\varrho}$ = elasticity of output with respect to capital, $v_t \equiv K_t/Y_t$ = capital : output ratio, $\varrho = (1 - \sigma)/\sigma$, σ = elasticity of substitution, $g_{Y,t}$ = output growth rate, $g_{K,t}$ = capital growth rate, and $g_{L^*,t}$ = growth rate of labour in man-hours, $t = 1951, 1952, \ldots, 1973$. Moreover, we shall assume that:

$$\lambda_{2,t} = \begin{array}{ll} \lambda_2 + \epsilon & \text{for } t = 1951, \ldots, 1961 \\ \\ \lambda_2 & \text{for } t = 1962, \ldots, 1973 \end{array} \tag{2}$$

The terms λ_1 and $\lambda_{2,t}$ in equation (1) are the rates of, respectively, the capital-augmenting and the labour-augmenting components of (disembodied) technical changes. In contrast to Weitzman's specification, we not only allow these rates to differ but also permit the possibility that the rate of the labour-augmenting component of technical change was in the years 1951–61 (sub-periods (a) and (b)) different by ϵ from that in the following years 1962–73 (sub-periods (c) and (d)). Of course, we expect ϵ to be positive. In this admittedly crude manner we want to meet our requirement (3). Equation (1) is estimated directly, using an algorithm similar to that employed by Weitzman. The results are as follows:

$\hat{\sigma} = 0.392, \hat{\lambda}_1 = 0.008, \hat{\lambda}_2 = 0.047, \hat{\epsilon} = 0.040, \hat{\delta} = 0.463$
$\hat{\gamma} = 0.986$, and ESS $= 2.34 \times 10^{-3}, \bar{R}^2 = 0.6823$

For comparison, the more restricted hypothesis $\lambda_1 = \lambda_2$, $\epsilon = 0$, which reduces equation (1) to Weitzman's specification, gives these results:

$\hat{\sigma} = 0.487, \hat{\lambda}_1 = \hat{\lambda}_2 = 0.030, \hat{\delta} = 0.579, \hat{\gamma} = 0.741$,
ESS $= 3.06 \times 10^{-3}, \bar{R}^2 = 0.6292$

It is seen here that the error sum of squares (ESS) is increased by 31 per cent. Applying the F-test we find that at the 95 per cent confidence level we would have to reject the hypothesis that the more restricted specification is the true functional form. Although the size of our sample of observations is such that we should not put too much confidence in the results of statistical tests designed for large samples, I am nevertheless inclined to interpret this particular result as an indication that equations (1) and (2) offer at least as good an explanation of the data as does the specification given by Weitzman. Moreover, we shall later be able to decrease the ESS considerably further.

The implied time series of imputed capital's share π_t is given in Table 7.2 of the original version of this paper, but not reprinted here. (See 2. Fallenbuchl (ed.), *Economic Development in the Soviet Union, vol. 2, Sectoral Analysis.*) Note a much slower decline in our π_t compared with that implied by Weitzman's hypothesis. This is despite the fact that our elasticity of substitution is also significantly less than one. This result is implied by the fact that the really essential variable affecting π is the type of technical change, not the elasticity of substitution. The type of technical change implied by Weitzman's hypothesis is strongly capital-saving in the Harrod sense, whereas under specification 1 it is almost neutral. We may note that when technical change is purely labour-saving and the capital/output ratio is constant, then the magnitude of the elasticity of substitution is irrelevant. This is so because then the capital/labour ratio, where labour is expressed in efficiency units, would be constant over time. It therefore follows that if technical changes in Soviet industry have actually been predominantly labour-saving, then in view of the relatively small changes in the capital/output ratio (small especially in the 1950s) the emphasis on difficulties in substituting capital for labour as a probable cause of slowdown would be misdirected. The emphasis should instead be on those factors that are likely to have contributed to a decline in the rate of this (predominantly labour-saving) technical change. This decline in our preliminary test is represented by ϵ. It is a decline between the 1951–61 period and the 1962–73 period. Its magnitude is 4.0 per cent. Another implication of our test production function is that the asymptotic growth rate of labour productivity would be 4.7 per cent. Thus the function also meets our requirement (2). We shall develop this test production function much further later in this paper. The error and sensitivity analysis is postponed until then.

3. ESTIMATION OF THREE 'EXTRA' GROWTH EFFECTS

Apart from the catch-up effect and the working-hours effect, there are at least three other factors that might have been captured by our ϵ. These are (1) a change in the branch composition of employment, (2) a change in the age composition of capital, and (3) a change in the rate of diffusion of the foreign-made technology. I call (1) the branch-composition effect, (2) the age-composition effect, and (3) the diffusional effect. Before proceeding with our search for a best specification of the production function, we shall attempt to obtain an approximate estimate of the magnitude of these three effects.

The branch-composition effect
The growth rate of aggregate labour productivity in industry as a whole could in the 1950s be relatively higher because labour employed in branches with a low level of labour productivity was then expanding relatively less rapidly than in the 1960s. My calculations show, however, that this branch composition effect was fairly minor. [14] It contributed only about -0.1 per cent annually in the 1950s and about -0.3 per cent annually in the 1960s. These calculations are based on Weitzman's value-added weights, [15] but the result does not change if Desai's weights are applied instead. The standard 11 industrial branches are distinguished. The relative difference of 0.2 per cent in favour of the 1950s could perhaps be increased if the level of disaggregation was higher. I did not have enough data to pursue such an inquiry, but my feeling is that the result would not be much different.

The age-composition effect
Assuming that technical progress is partly of an embodied type, the average level of labour productivity would be a function of the age composition of the capital stock. A decrease (increase) in the average age of this capital is then an extra factor contributing positively (negatively) to the labour productivity growth rate. In my calculations of this contribution I assumed (1) the age composition of machines matters only, so that the stock of structures is ignored; (2) machines are a constant fraction of the total stock of the fixed capital; (3) all machines have the same service life; (4) one-third of each capital vintage added to the capital stock before 1942 was destroyed during the war; and (5) there is a two-year delay before a newly-produced machine is actually employed. Assumptions (4)

and (5) are approximately consistent with the Soviet official investment and capital stock data from 1940. On the basis of all these assumptions I calculated the average life of machines:

$$u_i(t) = \sum_{\tau=t}^{t-n_i+1} (t-\tau)I_{\tau-2} \Bigg/ \left(\sum_{\tau=t}^{t-n_i+1} I_{\tau-2} \right) \tag{3}$$

where the time subscript is running from $t = 1948$ to $t = 1973$, and where n_i is the maximum service life, the subscript i referring to the i's alternative. Eight alternatives were considered: $n_1 = 12$, $n_2 = 13$, ..., $n_8 = 19$. The results are reported in Table 3 (of the original version of this paper). It is seen that for all these alternatives the average age was declining markedly from 1948, to reach a minimum sometime in the period 1954–58. That minimum was about 0.6 years below the 1948 level. Since 1956–58 the average age was increasing again to reach, in 1973, a level of some 0.3 to 0.7 above the 1948 level. These findings indicate that for slowdown in the growth of output the age-composition effect could have been a contributing factor. The actual size of this contribution depends on the extent to which technical changes in Soviet industry have been of embodied-type. It may be instructive to illustrate this point using Soviet investment data. Assume technical changes to be purely labour-augmenting and capital/output ratio the same for all vintages. Then we can find the labour productivity on vintage τ, expressed as a fraction of the labour productivity on vintage 1948,

$$y_\tau(t) = (1+\alpha)^{\tau-1948}(1+\beta)^{t-1948}$$
$$\tau \le t, \qquad \tau, t = 1948, 1949, \ldots, 1973 \tag{4}$$

where α is the rate of embodied technical change and β is the rate of disembodied technical change. We can also find the labour productivity for the industry as a whole:

$$y(t) = \sum_{\tau=t}^{t-n_i+1} (I_{\tau-2}) \Bigg/ \left\{ \sum_{\tau=t}^{t-n_i-1} [I_{\tau-2}/y_\tau(t)] \right\} \tag{5}$$

When $\alpha = 0$, then $y(t) = y_\tau(t)$ for all τ, so that the age composition of machines is irrelevant. I computed the growth rate of $y(t)$, denoted by $g_y(t)$, for six pairs of α, β, from $\alpha = 1$ per cent, $\beta = 5$ per cent to $\alpha = 6$ per cent, $\beta = 0$ per cent. In Table 4 (see original paper) a sample of the results is given. It is seen that $g_y(t)$ is at the bottom in the early 1960s and, generally, is higher during the 1950s than during the 1960s, the difference being in the range from about 0.1 per cent ($\alpha = 1$, $\beta = 5$) to about 0.8 per cent ($\alpha = 5$, $\beta = 1$). It would appear that this was the order of magnitude of the contribution of the age-composition change to slowdown in the labour productivity growth. The contribution could actually be even smaller if in the 1960s the average service life of machines was reduced. An approximate rule is that such a reduction by k years, $k = 1, 2, \ldots$, implies a reduction in the figures quoted above, 0.1 per cent and 0.8 per cent, by about $0.03\alpha k$ per cent.

Diffusional effect [16]

On the grounds of both theoretical arguments and empirical evidence it seems that for much of the world, with the notable exception of the United States, diffusion of foreign-made innovations is at present the single most important agent of technical change, and therefore also the key factor of the labour productivity growth. This 'law' seems to apply for the market-oriented economies as well as for economies of the Soviet-type, including the Soviet Union itself. [17] One thus has to explore a possibility that the collapse in the labour productivity growth in 1962 was a result of a sudden change in policy, or in socioeconomic environment, which has significantly reduced the growth rate of diffusion after 1961 compared with that prevailing until 1961. The growth rate of disembodied diffusion (licences, patents, technological espionage, scientific journals, exchange of personnel) could well be declining in the 1950s as the more readily available western advances in science and technology made during the war were gradually absorbed by Soviet research and development (R & D) sector. But there seems to be no evidence to indicate a sudden, large-scale decline in that rate by about 1960 or 1961.

There remains diffusion of the embodied type (import of investment goods incorporating new foreign-made technology). Elsewhere I made an attempt to compute the growth effect of Soviet imports of investment goods. [18] Table 5 gives six alternative sets of results. The absolute values of these results vary considerably, especially for the 1950s. But their common characteristic feature is a gradual decline of the growth effect in the 1950s, rather than a sudden jumpdown at the beginning of the 1960s.

We therefore reject the hypothesis that our ϵ in equation (2), estimated to be 4 per cent, captures a change in the diffusional effect. There is however some evidence for a gradual decline in that effect. This will be used in the next section to support our interpretation of the notion of 'post-war recovery trend'.

4. THE LONG-RUN TREND AND THE POST-WAR RECOVERY TREND

Let us come back again to the labour productivity data. These data are very important for two reasons. First, the growth rate of the labour/output ratio was in Soviet industry generally very high (in absolute terms) and subject to major changes over time. In contrast, the growth rate of the capital/output ratio was generally low and subject to relatively minor changes over time. Second, at the Soviet capital/output ratio changing slowly and at the technical changes predominantly Harrod-neutral, the productivity residual in the Hicks sense (respectively in the Harrod sense) is approximately proportional (equal) to the growth rate of labour productivity. Therefore a careful study of the dynamics of the latter growth rate should help greatly to specify more correctly the functional form of the technical progress terms, the labour-augmenting term especially.

The labour productivity per man-hour is denoted by y^*, and its 1937–73 long-run trend value by y_{tr}^*. The latter was already identified in Figure 7.4. The values of both y^* and y_{tr}^* are given in Table 7.1. Of particular interest is the difference $y_{tr}^* - y^*$, or rather the relative difference $(y_{tr}^* - y^*)/y_{tr}^*$. Let us denote it by x. Clearly x measures the relative distance of labour productivity from its long-run 'trend' path. The 'normal' state of affairs is when x is equal or close to zero. A significant deviation of x from zero level is brought about by factors which for a particular type of economy in a particular technological epoch are 'abnormal'.

The terms 'normal' and 'abnormal' should be used with care. They are meaningful only if the notion of the labour productivity 'trend' is meaningful. The assumption implicitly made in Figure 7.4 is that in the period 1937–73 the trend growth rate in labour productivity was constant. This may be questioned on the grounds that throughout that time the actual growth rate of capital, employment and output were highly unbalanced and that, as a result of destructive war, their trend growth paths must have changed permanently, as they no doubt did. However, what applies to such economic variables as capital, employment and output does not necessarily apply to their ratios, in particular to the capital/output ratio.

The following three observations can in fact be made in defence of the notion of the labour productivity constant trend.

1. Note that when technical changes are Harrod-neutral and

when returns to scale are constant, then:

$$Y_t = F(K_t, A_t L_t^*)$$

where A_t is the level of technical advance, L_t^* is employment in man-hours, K_t stands for capital, the Y_t is value-added. On dividing this equation by AL^* and solving the resulting equation with respect to $Y/(AL^*)$, we have:

$$y_t^* = h(v_t)A_t$$

where $y_t^* = Y_t/L_t^*$ and $v_t = K_t/Y_t$. Thus when the capital/output ratio v_t is relatively stable over time, the labour productivity is approximately proportional to the level of technical advance. From Figure 7.4 it is seen that in the period 1937–73 the Soviet industrial capital/output ratio was in fact fairly stable, though far from being exactly constant. In 1973 the value of v was only about 10 per cent below its 1937 level, implying about (-0.3) per cent annual average growth rate. Hence it follows that in the long run y_t^* is nearly proportional to A_t, so that the trend growth rates in labour productivity and in technical progress are about the same.

2. Observation (1) switches attention from labour productivity changes to technical changes. During the war the growth rate of Soviet technical changes was probably significantly depressed, especially in those sectors that were not of immediate importance to the war effort. This proposition does not apply, however, to the world technological environment in which the Soviet economy operates. Indeed, the average annual growth rate of output per man-hour in the US manufacturing sector in the years 1930–50 was about the same as it was in the following period, 1951–70 (2.1 per cent and 2.35 per cent, respectively).[19] This is despite the Great Depression in the 1930s and the fact that much of the world R & D sector in the years 1940–45 was at the service of the defence industries. Apparently most of the technical advances made then were later found useful also in civilian industries. So it does not seem unreasonable to suppose that the trend growth rate of the US (and possibly also Western European) technological level was not affected much by the war. This war could still have changed the trend growth path of the Soviet R & D sector. Consequently, it could have changed the trend growth rate of the Soviet technical advances, since probably most of the foreign-made and home-made technology is, respectively, transmitted and produced by that sector. However, the average annual growth rate of the Soviet R & D scientific personnel in the years 1914–50 was in fact about

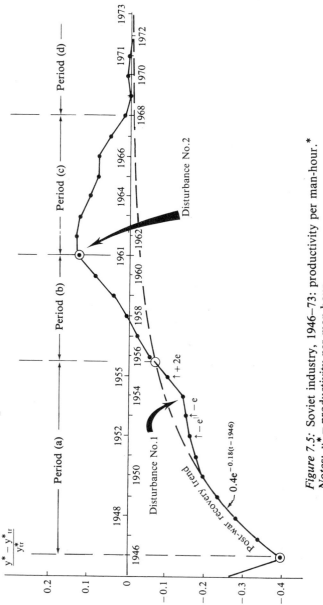

Figure 7.5: Soviet industry, 1946–73: productivity per man-hour.[*]
Notes: y^* = productivity per man-hour.
y^*_{tr} = the 1937–73 trend in y^* (6 per cent annual growth).
[*]Compiled by the author.

the same as in the years 1951–71 (8.0 per cent and 9.0 per cent, correspondingly).[20] The level of expenditure on R & D prior to 1941 is not available, but its growth rate in the years 1941–50 was not very different from in the years 1951–71 (respectively 12 per cent and 13 per cent).[21] We may thus conclude that there were present both external and internal factors conducive to a sustained (constant) trend in technological changes.

3. Finally, the war forced the Soviet Union twice to make rapid and large-scale changes in the composition of its industrial output and in the skill composition of the labour force, in 1941–42 and in 1945–46. These changes meant a great organisational disruption in industrial production. But they were mostly transitory and so resulted in something of a temporary aberration from the underlying trend in technical and organisational changes. After the 1946 switch from wartime to peacetime production, the utilisation of capital began to increase and the stock of innovations accumulated at home and abroad during the war had started to be gradually incorporated by civilian industries as new investment in plant and equipment proceeded.

Changes over time in the level of x are given in Figure 7.5. It is seen that in 1946 y^* was equal to $0.6y^*_{tr}$, so that $x = 0.4$. In the years 1946–50 this distance was diminishing at the annual rate of about 20 per cent. The time path of y^*_t in those years traces out what we shall call the post-war recovery trend path. However, after 1950 there seems to have been two 'shocks'—one relatively minor, the other relatively major—that greatly disturbed the evolution of y^* along that post-war recovery trend path. Disturbance no. 1 is located in the years 1951–55, with the performance rather poor in the years 1951–53 and 1955. The minor growth depression of 1951–53 may be interpreted as an imprint of increased production of arms during the Korean War (1950–53) combined with a crop failure in 1951. Both these factors no doubt caused a degree of transitional disruption in some industrial branches. Its subsequent removal in the years 1954–55 could then produce a minor 'growth recovery'. The big disturbance (no. 2 in Figure 7.5) begins in 1956, its first part marked with an above normal expansion. Its start coincides with the beginning of the programme, adopted in March 1956 by the 20th Congress of the CPSU, gradually to reduce the standard working week from 48 to 41 hours. The first part of the cycle ended in 1961, the year when the programme was completed, with the average annual number of working hours per man being actually reduced by about 20 per cent. During the years 1956–61

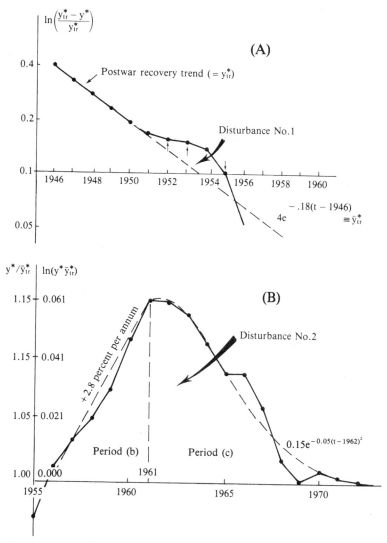

Figure 7.6: (A) The 1951–55 and (B) the 1956–73 deviations of the actual level of productivity (per man-hour) from its post-war recovery trend on the logarithmic scale.

the distance x was increasing again to reach in 1961 its maximum of about 0.15. But in the long run the labour productivity per man-hour may be expected to be largely independent of the number of hours worked per year. At this point let us note that Weitzman admits that 'in using hours worked as an index of labour inputs, we are in effect operating with a hidden assumption that labour efficiency per hour is unaffected by the reduction over time of total hours worked.'[22] On the basis of Figure 7.5, I adopt the same assumption for the long run, but in the short run (periods (b) and (c)) the assumption appears to be unacceptable. Disturbances 1 and 2 are shown more clearly on the logarithmic scale in Figure 7.6. On the basis of the 1946–50 data, the post-war recovery trend is estimated. The deviation from this trend for the years 1956–73 is presented in the bottom part of Figure 7.6 The type of asymmetry seen in disturbance no. 2, fairly linear changes in x in period (b) as opposed to bell-shaped or logistic-type changes in period (c), corresponds well to the nature of the different processes underlying these changes: a constant pressure applied in period (b) and a gradual relaxation of tension enjoyed in period (c).

5. VARIABLE TECHNICAL CHANGE VERSUS ELASTICITY OF SUBSTITUTION: A FURTHER TEST

The general form of a CES constant returns-to-scale production function to be fitted in our second test is also a standard one:

$$Y = \gamma [\delta_1 (BK)^{-\varrho} + (1 - \delta_1)(AL)^{-\varrho}]^{-1/\varrho} \tag{6}$$

where parameters γ, ϱ, and δ are constant, and where functions $A = A(t)$ and $B = B(t)$ represent (disembodied) factor-augmenting technical progress. The innovation in equation (6) is with a new specification of the technical progress terms, which are as follows:

$$B(t) = e^{\lambda_1 t} \tag{7}$$

$$A(t) = e^{\lambda_2 t}[1 - 0.4e^{-0.18(t - 1946)}]$$
$$[1 + 0.15\delta_{2t}e^{-0.05(t - 1962)^2}]e^{(\epsilon_t + \mu_t)t} \tag{8}$$

where time t runs from 1951–73 and where δ_{2t}, ϵ_t, and μ_t are dummy variables defined as follows:

$$\delta_{2t} = \begin{cases} \delta_2 \text{ for } 1962\text{--}73 \\ 0 \text{ otherwise} \end{cases}, \quad \epsilon_t = \begin{cases} -\epsilon \text{ for } 1952\text{--}53 \\ +2\epsilon \text{ for } 1955, \\ 0 \text{ otherwise} \end{cases} \quad \mu_t = \begin{cases} \mu \text{ for } 1956\text{--}61 \\ 0 \text{ otherwise} \end{cases} \quad (9)$$

In specification (8) λ_2 is the trend growth rate of the labour-augmenting technical progress. Expression in the first square brackets in equation (8), increasing from 0.6 for 1946 to 1 for large t, represents the post-war correction of the long-run trend in that type of progress, as implied by the post-war recovery trend. Note that by definition of the post-war recovery trend, $\bar{y}_{tr}^*$ is an estimate of the ratio $(y_{tr}^* - y_t^*)/:y_{tr}^* \equiv x_t$. Hence y_t^* is approximated by $(1 - \bar{y}_{tr}^*)y_{tr}^*$. As we noted in the previous section, if technical changes are predominantly neutral in the Harrod–Kalecki sense, then the index of the labour-augmenting component of technical advance $A(t)$ is in the long run approximately proportional to y_t^*. Hence the trend term $e^{\lambda_2 t}$ in the level of technical advance $A(t)$ is corrected to have the form $(1 - \bar{y}_{tr}^*) e^{\lambda_2 t}$. The expression for $\bar{y}_{tr}^*$ was estimated in the upper part of Figure 7.6. Expression in the second square brackets in equation (8), declining from 1.14 for 1962 to 1 for large t, represents the post-1961 gradual return of labour efficiency per hour to its long-run trend. Finally ϵ and μ are dummy variables covering, respectively, the 1952–55 cycle and the 1956–61 period of labour efficiency per hour being increasingly above its long-run trend corrected for the postwar recovery.

Equation (6) may be rewritten in terms of growth rates,

$$g_{Y,t} = \pi_t(g_{K,t} + \lambda_1) + (1 - \pi_t)\Bigg[g_{L^*,t} + \lambda_2 + \epsilon_t + \mu_t$$

$$+ \frac{0.0288 e^{-0.18(t-1951)}}{1 - 0.16 e^{-0.18(t-1951)}}$$

$$+ \delta_{2t} \frac{0.014(t-1962) e^{-0.05(t-1962)^2}}{1 + 0.14 e^{-0.05(t-1962)^2}} \Bigg] \quad (10)$$

where, as before, $\pi_t = \delta_1 \gamma^{-\varrho} e^{-\lambda_1 \varrho t} v_t^{-\varrho}$ and $\varrho = (1 - \sigma)/\sigma$.

Here eight parameters are to be estimated: λ_1, λ_2, δ_1, δ_2, γ, σ, μ and ϵ. Data used for this estimation (as well as in the subsequent final test) are, with one exception, the same data as used in the first test. The exception is the man-hours data for 1967–71, which are now changed to comply with Desai's revised index of working hours per man (see Table 7.1, col. 14). The estimation results are as follows:

$$\hat{\lambda}_1 = -3 \times 10^{-6}, \quad \hat{\lambda}_2 = 0.060, \quad \hat{\delta}_1 = 0.292, \quad \hat{\delta}_2 = -1.11,$$
$$\hat{\gamma} = 1.00, \quad \hat{\sigma} = 1.00, \quad \hat{\mu} = 0.030, \quad \hat{\epsilon} = 0.017,$$
$$\text{ESS} = 1.25 \times 10^{-3}, \quad \bar{R}^2 = 0.8076.$$

The technical change estimated is thus again predominantly Harrod-neutral. Compared with our previous test, the ESS is significantly reduced—from about 76 per cent to about 41 per cent of the ESS implied by the Weitzman-type specification. Also $\bar{R}^2$ is substantially increased—from 0.6823 to 0.8076. The elasticity of substitution estimated is almost exactly unity, and the (imputed) capital share almost exactly constant over time (equal to 0.292). However, only $\hat{\delta}_2$, $\hat{\mu}$ and $\hat{\epsilon}$ were found statistically significant. The sensitivity analysis revealed that there is a great deal of substitution between λ_1 and λ_2, as it in fact should be expected in the virtually Cobb–Douglas situation. The elasticity of substitution has a relatively large asymptotic standard error so that it could easily be anywhere in the range from 0.1 to 1.2. By fixing a few values of σ from this range and sub-minimising the ESS, it was found that the minimum was fairly flat, though σs close to unity were giving the best fit. These results, however disappointing in terms of standard errors, are nevertheless instructive since they indicate that there is likely to be no loss in the goodness of fit by directly fixing σ at 1. The number of parameters would then be reduced from eight to five, and by reducing the substitution possibilities between the remaining parameters their statistical significance should significantly increase.

6. COBB–DOUGLAS FUNCTION WITH VARIABLE TECHNICAL CHANGES: THE FINAL SPECIFICATION

After this long journey of preliminary descriptive interpretation of data and two intermediate econometric tests with CES production functions, we arrived at the point of formulating what will be our final specification of the production function for the Soviet industry. We shall fix σ at 1 so that $\pi = \delta_1$. Hence the form of the final specification:

$$
g_{Y,t} = \delta_1 g_{K,t} + (1 - \delta_1) \left[g_{L^*,t} + \frac{0.0288e^{-0.18(t-1951)}}{1 - 0.16e^{-0.18(t-1951)}} \right]
$$
$$
+ \lambda + \epsilon_t + \mu_t + \delta_{2t} \frac{0.015(t-1962)e^{-0.05(t-1962)^2}}{1 + 0.15e^{-0.05(t-1962)^2}}
\tag{11}
$$

The estimation results are now as follows (standard errors in the parentheses):

$$
\hat{\lambda} = 0.042, \quad \hat{\delta}_1 = 0.292, \quad \hat{\delta}_2 = 0.788, \quad \hat{\mu} = 0.021, \quad \hat{\epsilon} = 0.012,
$$
$$
(0.038) \quad\quad (0.332) \quad\quad (0.120) \quad\quad (0.009) \quad\quad (0.006)
$$
$$
\text{ESS} = 1.25 \times 10^{-3}, \text{ and } \bar{R}^2 = 0.8400.
$$

It may be seen that the ESS has remained at the previous level and, as a result of reducing the number of parameters, the value of $\bar{R}^2$ increased. The statistical significance of the estimated parameters is now also markedly improved.

At the conclusion of this section let it be emphasised that although our final specification is at $\sigma = 1$, this should not be taken to imply that the actual value of the elasticity of substitution is likely to be close to unity. After all, the ESS in the more general case (test no. 2) was found virtually insensitive to changes in σ. Therefore, rather than on a particular value of σ, the emphasis of this study is instead on the essentially labour-saving-type of technical changes in Soviet industry and on a rather complex dynamics of the growth rate of these technical changes during the post-war period. This study puts into question both the notion that in the context of slowdown in the Soviet industrial growth the basic parameter is the elasticity of (capital/labour) substitution and the related notion that the basic choice is between the two production functions: with σ close to unity and with σ significantly less than unity.

7. SUMMARY

The explanatory power of three hypotheses—Weitzman's, our preliminary one (test no. 1) and the final one—is indicated by the value of ESS and $\bar{R}^2$. In terms of these two statistical indicators the final specification is found to be significantly superior to the first two specifications. In particular, under this final specification the

ESS equals about 41 per cent of the ESS implied by Weitzman's specification. Morever, in 23 years there are five—1951, 1964, 1966, 1968 and 1972—that account for some 80 per cent of the remaining ESS. If these five years are excluded, the average deviation of the estimated from the actual annual output growth rate would be 0.37 per cent. As it is, the average deviation is 0.74. For comparison, under Weitzman's specification this deviation for the same 1951–73 period is 1.15 per cent. To assess their significance all these deviations should be compared with the average annual growth rate of output in that period, which was 9.85 per cent.

Three major propositions, together representing the main hypothesis of this study, may be articulated as follows:

1. Technical progress in Soviet industry was essentially neutral in the Harrod–Kalecki sense, that is to say, its labour-saving component was the dominant one.
2. The rate of this labour-saving technical progress was a sum of three components. Two of these were variable over time and transitory. One was produced by the post-war recovery, while the other was associated with the 1956–61 changes in the work year. Both these components were superimposed on a term representing the long-run trend in technical change. This trend term was constant until 1973, the end year of the period considered in this paper.
3. The error sum of squares was found almost insensitive to changes in the value of the elasticity of substitution from the range between 0.1 and 1.2. It is suggested therefore that the actual value of that parameter may be irrelevant in the search to explain the Soviet growth slowdown. This finding is really an implication of proposition 1.

Dynamics of the (estimated) productivity residual and the residual's three main components are given in Table 7.6 and in Figure 7.7. According to this estimate the PRF was quite important until about 1955, accounting in 1954 still for about one-tenth of the growth rate of output. The combined effect of the PRF and of the changes in the work year was to increase the output growth rate by about 2.2 per cent in the years 1951–61. However, the latter factor decreased this rate by (on average) about 1.4 per cent in the years 1963–69. This change from a positive (and declining) effect in the 1950s to a negative effect in the years 1963–69 accounts for the slowdown of the output growth in the years 1951–69 and, indeed,

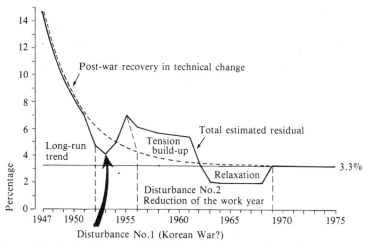

Figure 7.7: Soviet industry, 1951–75: actual versus estimated growth rates of output. Compiled by the author.
Source: ESS and $\bar{R}^2$ given for the period 1951–75. See note 4 for the definition of R_1^2 and R_2^2.

produces the jumpdown in the labour productivity growth in 1962–63.

Our interpretation of slowdown has two characteristics by which it may be viewed as an intermediate one between that of Weitzman and the traditional explanation. Common with the former but at variance with the latter is the notion of a constant trend component in the residual. On the other hand, the notion that the (imputed) capital share has been approximately constant is common with the traditional hypothesis, but at variance with that of Weitzman. Our computations of the effects of changes in the average age of machines are at variance with Brubaker's findings.[24] Consequently, the age-composition effect is in this study discounted as a major explanatory variable in the context of Soviet growth slowdown. Discounted are also both the effect of structural changes and the growth effect of embodied diffusion.

Table 7.6: Sources of Soviet industrial growth, estimated for 1951–73 and implied for 1947–50, under the 'final' specification

Year	Output growth rate	Capital's contribution	Labour's contribution	Components of the 'explained' residual			Total estimated residual*	Unexplained residual
				Post-war recovery	Changes in the work year	Trend		
1951	15.2	3.3	4.1	2.4	0	4.2	6.6	1.1
1952	11.4	3.7	2.6	2.0	0	4.2	5.0	0.1
1953	11.3	3.2	3.0	1.6	0	4.2	4.7	0.4
1954	12.3	3.2	3.4	1.3	0	4.2	5.6	0.7
1955	12.3	3.6	1.3	1.1	0	4.2	7.6	0.3
1956	9.9	3.5	-0.9	0.9	2.1	4.2	7.2	0.1
1957	10.1	3.1	0.2	0.7	2.1	4.2	7.0	0.2
1958	11.3	3.2	1.8	0.6	2.1	4.2	6.9	-0.7
1959	11.4	3.4	1.1	0.5	2.1	4.2	6.8	0.1
1960	10.4	3.4	-0.5	0.4	2.1	4.2	6.7	0.8
1961	9.6	3.4	-0.4	0.3	2.4	4.2	6.6	-0.1
1962	9.8	3.2	2.3	0.3	0	4.2	4.5	-0.3

1963	9.1	3.3	2.5	0.2	−0.3	4.2	3.5	−0.2
1964	8.1	3.4	3.0	0.2	−1.7	4.2	2.7	−1.0
1965	8.2	3.0	3.0	0.2	−2.1	4.2	2.3	−0.2
1966	8.9	2.7	1.8	0.2	−3.0	4.2	1.4	2.0
1967	9.9	2.5	4.8	0.1	−1.6	4.2	2.7	−0.1
1968	8.9	2.3	4.7	0.1	−1.1	4.2	3.2	−1.3
1969	7.1	2.3	1.3	0.1	−0.7	4.2	3.8	−0.1
1970	8.4	2.6	1.4	0.1	−0.4	4.2	3.9	0.5
1971	7.8	2.6	1.3	0.1	−0.1	4.2	4.2	−0.2
1972	6.4	2.7	0.9	0.1	0	4.2	4.2	−1.4
1973	7.3	2.5	0.9	0	0	4.2	4.2	−0.3

Sources of growth implied under the 'final' specification

1947	20.8	2.4	2.1	6.2		4.2	10.4	5.9
1948	26.9	3.7	7.7	4.8		4.2	9.0	5.5
1949	19.5	2.6	4.2	3.8		4.2	8.2	4.7
1950	22.7	2.7	7.8	3.0		4.2	7.2	5.0

Note: *Includes the estimate of the Korean War disturbance: −1.2 per cent in 1952 and 1953, and +2.4 per cent in 1955.

DATA APPENDIX

Table 1: *Basic facts of Soviet industrial growth, 1928–73*

	1	2	3	4	5	6	7	8	9	10
	Global product (index) X	Growth of global product g_x^a	Value-added (index) $Y^{(1)}$	Growth of value added $g_y^{a(1)}$	Value-added (billion 1955 roubles) $Y^{(2)}$	Gross investment (billion 1955 roubles) I	Capital Stock (billion 1955 roubles) K	Growth of capital stock g_k^a	Capital/output ratio (index) v	Employment (index) L
1928	8.95				0.93	0.33				28.33
1929	10.72	19.8			1.12	0.42				
1930	13.03	22.1			1.37	0.58				
1931	15.81	20.8			1.65	0.67				
1932	18.11	14.5			1.89	0.75				61.20
1933	19.06	5.2			1.99	0.92				
1934	22.73	19.3			2.37	1.00				
1935	27.88	22.7			2.91	1.24				
1936	35.89	28.7			3.74	1.4				
1937	39.90	11.2			4.16	1.6				76.00
1938	44.57	11.7			4.65	1.7				
1939	51.76	16.1			5.40	1.8				
1940	57.80	11.7			6.03	1.8	20.0		124.08	80.39
1941	56.65	-2.0			5.91	1.1				
1942	44.51	-21.4			4.64	1.5				
1943	53.02	16.9			5.43	1.6				
1944	60.12	15.6			6.27	1.8				70.37
1945	53.18	-11.5			8.04	2.0				69.63

Year										
1946	71.55	155.0		19.6^b		6.73			−16.3	44.51
1947	77.29	138.8	8.2^b	21.2^b	2.2	8.12			20.8	53.76
1948	85.71	123.3	12.7^b	23.9^b	2.6	10.31			26.9	68.21
1949	90.76	114.16	8.8^b	26.00	3.1	12.31			19.5	81.50
1950	100.00	101.87	9.3	28.49	3.6	15.11		100.0	22.7	100.00
1951	105.96	98.40	11.3	31.62	4.2	17.64	15.2	115.24	16.8	116.76
1952	110.16	99.51	12.6	35.63	5.0	19.65	11.4	128.39	11.4	130.06
1953	115.02	99.48	10.9	39.51	5.6	22.01	11.3	142.84	12.0	145.67
1954	120.79	97.61	11.1	43.90	6.2	24.78	12.9	161.27	13.1	164.74
1955	123.49	97.18	12.4	49.33	6.9	27.95	12.9	182.03	12.3	184.97
1956	127.71	98.96	11.9	55.22	7.7	30.92	9.9	200.10	10.6	204.58
1957	131.82	99.30	10.5	60.99	8.2	34.06	10.1	220.25	10.2	225.43
1958	135.87	98.97	11.0	67.68	8.7	37.56	11.3	245.23	10.3	248.56
1959	139.72	99.02	11.5	75.44	10.0	41.84	11.4	273.20	11.4	276.88
1960	147.69	100.00	11.5	84.13	11.8	45.77	10.4	301.67	9.4	302.89
1961	153.30	101.85	11.6	93.88	12.7	49.96	9.6	330.36	5.2	330.62
1962	158.60	103.04	11.1	104.26	13.1	54.76	9.8	362.90	9.6	362.41
1963	163.62	105.25	11.4	116.18	14.0	59.21	9.1	395.80	8.1	391.88
1964	169.30	108.84	11.7	129.82	14.9	63.58	8.1	427.75	7.4	420.78
1965	179.22	111.09	10.4	143.37	16.7	69.08	8.2	462.75	8.7	457.20
1966	186.14	111.40	9.2	156.59	17.7	75.11	8.9	504.10	8.7	497.08
1967	192.28	109.85	8.4	169.72	18.3	82.62	9.9	553.85	10.0	546.79
1968	198.68	108.89	7.9	183.73	19.5	89.43	8.9	603.05	8.2	591.87
1969	203.44	109.81	8.0	197.79	21.3	95.81	7.1	645.87	7.1	634.07
1970	206.25	110.20	8.9	215.37	22.0	103.93	8.4	700.12	8.4	687.82
1971	209.12	111.20	9.0	234.72	24.9	112.0	7.8	754.73	7.8	741.57
1972	211.87	114.23	9.3	256.60	25.9	119.2	6.4	803.03	6.4	788.97
1973	214.61	115.57	8.5	278.40	27.0	123.0	7.3	861.65	7.3	846.88

Table 1. (continued)

	11	12	13	14	15	16	17	18	19	20
	Working hours per man (index) h	Labour (in man-hours) $L^* = hL$	Growth of Labour (in man-hours) $gL_*^{(1)}$	Growth of Labour (in man-hours) $gL_*^{(2)}$	Investment in industry as percentage of total state investment I/Its	Total state investment rate in GNP (index) Its/GNP	Output per man-hours (index) y	Trend in output per man-hours (index) y_{tr}^*	(18)–(17) $y_{tr}^* - y^*$	(19)/(18) $(y_{tr}^* - y^*)/y_{tr}^*$
1928	87.2	24.70					36.25	34.34		
1929								36.40		
1930								38.58		
1931								40.88		
1932								43.34		
1933							34.41	45.94		
1934								48.70		
1935								51.62		
1936								54.72		
1937	84.7	64.37					61.95	58.00		
1938								61.48		
1939								65.97		
1940	92.4	78.90			38.0	100.0	73.26	69.08		
1941								73.23		
1942								77.62		
1943								82.28		
1944	122.0	85.85					70.03	87.22		
1945	112.0	78.04			47.5	107.2	68.18	92.45	24.27	0.263
1946	105.0	75.93			43.7	136.7	59.24	98.00	38.76	0.395

1947	100.0	77.29	2.9			69.56		103.88	34.32	0.330
1948	100.0	85.71	10.9			79.58		110.11	30.53	0.279
1949	100.0	90.76	5.9			89.80		116.72	26.92	0.239
1950	100.00	100.00	11.0		47.5	100.00		123.72	23.72	0.192
1951	99.98	105.96	6.0	5.8	46.8	108.97		131.14	22.17	0.169
1952	99.66	109.52	3.4	3.7	44.4	117.12	126.1	139.01	21.89	0.157
1953	99.57	114.26	4.3	4.3	44.7	124.88	121.2	147.35	22.47	0.132
1954	99.34	119.83	4.9	4.8	47.2	134.52	121.8	156.19	21.67	0.139
1955	99.12	122.01	1.8	1.9	47.0	148.99	123.3	165.56	16.57	0.100
1956	94.24	120.40	-1.3	-1.3	49.6	166.01	118.0	175.49	8.48	0.059
1957	91.41	120.76	0.3	0.3	47.3	182.26	123.0	186.01	3.75	0.020
1958	90.77	123.33	2.1	2.6	47.8	197.69	121.1	197.17	-0.62	-0.003
1959	89.27	124.73	1.1	1.5	44.1	218.90	125.6	209.00	-7.30	-0.038
1960	84.34	125.45	0.6	-0.7	41.2	241.08	133.6	221.54	-19.54	-0.088
1961	80.29	123.08	-1.9	-0.5	41.8	265.4	133.7	234.83	-30.5	-0.130
1962	80.06	126.98	3.2	3.3	44.2	282.0	139.7	248.32	-33.1	-0.133
1963	80.38	131.52	3.6	3.5	42.3	297.2	145.8	263.86	-33.3	-0.125
1964	81.02	137.17	4.3	4.2	41.1	308.9	145.0	279.69	-28.4	-0.102
1965	81.02	145.20	5.9	4.3	41.2	319.8	146.4	296.47	-23.3	-0.075
1966	79.97	148.82	2.5	5.9	41.3	339.5	149.4	314.26	-25.2	-0.080
1967	82.62	158.9	6.8	2.6	42.4	349.4	143.0	333.16	-16.5	-0.050
1968	85.28	169.4	6.6	6.8	41.5	355.8	151.2	353.15	-3.7	-0.010
1969	84.94	172.8	2.0	6.6	40.0	394.8	150.1	374.34	-0.5	-0.001
1970	85.28	175.9	1.8	1.8	39.5	399.5	149.0	396.80	-2.7	-0.007
1971	85.70	179.2	1.9	2.0	39.8	422.5	149.0	420.61	-1.3	-0.005
1972	85.70	181.6	1.3	1.8	39.4	443.6	148.2	445.85	2.3	0.005
1973	85.70	183.9	1.3	1.3	40.0	470.2	155.9	472.60	22.4	0.005

Notes:

Column

1: X = global product (index), Soviet estimate.

2: g_X = annual percentage rate of growth of global product.

3: $Y^{(1)}$ = value-added (index), Weitzman 'hybrid' index 1950–68, global product index 1969–73.

4: $g_Y^{(1)}$ = annual percentage rate of growth of value-added.

5: $Y^{(2)}$ = valued-added, billion of the 1955 roubles; $Y_t^{(2)} = (u/X1955) X_t$, where u = value-added in 1955 (J. Thornton), t = 1928, ..., 1973.

6: L = gross investment in fixed capital, billion of the 1955 roubles, in industry, Soviet estimate, author's interpolations.

7: K = gross fixed capital, billion of the 1955 roubles, Soviet estimate.

8: g_K = annual percentage rate of growth of gross fixed capital.

9: v = capital/output ratio, (index), $v = K/Y^{(1)}$ for 1950–68; $v = K/X$ otherwise.

10: L = total industrial employment (index), Soviet estimate.

11: h = annual working hours per man (index), Bergson–Weitzman–Desai index.

12: $L^* = hL$ man-hours (index).

13: $g_L^{(1)*}$ = annual percentage growth rate of labour L^*, given in col. 12.

14: $g_L^{(2)*}$ = annual percentage rate of growth of labour (in man-hours), Weitzman estimate for 1951–66, Desai estimate for 1968–71.

15: Industrial gross investment in fixed capital as percentage of total state investment in fixed capital.

16: Total state investment in fixed capital as proportion of GN(Material)P (index).

17: y^* = output per man-hour (index), equal to $Y^{(1)}/L^*$ for 1950–73, and to X/L^* otherwise.

18.: y_{tr} = 6.0 per cent growth trend in y^*.

Sources:

Columns 1, 2, 6, 10. Clarke, R. A. *Soviet Economic Facts*, London: Macmillian, 1972. These data were compiled from Soviet official publications, they are, therefore, referred to as 'Soviet estimates'.

Columns 3, 4, 7, 8, 11, 12, 14. The basic source is Weitzman, M. L., 'Soviet Postwar Economic Growth and Capital–Labor Substitution', *American Economic Review*, **60**, no. 4, 1970, 677, Table 1 for the years 1951–68. His output, capital and employment data are extended by Soviet official data.

Column 5. Thornton, J., 'Value-Added and Factor Productivity in Soviet Industry', *American Economic Review*, **60**, no. 5, 1970; pp. 863–71.

Column 11. Sources for the Bergson–Weitzman–Desai index of economic working hours per man are Bergson, A., *The Real National Income of Soviet Russia since 1928*, Cambridge, Mass.: Harvard University Press, 1961, p. 425, Table H-2, for years 1928, 1937, 1940, 1944, and 1948–50; Weitzman, *op. cit.*, p. 687, Table 4, for the years 1950–56; and Desai, P., 'The Production Function and Technical Change in Postwar Soviet Industry: A Reexamination', forthcoming, Table 1 for the years 1968–71. In her paper, Desai notes a difficulty, 'in deriving meaningful magnitudes of the index for the "transition" years 1967 and 1968'. She obtained a sharp rise of 20 per cent in 1967 and a decline of 3 per cent in 1968 in industrial man-hours. According to her, 'one possible reason [for this] is that while the change to a five-day work week (or 8.0 hours per day during the week) is announced on a given date in 1967, the change does not necessarily become effective on that date. The average length of the working day in 1967 is most likely to be somewhere between 6.67 hours (the figure for 1966) and 8 hours (as per the announcement).' I accepted this point and assumed, somewhat arbitrarily, that the average length of the working day in 1967 was $6.67 + \frac{1}{2} (8.0 - 6.67) = 7.34$ hours. I also assumed that there was no change in the number of annual working hours per man in the years 1972–73.

NOTES

1. Balassa, B., 'The Dynamic Efficiency of the Soviet Economy', *American Economic Review*, **54**, no. 3, 1964; pp. 490–506; Bergson, A., *Prospects for Soviet Economic Growth in the 1970s*, Brussels: Symposium, NATO, 1971, and 'Comparative Productivity and Efficiency in the Soviet Union and the United States', in *Comparison of Economic Systems: Theoretical and Methodological Approaches*, ed. Eckstein, A., Berkeley: University of California Press, 1973; Brubaker, E. R., 'Embodied Technology, the Asymptotic Behavior of Capital's Age, and Soviet Growth', *Review of Economics and Statistics*, **50**, no. 3 1968; pp. 304–11, and 'Soviet Postwar Economic Growth and Capital-Labor Substitution: Comment', *American Economic Review*, **62**, no. 4, 1972, pp. 675–8; Kaplan, N. M., 'Retardation in Soviet Growth', *Review of Economics and Statistics*, **50**, no. 3, 1968, pp. 293–303; Moorsteen, R. H. and Powell, R. P., *The Soviet Capital Stock 1928–1962*, Homewood, Ill.: Irwin, 1966; and *Two Supplements to the Soviet Capital Stock*, New Haven, Conn.: The Economic Growth Center of Yale University, 1968; Noren, J. H., 'Soviet Industry Trends in Output, Inputs and Productivity', in *New Directions in the Soviet Economy*, US Congress, Joint Economic Committee, Washington, D.C.: US Government Printing Office, 1966, pp. 271–326.
2. Weitzman, M. L., 'Soviet Postwar Economic Growth and Capital–Labor Substitution', *American Economic Review*, **60**, no. 4, 1970; pp. 676–92; and 'Soviet Postwar Economic Growth and Capital–Labor Substitution: Reply', *American Economic Review*, **62**, no. 4, 1972; pp. 682–4; Desai, P., 'The Production Function and Technical Change in Postwar Soviet Industry: A Re-examination', and 'Technical Change, Factor Elasticity of Substitution and Returns to Scale in Branches of Soviet Industry in the Postwar Period', in *On the Measurement of Factor Productivities: Theoretical Problems and Empirical Results, Papers and Proceedings of the Second Reisenburg Symposium*, ed. Altmann, F.-L., Kyn, O. and Wagener, H.-J., Gottingen: Vanderhoeck and Ruprecht, 1976).
3. Brubaker, 'Embodied Technology', *op. cit.*
4. Kaplan, *op. cit.*, p. 302.
5. Noren, *op. cit.*, p. 295; Bergson, 'prospects', *op. cit.*, p. 25.
6. Noren, *op. cit.*, p. 298.
7. Ibid., pp. 296–7.
8. Moorsteen and Powell, *Two Supplements*, *op. cit.*, p. 9.
9. The exception is Brubaker's attempt to estimate the effect of change in the average age of capital goods on changes in the productivity residual. However, our recalculation of the effect, which will be given in this chapter, largely discounts it as a main reason for the growth slowdown.
10. Most of the data in Table 7.1 are either based on or are directly the official Soviet data. The problems with quality of any Soviet data, official or non-official, are well known. But to secure comparability with Weitzman's paper I use above all his data (Weitzman, 'Soviet

Postwar Economic Growth'. *op. cit.*, Table 1, period 1950–68). My econometric tests cover the period 1951–73. The base year is thus 1950. The data for the period 1928–50 are used to formulate their descriptive, preliminary interpretation. Only the data for the period 1947–50 are used more directly to estimate the so-called post-war recovery trend in the labour-augmenting component of technical change. To estimate changes in the work year I used what I call the Bergson–Weitzman–Desai index of working hours per man-year. This index takes into account also the length of vacation time and the number of work holidays.

11. Recently in Poland there has begun a reduction in the work year. In 1974, 6 Saturdays were free, in 1975 their number was increased to 12. The principles upon which the reduction programme is based are spelled out by the Directive no. 41 of the Polish Council of Ministers, of 7 February 1974. Two of these principles (4 and 7) make it clear (1) that the 'introduction of additional free days is conditional upon an increase in labour productivity sufficient to fulfil the production targets without any additional increase in employment', and (2) that 'workers are not to be paid for additional free days'. The savings in the wage fund that result from the reduction in working days are to be used 'to pay for increased labour norms'. It seems thus that in Poland the additional free days are openly used as an instrument of pressure applied to decrease disguised unemployment below its long-run 'trend' level. If my interpretation of the Soviet experience is correct and if it can be applied generally to any Soviet-type economy, then a period of increased pressure when the work year is reduced, with a resulting increase in the growth of output per man-hour, will be followed by a period of relaxation of tension, with a resulting reduction in the labour productivity growth.

12. The relative stability of s_t also virtually eliminates the possible explanation of slowdown in the growth rate of labour productivity based on the notion of positive association of the growth rate of technical change and the investment ratio.

13. Weitzman (1970), *op. cit.*, pp. 676–92. For the purpose of comparability with Weitzman's results I retain his assumption of no change in the work year after 1966. Later in the paper this assumption will be relaxed and, instead, Desai's index of working hours adopted.

14. Let $Y_t = \sum_{i=1}^n Y_{it}$, $L_t = \sum_{i=1}^n L_{it}$, $y_t = Y_t/L_t$, $y_{it} = Y_{it}/L_{it}$, and $\varrho_{it} = L_{it}/L_t$, where i numbers industrial branches. Note that $y_t = \sum_{i=1}^n \varrho_{it} y_{it}$. Therefore, $\dot{y}_t = \sum_{i=1}^n \dot{\varrho}_{it} y_{it} + \sum_{i=1}^n \varrho_{it} \dot{y}_{it}$. The term $\sum_{i=1}^n \dot{\varrho}_{it} y_{it} \equiv \dot{y}_t^s$ represents a change in y_t brought about by a change in the branch composition of employment. By the branch composition (growth) effect, we mean the rate $\dot{y}_t^s/y_t$.

15. Weitzman (1970), *op. cit.*, p. 689, Table 6.

16. This brief section is based mainly on my macro models of inter-country technological diffusion developed in Gomulka, S., 'Extensions of the Golden Rule of Research of Phelps', *Review of Economic Studies*, no. 1, 1970, pp. 73–93, and Gomulka, S. and Sylwestrowicz, J. D., 'Import-led Growth: Theory and Estimation', in *On the Measurement of Factor Productivities: Theoretical problems*

and Empirical Results, Papers and Proceedings of the Second Reisenburg Symposium, ed. Altmann, F.-L., Kyn, O. and Wagener, H.-J. Gottingen: Vandenhoeck and Ruprecht, 1976.

17. Gomulka, S., *Inventive Activity, Diffusion and the Stages of Economic Growth*, Aarhus, Denmark: Economic Institute, 1971, Chapters 3 and 4, in particular the 'hat-shape relationship'.

18. Gomulka and Sylwestrowicz, *op. cit.*

19. Data from *Historical Statistics of the United States*, pp. 600, 601, and *Economic Report of the President*, 1972, p. 234.

20. Narkhoz, U.S.S.R. 1922–1972, Moscow, 1972, p. 103, puts the number of 'scientific workers' at 162, 500 in 1950 and at 1.003 million in 1971. Freeman, C. and Young, A., *The Research and Development Effort in Western Europe, North America, and the Soviet Union*, Paris: OECD, 1965, p. 140, give 10,200 as the number of 'scientists' in Russia in 1914. If we assume that the same 10.2 thousand were active in the Soviet Union in 1926 and that the term 'scientist' is fully equivalent to the term 'scientific worker' then the annual rate of increase of the number of Soviet scientists for the period 1927–50 would be 12.5 per cent.

21. U.S.S.R., 1922–1972, *op. cit.*, p. 483. These expenditures are put at 0.3 billion roubles in 1940, to 1.0 billion roubles in 1950, and at 13.0 billion roubles in 1971.

22. Weitzman (1970), *op. cit.*, pp. 687–88.

23. Brubaker, 'Embodied Technology,' *op. cit.*

8 Slowdown in Soviet Industrial Growth: 1947–75 Reconsidered*

The primary purpose of this paper is to report new results which somewhat modify the economics and and significantly improve the statistical features of the explanation of slowdown in Soviet industrial growth since 1946 offered in the previous chapter. Also the data base is further extended by two years to cover the 25-year period 1951–75. To make the paper self-contained, some of the main features of the data are first briefly related.

1. BASIC DATA AND THEIR PRELIMINARY INTERPRETATION

The data used in this paper for computation purposes are given in Table 8.1. Also two updated diagrams are reproduced from Gomulka (1976) (See Figures 7.3 and 7.4 in the previous chapter) which place the period 1951–75 in a longer historical perspective, and which originally were instrumental in formulating the 'third explanation'.

Figure 7.3 reveals a certain regularity in the growth rate of output per man-hour. It is seen that rather than a slowdown in this rate there was in fact a jumpdown from a high level of about 10 per cent, prevailing until 1961, to a level of about 5 per cent prevailing since 1962. However, the years 1947–61 were exceptional for both the pre-war and the post-war growth experience. They also follow

*The numerical work for this paper was done by Joanna Gomulka. I owe a great deal to her patience and advice. I also wish to thank Professor John Wise and Mr Jan Rostowski for their stimulating suggestions and comments. While the paper is a follow-up of Gomulka (1976), care was taken to make it reasonably self-contained. Reprinted with permission from *European Economic Review* **10** (1977), pp. 37–49, North-Holland Publishing Company, with the omission of the introductory section.

Table 8.1: Annual percentage rates of growth of output, capital, and labour, and index of capital output ratio (1960 = 1) for Soviet industry, 1951–75

t	g_Y	g_K	g_L	K/Y
1951	15.2	11.3	5.8	0.98
1952	11.4	12.6	3.7	1.00
1953	11.3	10.9	4.3	0.99
1954	12.9	11.1	4.8	0.98
1955	12.9	12.4	1.9	0.97
1956	9.9	11.3	− 1.3	0.99
1957	10.1	10.5	0.3	0.99
1958	11.3	11.0	2.6	0.99
1959	11.4	11.5	1.5	0.99
1960	10.4	11.5	− 0.7	1.00
1961	9.6	11.6	− 0.5	1.02
1962	9.8	11.1	3.3	1.03
1963	9.1	11.4	3.5	1.05
1964	8.1	11.7	4.2	1.09
1965	8.2	10.4	4.3	1.11
1966	8.9	9.2	2.6	1.10
1967	10.0	8.4	6.8	1.09
1968	8.2	7.9	6.6	1.09
1969	7.1	8.0	1.8	1.10
1970	8.4	8.9	2.0	1.10
1971	7.7	8.6	1.8	1.11
1972	6.5	8.1	1.3	1.13
1973	7.5	8.8	1.3	1.14
1974	8.0	8.1	1.7	1.14
1975	7.5	8.2	0.8	1.15

Sources: 1951–66, Weitzman (1970, Table 1); 1967–75, ouput–Soviet official; employment: 1967–71, Gomulka (1976a, Table 1.1, col. 14); 1972–75, Soviet official, no change in hours worked assumed; capital: 1969–70, Gomulka (1976, Table 1.1, col. 8); 1971–74, Narkhoz (1974); 1975, the author's estimate.

a six-year period (1941–46) of negative growth of output per man-hour.

In Figure 7.4 the period 1947–73 is divided into four separate sub-periods: (a) 1947–55, (b) 1956–61, (c) 1962–68, and (d) 1969–75. In 1946 the level of output was equal to about 0.74 of the 1944 level. In that year the level of output per man-hour was also at its minimum, being just about 0.85 of the 1944 level, and about

0.8 of the 1940 level. On the other hand, the capital/output ratio in 1946 was about 1.25 of its level in 1940. Apparently a switch from war to peace economy needed time, resulting in the fall of both ouput and labour productivity in 1946. But from 1947 the labour productivity was increasing again, though with a gradually declining rate of growth as the difference from the long-run trend was diminishing.

In period (b) there was, however, a significant increase in the growth rate of labour productivity. This is the same period of six years when the number of working hours per man was being reduced at an average rate of about 3.6 per cent. A possible interpretation is, therefore, that the planners' policy in period (b) was to link the decrease in the work-year with maintaining the old tempo of gains in the productivity per man rather than per man-hour; that is, to make the former conditional upon the latter. From this interpretation it follows that (b) was a period when overmanning, or hidden unemployment, was increasingly below its 1955 level. The increasing pressure applied by the planners to reduce the overmanning would end with the completion of the programme to reduce working hours in December 1961. A relaxation of tension in the following years should then result in at least partial, if not full, return of the overmanning (including intensity of work) to its long run equilibrium level. Hence it is suggested that periods (b) and (c) are interlinked in the sense that period (c) absorbed a delayed effect of what happened in period (b), and that this created a characteristic gap between above 'normal' performance in the year 1956–61 and below 'normal' performance in the following several years, this being what resulted in the 'jumpdown phenomenon'.

2. FITTING A CES PRODUCTION FUNCTION WITH A VARIABLE RATE OF TECHNICAL CHANGE

The general form of a CES constant returns-to-scale production function to be fitted is a standard one:

$$Y = \gamma \left| \delta_1 (BK)^{-\varrho} + (1 - \delta_1)(AL)^{-\varrho} \right|^{-1/\varrho}, \tag{1}$$

with $\sigma = 1/(1 + \varrho)$ being the (constant) elasticity of substitution, and $A = \mathrm{A}(t)$, $B = \mathrm{B}(t)$ representing the (disembodied) factor-augmenting technical change. To reduce the influence of trends in K, L and Y, the CES function to be estimated is expressed directly in terms of growth rates, rather than in terms of levels or log levels,

$$g_{Y,t} = \pi_t(g_{K,t} + \lambda_{1,t}) + (1 - \pi_{1,t})(g_{L,t} + \lambda_{2,t}), \tag{2}$$

where $\pi_t = \delta_1 \gamma^{-\varrho} e^{-\lambda_1 \varrho t} v_t^{-\varrho}$ is the (imputed) capital's share, or the elasticity of output Y with respect to capital K, $v_t = K_t/Y_t$, and g_Y, g_K, g_L, λ_1, λ_2 are the growth rates of Y, K, L, B, A, respectively. The authors estimating (1) or (2) are free to choose what they please for $A(t)$ and $B(t)$. However, it is known that the results can occasionally be highly sensitive to this choice, especially when the normally more or less exponential technical progress is seriously disturbed, e.g. by war or a major internal upheaval.

We shall later compare the explanatory power of the four different specifications of the technical progress terms: (i) by Weitzman (1970), (ii)—(iii) by Gomulka (1976), and (iv) the one which we shall now present and which will in fact emerge the winner.

Since the tests reported in Gomulka (1976), as well as in some other studies [1], indicate flatness of the ESS surface in the direction of σ, we fix σ at 1, so that $\pi = \delta_1$—the Cobb–Douglas case. We then specify $A(t)$ and $B(t)$ in (1) as follows:

$$A(t) = e^{\lambda t} \left| 1 - \xi\eta \exp[-\eta(t - 1951)] \right|^{1/\eta^2} \exp(\epsilon_t + \mu_t + \delta_{2t})t, \tag{3}$$

$$B(t) = e^{\lambda t} \exp(\epsilon_t + \mu_t + \delta_{2t})t, \tag{4}$$

where $t = 1951, \ldots, 1975$, and where ϵ_t, μ_t and δ_{2t} are dummy variables defined as follows:

$$\begin{aligned}
\epsilon_t &= -\epsilon & [1952\text{–}53], \\
&= 2\epsilon & [1955], \\
&= 0 & [\text{otherwise}];
\end{aligned} \tag{5a}$$

$$\begin{aligned}
\mu_t &= \mu & [1956\text{–}61], \\
&= 0 & [\text{otherwise}];
\end{aligned} \tag{5b}$$

$$\begin{aligned}
\delta_{2t} &= \delta_2 & [1963\text{–}68], \\
&= 0 & [\text{otherwise}].
\end{aligned} \tag{5c}$$

In specification (3)–(4), λ is the trend rate of technical change. The expression in the square brackets in (3) is superimposed on the trend. It increases to 1 for large t and its purpose is to capture the positive influence on technical change of the post-war reconstruction, including the partial replacement of women by men, and the gradual assimilation by civilian industries of the stock of product and process innovations accumulated at home and abroad during the war, as new investment in plant and equipment proceeded.

Parameter ϵ covers the 1952–55 disturbance.[2] Dummy variables μ and δ_2 cover the six-year periods (b) and (c), respectively. On computing $\lambda_{1,\,t}$ and $\lambda_{2,t}$, and on substituting them into (2), the equation to be estimated is as follows:

$$g_{Y,t} = \delta_1 g_{K,t} + (1 - \delta_1) \left[g_{L,t} + \frac{\xi \exp[-\eta(t-1951)]}{1 - \xi\eta \exp[-\eta(t-1951)]} \right]$$
$$+ \lambda + \epsilon_t + \mu_t + \delta_{2t} + u_t, \tag{6}$$

where u_t is the error term. An error sum of squares function is formed, $\phi = \Sigma u_t^2 \equiv \phi(x,\beta,t)$, where X is the data and β is the parameter vector. There are seven parameters in (6), and their values are estimated directly by minimising ϕ with respect to β.[3] The (hopefully global) minimum is found for the following values:[4]

$$\hat{\delta} = 0.401, \quad \hat{\lambda} = 0.0327, \quad \hat{\epsilon} = 0.0126, \quad \hat{\mu} = 0.0193, \quad \hat{\delta}_2 = -0.0133,$$
$$(0.171) \qquad (0.0127) \qquad (0.0063) \qquad (0.0102) \qquad (0.0082)$$

$$\hat{\eta} = 0.274, \quad \hat{\xi} = 0.0607, \quad ESS = 9.03 \times 10^{-4}, \quad R_1^2 = 0.9419,$$
$$(0.237) \qquad (0.0286)$$

$$R^2 = 0.8861.$$

Comparison of the actual growth rates of output and those estimated above is given in Figure 7.7.

3. FOUR HYPOTHESES: COMPARISON OF THE EXPLANATORY POWER

It is interesting to compare the explanatory power, indicated by the values of ESS and $\bar{R}^2$, of the specification (3)–(5) with that of the other three specifications mentioned above. These three specifications are as follows:

$$\lambda_{1,t} = \lambda_{2,t} = \lambda, \quad \text{all } t, \, \sigma \text{ any constant}; \tag{7}$$

$$\lambda_{1,t} = \lambda_1, \qquad \text{all } t,$$
$$\lambda_{2t} = \lambda_2 + \beta, \quad 1951–61,$$
$$\quad\;\; = \lambda_2, \qquad 1962–75, \, \sigma \text{ any constant}; \tag{8}$$

'Final Specification' [Gomulka (1976, eq. 11)]. $\qquad$ (9)

Equation (7) is the Weitzman (1970, eq. 5) specification and (8) is the 'preliminary specification' in Gomulka (1976). We denote (8), (9) and (3)–(5) by, respectively, G-1, G-2 and G-3. A summary of

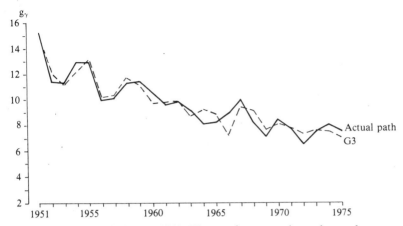

Figure 8.1: Soviet industry, 1951–75: actual versus estimated growth rates of output. Compiled by the author.
Source: ESS and $\bar{R}^2$ given for the period 1951–75. See note 4 for the definition of R_1^2 and R_2^2.

Hypothesis	$ESS \times 10^4$	$\bar{R}_1^2$	$\bar{R}_2^2$
Weitzman	31.03	0.8909	0.6648
Gomulka G-1	17.58	0.8441	0.7900
G-2	12.70	0.6700	0.8520
G-3	9.03	0.9419	0.8861

Source: *ESS and* R^2 given for the period 1951–75. See note 4 for the definition of $R_1{}^2$ and $R_2{}^2$.

the values of *ESS* and $\bar{R}^2$ is given in Figure 8.1. In terms of these two statistical indicators, this paper's specification is seen to be a clear winner from among the four. In particular, under G-3 the *ESS* equals about 30 per cent of the *ESS* implied by specification (7). The average deviation of the estimated from the actual output growth rates is 0.48 per cent. For assessing its relative weight, this deviation should be compared with the average annual growth rate of output, which in the years 1951–75 was 9.66 per cent.

In comparison with (9), specification G-3 performs better not only for the period 1951–75 but also for the years 1947–50. However, there is also another important reason why G-3 may be preferred; it is that $\lambda_{2,t}$ in (9) includes terms which were estimated in a rather ad hoc manner and, moreover, separately from the remaining terms though in part on the basis of the same data.

Table 8.2: Sources of Soviet industrial growth, estimated for 1951–75 and implied for 1947–50, under specification G-3

	Output growth rate	Capital's contribution	Components of the 'explained' residual				Total estimated residual[a]	Unexplained residual
			Labour's contribution	Post-war recovery	Changes in work year	Trend		
1951	15.2	4.5	3.5	3.7	0.0	3.3	7.0	0.2
1952	11.4	5.1	2.2	2.8	0.0	3.3	4.8	-0.7
1953	11.3	4.4	2.6	2.1	0.0	3.3	4.1	0.2
1954	12.9	4.5	2.9	1.6	0.0	3.3	4.9	0.7
1955	12.9	5.0	1.1	1.2	0.0	3.3	7.0	-0.2
1956	9.9	4.8	-0.8	0.9	1.9	3.3	6.1	-0.2
1957	10.1	4.2	0.2	0.7	1.9	3.3	5.9	0.2
1958	11.3	4.4	1.6	0.5	1.9	3.3	5.7	-0.4
1959	11.4	4.6	0.9	0.4	1.9	3.3	5.6	0.3
1960	10.4	4.6	-0.4	0.3	1.9	3.3	5.5	0.7
1961	9.6	4.7	-0.3	0.2	1.9	3.3	5.4	-0.2
1962	9.8	4.5	2.0	0.2	0.0	3.3	3.4	-0.1
1963	9.1	4.6	2.1	0.1	-1.3	3.3	2.1	0.4
1964	8.1	4.7	2.5	0.1	-1.3	3.3	2.0	-1.2
1965	8.2	4.2	2.6	0.1	-1.3	3.3	2.0	-0.6

1966	8.9	3.7	1.6	0.1	-1.3	3.3	2.0	1.7
1967	10.0	3.4	4.1	0.0	-1.3	3.3	2.0	0.6
1968	8.2	3.2	4.0	0.0	-1.3	3.3	2.0	-0.9
1969	7.1	3.2	1.1	0.0	0.0	3.3	3.3	-0.5
1970	8.4	3.6	1.2	0.0	0.0	3.3	3.3	0.4
1971	7.7	3.5	1.1	0.0	0.0	3.3	3.3	-0.1
1972	6.5	3.5	0.8	0.0	0.0	3.3	3.3	-0.8
1973	7.5	3.3	0.8	0.0	0.0	3.3	3.3	-0.1
1974	8.0	3.3	1.0	0.0	0.0	3.3	3.3	0.5
1975	7.5[b]	3.3	0.5	0.0	0.0	3.3	3.3	0.5

Sources of growth implied under specification G-3[c]

1947	20.8	3.3	1.7 (2.9)	11.4		3.3	14.7	1.1(-0.1)
1948	26.9	5.1	6.5(10.9)	8.6		3.3	11.9	3.4(-1.0)
1949	19.5	3.3	3.5 (5.9)	6.5		3.3	9.8	2.9 (0.5)
1950	22.7	3.7	6.6(11.0)	4.9		3.3	8.2	4.2(-0.2)

NOTES:

[a]Includes the estimate of the 1952–55 disturbance (Korean War): -1.26 per cent in both 1952 and 1953, and +2.52 per cent in 1955.

[b]Preliminary.

[c]Numbers in parentheses refer to the case when labour's contribution to output is proportional to employment.

4. THE ECONOMICS OF SLOWDOWN

The dynamics of the (estimated) productivity residual and the residual's three main components are given in Table 8.2 and in Figure 7.7. According to this estimate the catch-up phenomenon was quite important until about 1955, accounting in that year for about one-tenth of the growth rate of output. In the years 1951–61 the combined effect of the catch-up phenomenon and of the changes in the workyear increased the growth rate of output by about 2.5 per cent above its trend value. By 1962 the catch-up was completed, so it ceased to play a role any more. But then, according to the estimate, the negative effect of reduction in the work year just began to be felt, decreasing the growth rate of output in the years 1963–68 by about 1.3 per cent below its trend. It thus follows that it was this sudden change from a positive value to a negative one in the non-trend component of the residual which produced the phenomenon of jumpdown in the growth of labour productivity in 1962–63.

While the main features of the explanation of slowdown implied by specifications G-2 and G-3, respectively, are the same, there are two notable differences. One is that under G-3 the growth effect of catching up is greater from the beginning of the recovery process in 1947 until about 1955, and it decreases more rapidly over time. The other is that the trend component in the residual is significantly lower, it is 3.3 per cent compared with 4.2 per cent under G-2. However, the really important determinant of the growth potential of labour productivity, output and capital is not λ, but the Harrod–Kalecki rate of technical change $\lambda/(1-\delta_1)$. This rate is equal to 5.97 per cent under G-2 and 5.45 per cent under G-3. From $g_Y = \delta_1 g_K + (1 - \delta_1)g_L + \lambda$, which is the form of G-3 for the post-1969 years, it follows that, at $\delta_1 = 0.4$ (growth rates in per cents), $g_Y = (2/3)g_{K/Y} + g_L + 5.45$. Since g_K must with time follow g_Y, the growth rate of Soviet industrial output (as well as the growth rate of capital) to be expected on the basis of this paper's findings is close to $g_L + 5.5$ per cent, that is 0.5 per cent less than the prediction given in Gomulka (1976). It may be recalled that Weitzman's paper implied that the Soviet growth slowdown would continue in the future until g_Y decreases to about $g_L + 2.0$ per cent. Applying his specification (eq. (7) above) to the data in Table 8.1 gives essentially the same result: $\lambda = 2.1$ per cent and $\sigma = 0.51$ implying the limit growth rate of output to be $g_L + 2.1$ per cent.

Finally there is the question of what we can really deduce from the above findings about the nature of technical change in the Soviet Union, and about the value of capital labour elasticity σ and its role in generating the growth slowdown. In Gomulka (1976) it was emphasised, and this emphasis applies fully also in this paper, that although the preferred specification is at $\sigma = 1$, this should not be taken to imply that the actual value of the elasticity of substitution is in fact close to unity. Instead of pointing to a particular value of σ, both the above mentioned study and this paper suggest that σ should be considered jointly with the direction of technical change λ_1/λ_2, and that in the case in hand there are in fact only two possibilities: either technical change is predominantly labour-augmenting, that is $\lambda_2 \gg \lambda_1$, and then the actual value of σ remains unknown, or σ is approximately 1, but then the actual direction of technical change remains unknown. There is also a negative result, that Weitzman's preferred combination: $\lambda_1 = \lambda_2$, $\sigma \ll 1$, which incidently would be sub-optimal in an innovation possibility frontier model of the Kennedy–Samuelson-type, is in fact not a very likely possibility. It is of course this latter result which puts into doubt the notion that the basic cause of slowdown was that during its post-war transition from a labour-surplus state to a labour-deficit one the Soviet economy suffered from the combination of a low substitutability of capital for labour and an inability of the Soviet planners to induce a gradual increase in the rate of labour-saving innovations at the expense, if necessary, of the capital-saving innovations. This paper suggests that there is nothing specifically Soviet, nothing 'systemic', which is likely to have been underlying growth slowdown. In my view the explanation is much simpler; it is, in a nutshell, that slowdown is the reflection of two major shocks: the second world war (above all), and the reduction in the work year, which together produced a rather complex dynamics of the rate of technical change during the post-war period.[5]

NOTES

1. Gapinski and Kumar (1976), note 5.
2. See Gomulka (1976) p. 31 for its description (chapter 7, p. 120, this volume).
3. An algorithm devised by Torn (1975) was used. It differs from the so far commonly used procedure of running an optimisation algorithm successively from a number of different initial points in its much more efficient use of the information gained during the optimisation process.

This allows one to take into account a relatively large number of initial points, thus increasing considerably one's confidence that the best point obtained is in fact the global minimum. In our particular case the number of such initial points was 30. They were random points, uniformly distributed in the permissible range of the parameters. The algorithm was tested at the Numerical Optimisation Centre, Hatfield, and the results are reported in Gomulka (1977).

4. R_1^2 is defined in the usual way as the ratio $\Sigma(\hat{g}_{Y,t} - \bar{g}_{Y,t})^2/\Sigma(g_{Y,t} - \bar{g}_{Y,t})^2$, where $\bar{g}_{Y,t}$ is the sample mean of g_Y. R^2 reported in Gomulka (1976) (Chapter 7, this volume) was defined as the difference: $1 - ESS/(\Sigma\, g_{Y,t} - \bar{g}_{Y,t})^2$, which in this paper is denoted by R_2^2 and is preferred as a measure of goodness of fit, since R_1^2 could in a non-linear model exceed 1. As usual, $\bar{R}^2$ is R^2 corrected for the degrees of freedom. Numbers in parenthesis denote the standard linearised errors. For a comment on these errors, see Weitzman (1970, footnote 11).

5. Green and Levine (1976) suggest that machinery imports from the West might have been a much more powerful source of Soviet industrial growth than my own estimate (Gomulka (1976, Table 1.5) appears to indicate. They estimate the contribution of these imports to growth for the period 1961–74, and found it to be, on average, about 1.3 per cent in the period 1961–68, rising to about 2.1 per cent in the years 1969–74. If these estimates are correct, we may have an additional factor contributing to the upswing in the labour productivity growth in the post-1968 years. However, the Green–Levine specification of the (Cobb–Douglas) production function has no separate term for technical progress. Consequently, the growth effect of that progress has to be captured by physical inputs. Since, according to this paper, technical progress was low in the years 1963–68, that is when Soviet machinery imports happened to be also low, it is possible that in their exercise it was the imported input which captured more of that progress than is its 'fair' share.

REFERENCES

Brubaker, E. R., 'Embodied Technology, the Asymptotic Behaviour of Capital's Age, and the Soviet Growth, Review of Economics and Statistics, **50**, no. 3, 1968, pp. 304–11.

Gapiński, J. H. and Kumar, T. K. 'Embodiment, Putty-clay, and Misspecification of the Directly Estimated CES', *International Economic Review,* **17**, June, no. 2, 1976, pp. 472–83.

Gomulka, J., 'Numerical experience with the Torn's clustering algorithm, in Dixon, L. C. W. and Szego, G. (eds), *Global Optimization II,* North-Holland, Amsterdam, 1977.

Gomulka, S., 'Soviet Post-war Industrial Growth, Capital Labour Substitution, and Technical Changes: A Re-examination', in Fallenbuchl, Z. M. (ed.) *Economic Development in the Soviet Union and Eastern Europe,* vol. 2 (Praeger, New York) pp. 3–47, 1976.

Green, D. W. and Levine, H. S. Macro-econometric Evidence of the Value of Machinery Imports to the USSR, Paper presented to the NSF/GWU Workshop in Soviet Science and Technology, 1976.

Rostowski, J., 1976. A Sectoral Test of Alternative Interpretations of the Slowdown in Soviet Industrial Growth, mimeo, 1976.

Torn, A., Cluster Analysis as a Tool in a Global Optimisation Model, mimeo. 1975.

Weitzman, M. L., 'Soviet Post-war Economic Growth and Capital Labour Substitution', *American Economic Review,* **60,** September, no. 4, 1970, pp. 676–92.

Afterword

Over the last ten years, from 1975–1985, the slowdown in Soviet industrial growth has continued, by the mid-1980s the growth rate stabilising at a level of between 3 per cent and 4 per cent, which happens to be also the trend growth rate of US industry in the post-war period. In these ten years several new studies of the slowdown phenomenon have been published, some of them—in particular Bergson (1979) and Hanson (1981)—noting and contrasting its interpretation by Weitzman (1970) and Desai (1976) with that of my own (Chapters 7 and 8, this volume). To help the reader to follow this literature, it may be useful to comment on two matters that have emerged as crucial: one concerns the economic significance of the ease with which capital can be substituted for labour, the other relates to the dynamics of the innovation rate.

In Chapters 7 and 8, it has been already noted that the economic significance of the capital-labour elasticity of substitution, σ_{KL}, depends on its magnitude and on the nature of the technological change: whether the labour-saving innovation dominates, as many (perhaps most), economists think is the case with reference to western economies, or it does not dominate, as Weitzman and Desai suggest is the case with reference to the USSR. There are good grounds for supposing that the magnitude of σ_{KL} is low in the USSR as well as worldwide. The reason is that the capital which is already in place cannot be, or cannot be easily, substituted for labour, and that practically the only way to effect such substitution is through new additions to the stock of capital. But in this case we have that (make note that $v = K/L$ and $k = I/L'$):

$$\sigma_{KL} = \left(\pi \frac{L'}{L} + (1 - \pi) \frac{I}{K} \right) \sigma_{IL'} = \left(\pi \frac{v - k}{k} + 1 \right) \frac{I}{K} \sigma_{IL'} \qquad (1)^*$$

where K is total capital stock, I is the newly added capital stock which I take to be last year's gross investment, L' is the (new) labour associated with I, $\sigma_{IL'}$ is the *ex-ante* substitution elasticity between I and L', given the size of new output, and π is the capital elasticity of the new output. There are two implications of this relation. One is that σ_{IL}' would have to be quite high, perhaps more than 10, for σ_{KL} to be unity or more. But if actual σ_{IL}' is less than 10, then σ_{KL} would be, with $k \geq \nu$ and the ratio I/K usually less than 0.1, in the range between 0 and 1. The other implication is that, assuming σ_{IL}' constant over time, the Soviet σ_{KL} would have been declining over time in line with the I/K ratio. If σ_{KL} were a parameter of consequence, a fall in I/K would have compounded Soviet problems.

However, if the labour-saving innovation dominates, then the value of σ_{KL} is of little significance. In the case when $Y = F(K, TL)$, so that innovation is purely labour-saving, the ratio K/TL plays the same role as does the (K/L) ratio under the Hicks-neutral technological change. Assuming constant returns to scale, the marginal input productivities and input shares depend, then, on K/TL instead of K/L. Since T increases approximately as fast as does the labour productivity, the ratio K/TL would change little over time. Consequently these marginal input productivities and input shares would also change little over time even if σ_{KL} were significantly less than one. It follows that if for some reasons, Soviet-specific or world-common, the Soviet σ_{KL} were low, this should have induced Soviet planners to direct R & D resources to the production and assimilation of the labour-saving inventions. The basic inefficiency that is (implicitly) claimed by Weitzman is, therefore, that they have failed to do so and instead continued to give equal weight to labour-saving innovation and to capital-saving innovation, this having been the case despite the rapid transformation of the Soviet economy since 1928 from one with capital shortage to that with labour shortage. It is thus apparent that at the centre of our debate is the question of the type of Soviet innovation. My attempt to answer that question has led me to suggest that the Soviet growth data are better explained if one allows that, in fact, the labour-saving innovation has been the dominant type. According to this suggestion, the type of Soviet innovation has been, and is, similar to that which, it appears, has been prevailing in the developed West; something which should not be surprising if the former has been and is largely a part of the latter.

It may also be noted that Weitzman (1970) suggests that there operates a law of development by which, in the course of industrialisation of any less-developed country, the capital's imputed share of output would be falling as the capital input becomes plentiful and the agricultural labour reserve becomes exhausted. Soviet slowdown in the 1950s and the 1960s would be simply a manifestation of that general law. However, the generality of this interesting suggestion remains still to be demonstrated and, in any case, seems to be at variance with the experience of other CPEs, such as Bulgaria, Romania and Poland, where no industrial slowdown of the Soviet-type had been observed in the years of rapid transformation, 1950–75.

The other matter is the cause, or causes, of the post-1975 slowdown. In my interpretation, the latter slowdown is qualitatively different from the one observed until the mid-1970s. The difference is explained in Chapter 3. While in Chapters 7 and 8 it was suggested that, until 1975, the Soviet trend rate of industrial innovation was constant over time, this rate seems to have since decreased to the level of the corresponding US innovation rate. However, the more fundamental reasons of the recent growth slowdown appear to be many in number and difficult for any quantitative assessment of their relative weight. For good discussion of this topic the reader may consult Levine (1983), Levine *et al.* (1983), and a collection of studies edited by Bergson and Levine (1983).

NOTE

*Proof of equation (1). Let $K = \bar{K} + I$, $L = \bar{L} + L'$ and $Y = \bar{Y} + F(I,L')$, where $\bar{K}$, $\bar{L}$ and $\bar{Y}$ denote, respectively, capital stock, employment and output of the 'old' economy, I is gross investment of the last year and L' is the corresponding employment, and where $F(I,L')$ is the output of the 'new' economy. It follows that $Y = \bar{Y} + F(K-\bar{K}, L-\bar{L}) = G(K,L)$, say. Hence $G_K = F_I$ and $G_L = F_{L'}$, and therefore $F_{L'}/F_I = G_L/G_K = \omega$, where ω is the ratio of competitive factor prices, w/r. By definition,

$$\sigma_{KL} = \frac{\omega}{v} \frac{\partial v}{\partial \omega} \quad \text{and} \quad \sigma_{IL'} = \frac{\omega}{k} \frac{\partial k}{\partial \omega}$$

where $v = K/L$ and $k = I/L'$, and where both $\partial v/\partial \omega$ and $\partial k/\partial \omega$ are calculated along an output isoquant, i.e. while keeping $F(I,L') = Y' = \text{constant}$. Since

$$\sigma_{KL} = \frac{k}{v} \frac{\partial v}{\partial k} \sigma_{IL'}$$

we need to calculate $\partial v/\partial k$, given Y'. But

$$v = \frac{K}{L} = \frac{\bar{K} + kL'}{\bar{L} + L'}$$

where L' is implicity related to Y' and k by the relation: $Y' = F(I, L') = F(kL', L')$. Assuming constant returns to scale, $Y' = L'F(k, 1)$. On differentiating with respect to k, given Y', one obtains that $0 = L_k F(k, 1) + L'F_k$. Hence

$$L_k = -L' \frac{F_k}{F} = -\frac{L'}{k} \frac{kF_k}{F} = -\frac{L'}{k} \pi.$$

Now we are ready to calculate $\partial v / \partial k$. We have that

$$\frac{\partial v}{\partial k} = \frac{L'}{L} \left(1 + (k - v) \frac{L_k}{L'} \right) = \frac{L'}{L} \left(1 - \pi + \pi \frac{v}{k} \right).$$

Hence

$$\frac{k}{v} \frac{\partial v}{\partial k} = \frac{I}{K} \left(1 - \pi + \pi \frac{v}{k} \right) = \pi \frac{L'}{L} + (1 - \pi) \frac{I}{K}$$

and

$$\sigma_{KL} = \frac{k}{v} \frac{\partial v}{\partial k} \sigma_{IL}' = \left(\pi \frac{L'}{L} + (1 - \pi) \frac{I}{K} \right) \sigma_{IL}'.$$

The expression in parenthesis may be interpreted as weight of the economy's new segment, in which the capital-labour substitution elasticity equals σ_{IL}', in the total economy.

REFERENCES

1. Bergson, A., (1979), 'Notes on the Production Function in Soviet Postwar Industrial Growth', *Journal of Comparative Economics* **3**(2), June, pp. 116–26.
2. Bergson, A. and Levine, H. (eds)(1983), *The Soviet Economy Toward the Year 2000,* London: Allen & Unwin.
3. Desai, P., (1976), 'The Production Function and Technical Change in Postwar Soviet Industry', *American Economic Review,* **66**(3), June, pp. 372–81.
4. Hanson, P., (1981), *Trade and Technology in Soviet-Western Relations,* London: Macmillan.
5. Levine, H., (1983), 'On the Possible Causes of the Deterioration of Soviet Productivity Growth in the Period 1976-1980', in Joint Economic Committee, *Soviet Economy in the 1980s: Problems and Prospects,* Washington, DC: US Government Printing Office.
6. Levine, H., Bond, D. L., Movet, C. and Goldstein, E. (1983), *The Causes and Implications of the Sharp Deterioration in Soviet Economic Performance, Centrally Planned Economies Projects,* Washington, DC: Wharton Econometric Forecasting Associates, Inc.
7. Weitzman, M. L. (1970), 'Soviet Postwar Economic Growth and Capital-Labour Substitution', *American Economic Review* **60**(4), September, pp. 676–92.

9 Poland's Industrialisation*

1. INTRODUCTION

This paper deals primarily with Poland's industrialisation in the 1945–1982 period. In order to assess the scale of progress that has been made in that period, it is essential to place it in a longer historical perspective. The starting point that has been chosen is the year 1860. Since that time several major border changes have taken place. If our intertemporal comparisons are to be meaningful, they must relate consistently to the same area of land. For obvious reasons we have chosen it to be the post-war Poland.

The novel element in our analysis of the sources of economic growth in the post-1945 years, given in section 3, is an attempt to separate the impact of transitory phenomena, associated with activation of the growth reserves that were present in 1946, from the actual growth rate, in order to identify the rate that has been truly characteristic for the post-war period. The phenomena we look at are well known, but have not been given proper weight in the academic literature, and tend to be overlooked or misinterpreted in official accounts of the period.

*This was an invited paper presented at an International Conference on 'Contemporary Poland in Historical Perspective', held at Yale University, New Haven, 22–25 May 1984. I wish to thank Michael Montias and Piotr Wandycz, the main organisers of the conference, for their invitation and encouragement. The paper is a part of an SSRC-financed project on Economic Growth in Eastern Europe 1946–1975: The causes of variation over time and between countries. The present version of the paper benefited much from criticisms and suggestions of the following colleagues: John Farrell of the Oregon State University, Maria Hirszowicz of Reading University, David Kemme of the University of North Carolina, Kazimierz Laski of Linz University, Austria, and Jacek Rostowski of Kingston Polytechnic, London. I am particularly grateful to Mark Schaffer of the London School of Economics and Stanford for editing the paper as well as for comments of substance. Needless to say, I alone am responsible for the final outcome.

There is little doubt that Poland's industrialisation has been influenced much by 'systemic' factors—the particular economic system and development strategy that the communist authorities have adopted. The forms and extent of that influence have been subjected to close scrutiny by many authors, from both Eastern Europe and the West. Nevertheless the full impact of the systemic factors still remain somewhat elusive. We raise this subject in section 4, emphasising three aspects: sources of financial accumulation, sectoral composition of investment, and economic efficiency. In particular it is argued that, in the face of system-induced micro decisions of individual enterprises to adopt resource-intensive methods of making things, the ability of the centre to control the branch composition of industrial output is more apparent than real.

The industrialisation of a country means the expansion of industrial activity, both in absolute terms and as a proportion of the country's total economic activity. However, industrialisation may also be seen as necessary to propel the expansion of sectors other than industry itself. In section 5 we discuss to what extent this was the case in post-1945 Poland. In that section we also assess the impact of industrialisation on the standard of living.

Industrialisation needs qualitative changes to be sustained, and it also helps to produce them. These interactions between quantitative and qualitative changes are discussed first in section 6, with emphasis on education and technological change, and then in section 7, where wider issues of industrialisation and social change are raised. Finally, in section 8, we relate the progress Poland has made so far to that of some other countries, and review briefly the development constraints that have emerged recently and which are likely to exert major impact on the country's economic fortunes in the decades to come.

All major tables containing data and estimates are in the Appendix—A preceding a number reference to a table indicating that the table is to be found there.

2. EXTENT AND CHANGING PACE OF INDUSTRIALISATION, 1860–1980

Possibly the most accurate measure of the extent of industrialisation is the proportion of gross national product (GNP) which originates in industry. However, in the nineteenth century the quality of output data was poor. Better was the quality of data on population and employment. When output per worker varies little between major types of economic activity, which is usually the case, the proportion of the labour force engaged in industry is a good proxy for the corresponding output measure. In Table A1 we make a further assumption, namely that employment is a constant proportion of the total population, and use as a measure of industrialisation the ratio of industrial employment to total population.[1] In Table A1 we also give the progress of urbanisation on Poland's present lands since 1860 as measured by the proportion of urban population, and the composition of total industrial employment by branches.

The 120 years are seen to fall into three distinct periods: 1860–1914, 1914–1945 and 1945–1980. The trend growth rate established in the first period was high, but the growth process (curve C in Figure 9.1) was stopped in the second period by two world wars and the interwar economic depression. The growth was resumed in 1945 with great vigour, but continued at a rate that was declining as the distance between 'potential' growth path (C^* in Figure 9.1) and the actual one declined. The path C^* indicates what would possibly have happened in the absence of wars and depression.[2] Yet some economic development did occur in the period 1914–1945. Curve A in Figure 9.1 indicates that urbanisation was progressing at the trend growth rate of 1 per cent per annum until 1939. Since urbanisation is a base which is necessary to support industrialisation, the increase in this base in the period 1914–45 represented a growth reserve, enabling the post-1945 industrialisation to proceed somewhat faster than would have been possible otherwise. During the second world war a large proportion of urban population perished. Nevertheless, as a proportion of total population, it already reached the trend path by the late 1950s. The urban infrastructure of 1939 was apparently sufficiently intact to sustain the previous urbanisation trend, given the much smaller total population of the 1946–1960 period. The capital stock in industry and in other 'productive' sectors was underemployed in the first several years after 1945, as it will be clear from the evidence presented in section 3. The true extent of industrialisation in those years was therefore above the C-path. It was almost certainly below the C^*-path, although theoretically the war could have increased the ratio of industrial employment to population, if the non-industrial sector suffered proportionately more than the industrial one, which probably it did not.

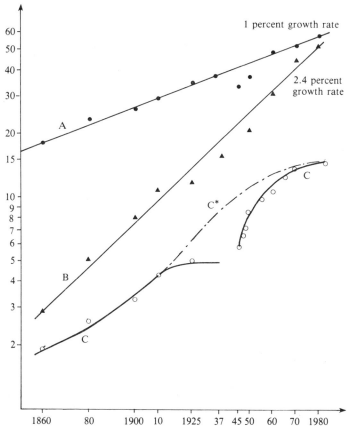

Figure 9.1: Urban population (A) and industrial employment (C) as per cent of total population, and industrial employment as such (B), Poland in post-1945 boundaries 1860–1980.
(.—.—.) Hypothetical extrapolation of the C-path, as established in the years 1860–1910, for the years 1910–1980. The difference between C and C is indicative of the effects of two world wars and the inter-war economic depression.

The data in Table A1 also give the distribution of industrial employment on Poland's lands among Russia, Prussia and Austria before 1918, and between Poland and Germany in 1938. Industrialisation of the lands under Prussia was fastest and, in 1910, about 63 per cent of total industry was on those lands, with their population standing at about 44 per cent of the total. Employment data for the 1920s and the 1930s indicate that about half of Polish industry in 1945 was on German lands.[3] According to Secomski,

Table 9.1: Fixed capital assets in Polish industry, 1938 and 1946

	1946 Poland		1938 Poland
	German lands before 1939	Polish lands before 1939 and after 1945	Soviet lands after 1945
Assets in 1938	45	55	10
Assets in 1946		65	

Note: Assets in 1938 on lands belonging to Poland in 1946 are taken as 100.

war losses of industrial fixed assets on post-war lands were 35 per cent.[4] How did the remaining 65 per cent compare with the total value, in 1939, of industrial assets within the pre-war borders? From the figures in Table 9.1 the answer would appear to be that the value of fixed industrial assets under Polish administration was about the same in 1946 as in 1938. It follows that these assets per head of population increased from 1938 to 1946 by about 50 per cent.

3. SOURCES OF ECONOMIC GROWTH IN THE POST-1945 PERIOD

In this section we shall attempt to account for the growth of Poland's economy in the post-war period. The emphasis is on industrial growth, but the growth of other sectors is also looked at.

(i) Changes in inputs and in their separate and joint productivities

The basic industrial growth data are presented in Table A2 and in Figures 9.2A, 9.2B and 9.3. It is useful to begin by surveying and interpreting changes over time of the key five ratios and growth rates presented in the two diagrams: capital/output ratio, investment/output ratio, incremental capital/output ratio, the growth rate of capital stock and the growth rate of investment.

From the point of view of growth accounting the most interesting of the five are changes in the average and incremental capital/output ratios, both shown in Figure 9.2B. Changes in the average capital/output ratio follow a distinct U curve: declining sharply in the years 1946–53, declining marginally in the years 1954–65, nearly perfectly constant in the years 1965–77, and again rising

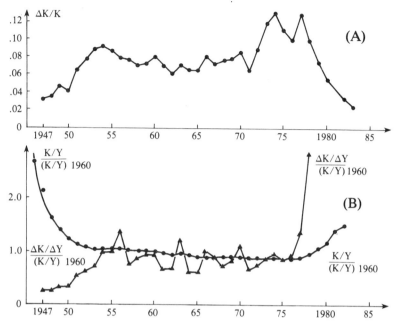

Figure 9.2: Polish industry. (A): The growth rate of capital stock, (B): the average capital/output ratio and the incremental capital/ratio, 1947–1982.

sharply in the years 1978–82. The incremental capital/output ratio was low but rising in the years 1947–54, fluctuating around the (nearly constant) average (K/Y) ratio in the years 1955–76, and virtually exploding during the crisis 1979–82.

This pattern of changes is instructive in so far as it reveals clearly the years 1947–53 as those when the post-war reconstruction was a powerful source of growth of industrial ouput. Not surprisingly, in the four years 1946–49 industrial investment was very low as a proportion of the existing capital stock. These investments were rather high in the years 1950–53, but a large proportion went into projects with long gestation periods.[5] However, in many enterprises investments did not have to be large to alleviate or eliminate the output bottlenecks that the war losses had created. In addition, industrial output was increased by non-industrial investment (e.g. in restoring electric power supplies or repairing transport and communications), and was coupled with the employment of new labour and the introduction of overtime in some enterprises, second and third work shifts in others. Output was probably also increased, perhaps even significantly, by reducing the pre-war technological and technical standards, that is, by trading off quality for quantity. Because all these measures enabled more output to be produced out of the essentially unchanged capacity, they come under our umbrella term of the 'post-war reconstruction factor' (PRF).

What was the growth contribution of the PRF? In the year 1953, industrial stock of fixed capital assets stood at 1.45 of the 1946 level, but net industrial output was four times greater than its 1946 level. It follows that the PRF probably accounted for as much as 85 per cent of the output increase during that period $[(300-45)/300 = 0.85]$. As such, it was therefore *the* growth factor.[6] Its significance, of course, declined with time. Even so, using the same method we find that the PRF has accounted for 60 per cent of the output increase during the first four years of the six-year plan, from 1949 to 1953.

The dominant role of the PRF as a source of growth in the 1946–53 period has not been fully recognised by the official economic history, especially in relation to the years 1949–53. On the other hand, such a role should not lead one to underestimate the success of the new communist-led authorities in organising the recovery effort after a disaster in which, as a country, Poland suffered proportionately far more than any other war partic-ipant. Nevertheless, the PRF was essentially the activation of idle resources, and as such was of a different category than the expansion of resources through accumulation, education and technological change, the key sources of industrial growth after 1953.

Another aspect of any industrialisation is the size of the invest-ment effort. Diagrams in Figure 9.3 tell us the relevant story, in terms of the growth rate of industrial investment, g_I, and the ratio of that investment to net industrial output, I/Y. The period 1955–71 was one of remarkable stability in the I/Y ratio. Although the growth rate of investment fluctuated from year to year, these fluctuations do not appear to form any clear pattern.[7] We also see two distinct 'humps', corresponding to two attempts at accelerated industrialisation, in the early 1950s and the mid-1970s. The latter attempt was greater, and so have been its aftermath effects in terms of economic efficiency and stability. The ratio prevailing in the period 1955–71 probably corresponds to the maximum investment effort which the country could have absorbed, given the size and quality of its labour force, its infrastructure and ability to export.

The rate was rather high and, as a result, the weight of industry as a sector of Polish total economy was increasing until 1980. In

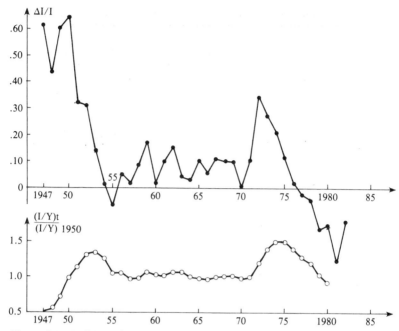

Figure 9.3: Polish industry. Variation over time in the growth rate of (gross productive in fixed capital) investment and in the ratio of investment to net output, 1947–83.

terms of resources employed and net outputs produced it gained at some expense of 'other material' sectors, but especially at the expense of the 'non-material' part of the economy, the largest segment of which is housing. Changes in the distribution of labour L, capital K, and net output Y among the three parts of Poland's economy that occurred from 1950 to 1980 are given in Table 9.2. A still better indicator of the emphasis which the Polish communist authorities have given to industrial growth is the distribution of new fixed capital assets that were *added* in the period 1950–80 to the initial capital stock. The share of industry in these new assets has been 39 per cent, against only 25 per cent allocated to all the 'non-material' sectors. These data are striking, since market-oriented countries of whatever level of development tend to devote significantly more to housing, education, health services and other 'non-material' sectors than to industry. This emphasis on industry is thus a distinct characteristic of communist development strategy. (It also leads to a statistical bias which inflates the overall growth rate, about which later.)

Table 9.2 Shares of inputs and net outputs by activity, in per cent of total

		Industry	Other material sectors	Non-material sectors	Total
	L	19	68	13	100
1950	K	10	34	56	100
	Y	22	41	37	100
	L	29	53	18	100
1980	K	30	35	35	100
	Y	43	37	20	100

Source:
Tables A2, A4 and A5 of the Appendix, in A5 columns corresponding to 8 per cent as the imputed capital rent.
Note:
The capital rent assumed for the purpose of calculating Y originating in non-material sectors need not have been 8 per cent nor constant. Taking 4 per cent as the rent, our estimate of the sectors' share in total Y, meaning GNP, would drop to 26.7 per cent in 1950 and to 15.6 per cent in 1980.

In order to relate industrial growth to that of the whole economy, I have taken the output of the non-material sector to be the imputed payments to capital and labour employed in that sector. This output series is presented in Table A5. In turn Table A6 gives the average annual growth rates for industry, all material sectors and total economy. Industrial output is seen to have been increasing significantly faster than that of total economy, as well as that of other 'material' sectors. Some of this increase was due to the quantitative growth of primary inputs (taken here to be labour and capital), while the residual is the contribution to output growth of changes in quality and utilisation of all the inputs. Assuming constant returns to scale and a Cobb–Douglas production function, the residual term is reported in Table A7 for industry and the total economy. The division for sub-periods reflects our earlier point on the significance of 1953 as the year when the post-war recovery period came to an end. With decline in importance of the PRF, the residual dropped sharply from a high level in the period 1949–53 to a low one in the years 1954–55. It rose again above the long-term average in the years 1956–65, but fell below this average in the last five years of Gomułka's rule. The changes in the 1970s reflect, of course, the stimulating role of fast-increasing imports in the earlier part of the period and the effect of heavy import restrictions in the later part.

Taking as an example 0.3 for the imputed capital share, the

average residual for the 1953–80 period was 3.4 per cent in both industry and the economy total. This is thus one possible estimate, in terms of their output effect, of the rate of qualitative changes in Poland's industry and economy. (We assume utilisation rates for labour and capital to be about the same in 1953 as in 1980, which may not be quite true. As in any aggregate-type analysis, we also disregard the impact on aggregate output of changes in the branch composition of inputs and outputs.) That estimate gives us the contribution to growth of the so-called 'intensive factors of growth'. The average annual growth rate of output in the period 1953–80 was 7.7 per cent in industry and 5.8 per cent for the economy total. Therefore the 'extensive factors', meaning the purely quantitative growth of capital and labour, accounted for 4.3 per cent growth in industry (nearly 56 per cent of the actual growth rate), but for only 2.4 per cent growth in the economy total (about 41 per cent of the actual growth rate). These illustrative estimates indicate that industrial growth was possibly predominantly extensive, while non-industrial growth might have been predominantly intensive.[8]

(ii) Unusual growth factors in the post-1945 period

The growth data of the foregoing section portray a progress of industrialisation in the post-1945 period that, while not nearly as spectacular as that in some of the Far East countries, would appear to have been very respectable by the standards established among medium-developed countries in the same period. However, any sound assessment of the progress that has been made must look for and take proper account of unusual factors which raised (or conceivably lowered) the rate of industrial growth above (or below) what would have been the rate in their absence. The purpose of such an inquiry is to identify the growth rate which was, or is, sustainable in the longer term and which reflects more accurately the inner growth dynamics that were present in a particular period and is characteristic for a particular economy. In the section above we have already discussed two such unusual factors operating in Poland in the post-1945 period, the PRF and the impact of border and population changes, the latter having increased, in per capita terms, both the stock of industrial assets and the stock of infrastructure. There were three other factors of such unusual type.

Industrial bias: In the period 1953–80 a high rate of industrial growth was sustained by an exceptional concentration of investment effort on industrial activities. That such a highly unbalanced growth strategy was feasible is consistent with the possibility, already mentioned, that some (perhaps considerable) spare capacity in the infrastructure sector was present in the early 1950s. That capacity would have been inherited by post-war Poland, and represented a growth reserve which would have served to sustain the industrial growth during the period 1946–80. An illustration of this point is the fall in the ratio of fixed (productive) capital assets in transport and communications to that of industry from 69 per cent in 1950 to 32 per cent in 1980. The share of Poland's transport and communications in all fixed capital assets, at 9.2 per cent in 1980, was lowest among the seven European CMEA countries. (For comparison, the share was 15.2 per cent in both Bulgaria and Hungary, 15.3 per cent in Czechoslovakia, 13.7 per cent in the USSR, 13.5 per cent in Romania and 9.7 per cent in the GDR.) Consequently, the infrastructure sectors, such as transport, communications and housing, appear to have become a binding constraint on further growth. This was apparently not so in the 1950s and the 1960s.

It is hazardous to speculate what would have been the growth of industrial output if the development strategy was more balanced. Since the average (and incremental) capital/output ratio was nearly constant for the best part of the post-1953 period, industrial growth rate in year t, $g_{Y,t}$, was given approximately by the following rule:

$$s_{t-2} = \frac{\Delta K}{\Delta Y} \cdot g_{Y,t} + \delta_t \tag{1}$$

where we take two years as the average time-lag between investment and output, and where $s = I/Y$, the ratio of gross investment in industry to industrial net output, and δ is the ratio of replacement investment to net output. The investment ratio was nearly constant in the period 1955–71, standing at about 23 per cent. In the period 1952–73 the average annual g_Y was 8.6 per cent. Taking $(\Delta K/\Delta K)_{1955-71}$, equal to 2.24, for $\Delta K/\Delta Y$, it follows from (1) that $\delta = 3.7$. Hence:

$$s_{t-2} = 2.24 \, g_{Y,t} + 3.7 \tag{1a}$$

or that:

$$g_{Y,t} = .45 s_{t-2} - 1.7 \tag{2}$$

where both s and g_Y are in per cent.

In mature economies, such as those of Western Europe, industrial investment absorbs usually about 25 per cent of total investment. Assuming that the long-term equilibrium share which Poland and other centrally-planned economies would have to adopt is also about that level, we can find from (2) the growth rate of industrial output corresponding to such an equilibrium share. The share of 25 per cent would be equivalent, in the years 1955–80, to the (I/Y) ratio of 16 per cent. Therefore, if infrastructure was given a 'proper' share of investment outlays, Poland's industrial growth rate would have been, in the period 1957–73, some 3 percentage points lower than it had been; that is, about 5.4 per cent rather than the actual 8.6 per cent. Needless to say, one cannot be quite certain about the precise size of this particular effect, but our illustrative estimate does seem to suggest that it might have been very significant.

Labour and technological reserve: In the 1950s and 1960s it was also fashionable among Poland's government officials and economists to compare the growth rate of industrial output in Poland (and other communist countries) with that in advanced capitalist countries. Such comparisons tended to overlook the universal law of development, according to which medium-developed countries grow fastest. These countries are yet to make full use of the two major growth reserves: the underemployed labour of their agricultural sector and the underemployed technology of the most advanced countries. Moreover, they have already developed sufficient infrastructure to be able to activate these reserves quickly. The activation process is transitory, but as long as it lasts the growth rates of both employment and technological change are naturally higher than those in the most advanced countries.

Human losses during the war: The one 'unusual' fact which has hindered Poland's progress after 1946 was an almost total loss, due to war, emigration and post-war terror, of the pre-war intelligentsia. It is perhaps remarkable how the country managed to progress as it did in the first years after the war with so few able to offer expertise in the areas of technology, management and education.

4. INFLUENCES OF THE 'SYSTEMIC FACTOR'

(i) The branch composition of investment and profitability

While the concern of the section above was with the dynamics of Poland's industrial and overall growth over time, in this section we shall look into the branch composition of inputs, outputs and profits in two years only, 1960 and 1975. The primary purpose of this investigation is to identify the branches which were financing the investment effort in industry.

The relevant data are presented in Table A3a for 1960 and Table A3b for 1975. The ratio of investment to capital and capital profitability for each of the nine branches and industry total are also presented in Figure 9.4. In market-oriented economies branches which earn more profits per unit of capital usually attract more investment per unit of capital. In Poland the relationship between the two ratios was rather different; the most profitable branches investing relatively less than other branches. This may well be a common characteristic for other centrally-planned economies.

But whether common or not, the relationship should not be interpreted as evidence of resource misallocation. Rather, it has to do with the way investment has been financed. In 1960, the branch producing foodstuffs, alcoholic beverages and tobacco products made about half of total industrial profits, but was allocated only 10 per cent of all industrial investment. The second most profitable branch in that year, textiles and clothing, accounted for a further 18.4 per cent of all profits made by industry, but attracted 6.7 per

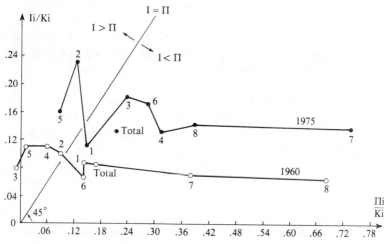

Figure 9.4: Polish industry. The (negative) relationship between capacity expansion and profitability, 1960 and 1975. 1 = energy and fuels; 2 = metallurgy; 3 = machine-building; 4 = chemicals; 5 = building materials; 6 = wood & paper; 7 = textiles & clothing; 8 = foodstuffs.

cent of all industrial investment. Profits made by the first of the two consumer branches were, in 1960, about sufficient to finance all industrial investment. Among particularly profitable consumer goods has been (and is) alcohol. The sales of that product alone have been in the 1960s and the 1970s equal to as much as between 50 per cent and 60 per cent of total industrial investment in fixed capital.

Of course, when prices are fixed by the state, profits are not really earned, but rather adminstratively imposed. Profitability in any centrally-administered economy need not be, and usually is not, an indicator of economic efficiency, but rather of the price policy of the government. In Poland the cost mark-ups have clearly been much higher for industrial consumer goods (the buyers of which were largely those financing industrialisation) than for intermediate inputs and investment goods. This practice had the effect of inflating the share of consumption in gross national product (GNP), and understating the share of investment.

The two consumer branches were again most profitable in 1975, although their joint share of total industrial profits declined from about 70 per cent in 1960 to about 38 per cent. Large-scale production of cars, consumer chemicals and household appliances lifted the profitability of the machinery branch and the chemicals branch, the latter also including petrochemicals. Between 1960 and 1975 the branch composition of employment and capital stock had changed significantly, away from energy and fuels, building materials, chemicals and metallurgy. The branches which in both years were investing more than their profits were building materials and metallurgy.

The Polish price system, imposing mark-ups that vary widely among products, puts into question the value of any inter-branch comparisons of capital/output ratios and labour productivities. In general, the system tends to inflate net outputs of consumer goods and understate net inputs of the branches producing investment goods and intermediate inputs. Consequently, branches supplying consumer goods are, on paper, much more efficient than they would be under a uniform tax rate. The practice of taxing these and some other industrial goods much more highly than non-industrial goods, and the fact that all the taxes are included into net outputs, overstate the contribution of industry total to GNP. One effect of this is to reduce the industry's average capital/output ratio. This ratio, between 2.4 and 2.7 for most of the period 1953–77, nevertheless, has been and still is about twice as high as the average industrial capital/output ratio for the 24 OECD countries, although similar in magnitude to that observed in industries of other centrally-planned economies. (In 1975 the ratios were 1.97 in Bulgaria, 2.78 in Czechoslavakia, 2.61 in the GDR, 2.78 in Hungary, 1.81 in Romania, and 2.30 in the USSR.) Another effect is that, within industry, value-added per worker may be lower in more capital-intensive branches. From Table A3a it can be seen that, in 1960, machinery, chemicals and building materials were the branches needing more of both capital and labour, to produce a value unit of net output than the industry as a whole. However, by 1975 only the building materials branch remained in this category.

(ii) The communist pattern of industrialisation

In the academic literature there seems to be little disagreement that apart from inevitable common factors and in addition to country-specific factors, there are important aspects of communist-led industrialisation which form a pattern quite distinct from that observed in countries under different economic and political systems. The lists of such aspects that have been composed by several authors usually overlap to a remarkable extent. However, not all the aspects are equally important and some appear to be implications of others. Assessing the relative weight of the various aspects and their mutual interrelations are clearly the more difficult tasks. The trouble is that such analysis has in the past not always been convincing.

It will be useful to begin our discussion of the topic by listing the four aspects of the communist pattern of industrialisation which were proposed by Fallenbuchl (1970). They are as follows:

(a) It is taken as a principle of development during industrialisation that the rate of expansion of output of producer goods must exceed that of consumer goods. The principle has been interpreted to mean that 'as much investment as possible should be allocated for the so-called "productive investments" ... [hence that] the rate of growth of industry should exceed the rate of growth of other sectors, [and within industry the emphasis should be] almost exclusively on iron and steel, coal and machines' (pp. 459–60).

(b) The total investment effort must be high, since 'a linear relationship has been assumed between the share of national income allocated for investment and the rate at which national income will increase' (p. 459).

(c) Preference is to be given for 'expanding domestic production of the commodities which had to be imported previously rather than through expansion of exports' (p. 458).

(d) Finally, 'in order to implement these rules', (i.e. (a) to (c) above), planning and economic administration must be highly centralised, market forces suppressed, and the planned targets ambitious (p. 460).

It may be noted that in Fallenbuchl's view the centralised system of planning and management was not seen by the communist leaders as an end in itself, essential in its own right in any socialist (communist) society at all times, but as an instrument necessary for the specific purpose of conducting industrialisation at an accelerated pace, and hence presumably not essential once industrialisation is completed. The direction of causality is suggested to run from (a), (b) and (c) to (d).

A similar view was offered earlier by Kurowski (1957), who in a paper on 'The model and the ends' argued, in Michael Montias's interpretation, that

the planners, by imposing a pattern of allocation during the Stalinist era that was in flagrant conflict with the preferences of consumers, had been forced to rely on centralized controls. The *ends*, the armaments build-up and the rapid expansion of heavy industry to support it, had *determined the means,* administration of the economy by fiat and the relegation of the price system to cost-accounting and record-keeping. (Montias, 1962, p. 223; emphasis added)

Kurowski also argued that in addition to centralised economic system, the creation of an apparatus of political repression was necessary in order to overcome the resistance of society to resource allocations that express the preferences of communist planners rather than those of individual consumers. This argument underlined his notion of the link between political repression and centralised planning. Consequently 'economic decentralization, democracy, and consumer's sovereignty were [seen by him to be] inseparable' (ibid., p. 273). This view of the necessity for centralised economic control may be appealing, but is it correct? What would be an alternative view of the link (if any) between (d) on the one hand, and (a), (b) and (c) on the other?

The initial point to note is that apart from economic and military strategic aims there were and are also political and ideological considerations. In the USSR under Lenin and Stalin, and later in Eastern Europe, the political system had to be extremely repressive whatever economic policies the communist authorities would have chosen to adopt. In the economic field (excepting agriculture) there was in fact much common ground between the communist rulers and the ruled. However, the rulers wished not only to increase material consumption and military power, but also to change radically the ideological and political make-up of their citizens, and to remain in absolute power in the process. Retaining full control in a politically hostile internal environment, therefore, was and had to be the supreme aim. In this there has so far been no compromise, no real power-sharing of any kind. Other aims, economic and ideological, were and continue to be important, but they have been allowed to become a subject of bargaining and debate.

The next point concerns the link between the political system, which with the priorities as above has to be repressive, and the system of economic management. In principle the latter need not be highly centralised, as the Yugoslavs have shown, in order to conduct industrialisation at a high speed. A repressive political system alone is sufficient to extract a high rate of savings through taxes, and the savings could be channelled to heavy industry or the arms sector if that was the wish of the central authorities. This is the way the state had influenced industrialisation very successfully in Japan and Germany before 1945. But Stalin must have been impressed by the point that political control is far more complete when the economy is under direct administrative control. In addition to this key political consideration he must have thought of such a centralised system as, on ideological grounds, the right way to proceed towards the goal of a communist (Marxian type) society. For an ideology which was intensely anti-market, the administrative system was quite natural to adopt. The purely economic considerations—that it would be easier for the centre to impose its wishes over the society and enterprises in the areas of growth, structural change, and efficiency—could have entered his mind as well, but need not have been the dominant reason for adopting a command-type economic system. Moreover, the history of resistance to economic reforms suggests that irrespective of whether or not the initial stimulus to adopting the administrative economic system was mainly to serve the purpose of accelerated industrialisation, the really important reasons for maintaining it in *the course* of industrialisation have been political and ideological.

Now I am ready to make my main point, which is that the aspects (a), (b) and (c) of the communist pattern of industrialisation have been to a great extent *caused* by the choice of the administrative economic system, rather than being aspects independent of that choice. The new system has been inducing enterprises to adopt production methods that are highly resource-intensive (Chapters 3 and 5, this volume). Therefore, in order to sustain the production of a particular volume of final consumer and military goods, a much larger base of intermediate inputs was needed than would have been the case under a market-based system. The demand for these inputs was originating in enterprises. The central planners were on the receiving end. No doubt they were bargaining hard to reduce some investment and other inputs, but the technologies which have emerged as a result of the choices made by enterprises were still highly material, capital and energy-intensive. The branch composition of outputs and investment at the macro level had to reflect these microeconomic choices. The planners might have thought themselves to be the main actors. They may have even been perceived as such by the general public and individual managers. But in fact, exaggerating somewhat, they were merely the prisoners of the system, the national book-keepers drawing input–output balances and ensuring that these remained in equilibrium. The only instrument under the planners' control, and admittedly a very important one, was the composition of final goods for consumers, for the military, and for net export purposes. There is little evidence to suggest that this composition was particularly material- or capital-intensive. On the contrary, the supply of material-intensive final goods, such as housing or cars, have been highly restrained.[9]

The point above describes what may be the main systemic factor in communist-led industrialisation. The factor may not explain fully the changes in the sectoral and branch compositions of outputs in Poland and in other East European countries. It may be noted that with the exception of Czechoslovakia and the GDR, these countries had a large labour surplus in their agricultural sector. Industrialisation was a means to activate that surplus. The activation required an increased investment effort in industry and in productive and social infrastructure. The sectors producing investment and other producer goods had to expand faster than the economy as a whole. This is a common feature in all countries in the process of industrialisation, and therefore the tendencies to which aspects (a) and (b) allude are not specifically communist.[10] The intensity of these tendencies does appear to have been greater in the USSR and Eastern Europe than elsewhere; that is, the emphasis on the expansion of producer goods has been rather unusual. However, this unusual emphasis could have been caused primarily by the systemic factor we have discussed above, rather than being a deliberate policy choice. The same observation applies to aspect (c). The small East European countries have been eager to expand exports in the 1960s and especially the 1970s, but the systemic factor is now widely acknowledged throughout the area to have acted as a powerful disincentive at the enterprise level.

To summarise, I do not question the validity or the importance of the aspects (a), (b) and (c), but suggest, first, that the aspects are *in part* a common feature of industrialisation whatever the system and, secondly, that the communist-specific input in those three aspects could have been largely the outcome of (d), the centralised economic system. Furthermore, this system was, I think, adopted not so much (or not only) in order to assist in implementing (a), (b) and (c), but in part (and perhaps mainly) for two reasons: an ideology about how the new communist societies should function; and in order to serve as a convenient instrument of central power in the exercise of full political control under hostile domestic and international circumstances in which such full control was deemed essential.

5. EFFECTS ON GROWTH AND CONSUMPTION

(i) Industrialisation and the rate of growth of total economy

There are good arguments for regarding the industrial sector as the 'engine of growth' in all countries in the period, from 'take-off' to 'maturity', to use Rostow's terminology. On the supply side, industrial activity may stimulate the economy's overall production in three ways. First, it may activate the resources that remain idle, especially the labour surplus in agriculture and natural resources such as minerals. Second, innovation, which tends to be faster in industry than in other sectors, raises the productivity of some of the economic resources that are already employed. Third, economies of scale are particularly easy to exploit in industry, partly through the medium of international trade. The growth-stimulating role of these three supply side factors may be reinforced by changes in the composition of total (consumption, investment and export) demand in favour of industrial goods. Changes in consumption demand take place in response to the arrival of attractive new goods and cheaper methods of making old goods, and as a result of increases in real income per head.

The extent to which the industrial sector stimulated overall economic growth in Eastern Europe in the post-war period has been the subject of several studies, such as those of Nasilowski (1974) and Roman (1982). In my own study of this topic (Gomulka, 1983; Chapter 6, this volume), I found industrial employment and labour productivity increasing most rapidly in the (initially) least developed countries of the region: Bulgaria, Romania, Yugoslavia and Poland. This was due largely to the ability of the industrial sector to activate significant parts of the two major growth reserves: their agricultural labour surpluses and the accumulated technology of their more advanced neighbours. However, 'it was the variation in the rate of expansion of the industrial sector alone rather than the influence of its output (or output growth) upon the growth of other sectors, that had differentiated the overall output growth rate among the seven [East European] countries in the years 1955–75' (p. 101). This finding is consistent with the view of central planners having placed unusually strong emphasis on the growth of the sector alone, and of other sectors having as yet not benefited fully from that industrial growth. The picture which emerges is one of industry producing intermediate, investment and export goods mainly for its own needs. (This generalisation applies particularly to Romania and Bulgaria, less to Poland and Hungary, and still less to Yugoslavia, East Germany and Czechoslovakia.)

In section 3(i) above we related the growth of industry to that of other sectors of the Polish economy. Progress, at least in terms of absolute magnitude of flows or stocks of goods per capita, has been in evidence in all major sectors, including social infrastructure. However, in many important areas the gains have been small in relation to those in developed western countries, or in relation to Poland's own progress in industrial development. These areas include, above all, housing, water supplies, environment protection, transport and communications, and industrial supplies for private agriculture. In some specific instances, such as water, soil and air pollution and the level of ground water in agricultural soil, the situation has been allowed to deteriorate in absolute terms, and in parts of Silesia and lands near open-cast mines of coal and sulphur, apparently to a truly alarming extent.

We have already noted in section 3(i) a much slower growth of the capital stock in the sector of non-material services than in the material part of the economy, and of transport and communications services within the latter. It may be useful to illustrate this point with data pertaining to the state of housing services (Table 9.3) and telecommunications services (Table 9.4).

Table 9.3: Housing services in Poland's cities, 1950 and 1980

	Population	Households	Housing units	Rooms	Persons per room	Area per person (m^2)	Excess of households over units (%)
		('000s)					
1950	9151	3220	2445	5971	1.53	13.3	31.7
1980	20135	7248	6232	19408	1.05	15.2	16.3

Sources: For 1950 *Rocznik Statystyczny* 1956; for 1980 *Rocznik Statystyczny* 1983.

Table 9.4: Telecommunications services in Poland and other countries, per 100 persons 1978

	Telephone sets	Telephone subscribers	Conversations per annum within country	abroad
Poland	8.8	5.0	2 538	7.4
USA	77.0	39.3	102 072	23.3
France	37.2	18.8	73 510	
UK	44.7	25.2	28 704	99.7
W. Germany	44.4	25.7	26 241	253.0
GDR	17.6	7.4	11 028	50.9
Czechoslovakia	19.6	10.0	27 625	12.3
USSR	8.0	6.2	369	0.9

Source: J. Stepień, after *Biuletyn KPZK PAN* no. 123, 116, Warsaw, 1983.

In the period 1950 to 1980 some improvement occurred in the size and quality of housing per person, but there are still 16.3 per cent of households which have no accommodation of their own and the living area per person, at about 15 m^2, is still far below the average level for the OECD countries, which is about 40m^2.

The distance between Poland and other countries, especially in terms of the volume of telephone service, is seen from Table 9.4 to be great, although not as startling as the case of the USSR.

(ii) Changes in consumption, material and total

In any East European statistics, and especially in consumption data, there is the well-known problem of hidden price increases being ignored by the official price index, and therefore of the reported increases in consumption being overstated. Since the extent of the statistical bias involved is not known, we shall use the official data as a starting point.

The purpose of Table 9.5 is to show the impact of giving a proper weight to non-material services, in which housing services are the

Table 9.5: Consumption per head of Poland's population, 1950–82
(In 1 January 1977 prices; levels in thousands zl, growth rates in per cent)

	Material consumption		Non-material services		Total consumption	
	level	growth rate	level	growth rate	level	growth rate
1950	8.16	5.5	6.28	0.5	14.44	3.6
1960	13.95	4.3	6.58	2.9	20.53	3.9
1970	21.23	5.6	8.78	3.9	30.01	5.1
1980	36.64	3.0*	12.86	3.6*	49.50	3.2*
1982	30.33		13.46		43.79	

* Period 1970–82, otherwise growth rates refer to 10-year periods.
Sources:
Material consumption is the officially reported part of NNP distributed which goes to consumption. Non-material services come from Table A5, as the imputed income of the non-material part calculated at $r = 8$ per cent.

most important component, upon our evaluation of changes in total consumption. The official (material) consumption per head increased from 1950 to 1982 3.7 times, or 4.2 per cent per annum, while our suggested estimate of total (material and non-material) consumption increased 3 times, or 3.5 per cent per annum. If hidden price increases were adding some 1 to 2 per cent to the inflation rate, the pace of improvement in the total consumption would have been of the order of 2 per cent per annum, with the level of consumption in 1982 about twice that in 1950. It may also be noted that a part of our consumption is accounted for by public consumption of the kind which does not contribute to the standard of living, such as national defence or internal security. But if this kind of consumption was the same proportion of total consumption in 1950 as in 1982, then the 2 per cent figure would also apply to changes in the standard of living.

Although the slow growth of social infrastructure has had a depressing effect on overall progress in the material standard of living and the quality of life, gains in many typical indicators of material consumption have been much faster in the period 1945–80 than in any other 35 years of Poland's history, an unusual experience Poland has shared with much of the world in the same period. A truly revolutionary change has been brought by the spread of electric power to almost all villages for consumption and productive use. This has been followed by a rapid spread of electricity-using appliances and cars, as the following data illustrate:

Table 9.6: Polish households which own major consumer items, 1982
(% of total)

	Workers	Peasants	Peasant-workers	Retired
TV sets: black/white	98.3	89.6	99.6	88.3
colour	12.5	1.9	3.6	4.3
Washing-machines:				
standard	87.3	92.2	88.3	83.9
automatic	24.3	3.9	4.5	7.1
Fridges and freezers	99.3	75.5	89.2	81.6
Cars	24.1	12.5	15.2	3.5

Source:
Rocznik Statystyczny 1983, pp. 128–9.
Note:
The characteristics of quality and performance of these items are usually below western standards.

6. INDUSTRIALISATION AND QUALITATIVE CHANGES

(i) Education and R & D

Attainment of nearly complete literacy, great expansion of educational opportunities and vast training in skills have been at once objectives in their own right and means towards other aims, among which sustaining the industrialisation drive is probably the primary goal. In pre-war Poland educational standards were high, but large sections of the community had access to only very basic education. The demand for skilled personnel was also low, being limited by the modest spread of skill-intensive economic activities. The data in Table 9.7 illustrate that the educational progress has since been impressive, at least in quantitative terms.

Of those employed in the socialised sector in 1982, 8.7 per cent had higher and 28.6 per cent full secondary education. A further 25.7 per cent had formal vocational training of some kind. On the basis of these data, it appears that by 1980 the Polish population reached education standards comparable to those of the world's most developed nations.

This conclusion has to be qualified in view of the rich evidence indicating that the composition of the graduates and the quality of their education have in some fields been affected by the political and systemic factors. These factors resulted in pressure to trade quality for quantity, the limitation of access of Polish students and teachers to western publications, and restrictions on the curricula

Table 9.7: Graduates and accumulated graduates in Poland, 1938–80 ('000s)

	1937–38	*1949–50*	*1979–80*
Children age 7–14	5165	3108	4100
Graduates per annum:			
7 grade primary	127	217	490
2 or 3 grade vocational	60[c]	65	530
4 or 5 grade secondary			
vocational and general	30[c]	59	399
all higher education	6.1	6.8	84.0
Ph D degrees	0.2	0.1	3.1
Accumulated graduates:			
Secondary education	200[c]		3168[a]
Higher education	100[c]	199[a,b]	938[a]
Ph Ds			40[c]

Source:
Rocznik Statystyczny (1956, 1983).
Notes:
[a] employed in socialised sector; [b] 1956; [c] rough estimate by this author from various Polish sources.

for reasons of politics and official ideology. It may be tempting, but is clearly impossible, to give any trustworthy estimate of the economic cost of these system-related implications. It seems plausible that they did little damage in fields such as sciences and medicine, more damage in technical fields, and still more in social studies, law and humanities. Another observation that can be made concerns the number of engineering graduates. Their share of total university-level graduates, at about 35 per cent in 1980, is significantly higher than in western countries, where it usually ranges between 10 and 15 per cent. This technical bias in education is an interesting aspect of Poland's industrialisation and modernisation that appears to be common to all countries under centrally-planned economic systems. The explanation seems to be that a high proportion of engineering graduates perform administrative and managerial jobs, as it indeed should be in economies where the key daily problems for enterprise managements are those of maintaining maximum production rather than making economic choices or winning customers.

Apart from the education sector, Poland has also developed a sizeable R & D sector. However, there is evidence to suggest that the low level of internal competition, inadequate incentives (including low demand from industry), and poor access to the world's major centres of research have all had an impact on the sector's productivity. Pooling all the developed OECD and CMEA countries together, in 1978 Poland's share of the total was 3.3 per cent for R & D personnel, 1.5 per cent for domestic patent applications by residents, and only 0.2 per cent for foreign patent applications (Slama, 1983, Table 8). The combined R & D sector of the OECD countries was, in 1978, 3 times as productive as Poland's sector in terms of domestic patent applications by residents and 33 times as productive in terms of patent applications abroad. (Incidentally, these productivity indicators for the Polish R & D sector are found by Slama to be very similar to those for the other six CMEA countries in the sample, including the USSR.) In spite of the large size of its R & D employment, Poland continues to be a disproportionately insignificant contributor to the world's new technology.

(ii) Technological change

In this vital area there are again features that are common to all newly-industrialised countries and others that are system-specific. In any country the level of technological sophistication varies considerably among sectors and among enterprises within sectors. Less-developed countries tend to have a dual economy, a small, highly advanced sector, and a large traditional sector. Technological change in such countries comes in two ways: as a result of expanding the modern sector faster than the traditional one, and as a result of upgrading technologies in each sector mainly through the transfer of technology from more advanced countries. Both methods require capital accumulation. Indeed, the rate of technological change may be related positively to the rate of growth of the capital stock, especially at the beginning of the industrialisation process when the two technology gaps, one between the modern sector and the traditional sector and the other between the country concerned and the developed world, are both high. Once the scope for unusually rapid internal diffusion is used up, the aggregate rate of technological change may be expected to decline. It should also decline once the international gaps are reduced to levels near to their long-term equilibrium, the latter to be determined by factors which tend to change little, such as those pertaining to economic system and culture (Chapters 1 and 4, this volume).

All these aspects have been in evidence in Poland during the industrialisation process since 1860. An acceleration of capital accumulation in the post-1946 period should have had a positive effect on the aggregate rate of technological change, while the system-related resistance to innovation was pulling in the opposite direction. The two effects cannot be estimated separately, but the productivity residuals we discussed in section 3(i) can be taken as measuring their combined effect.

Since Poland's own inventive activity is a very insignificant part of the world's total inventive activity, the country's industrialisation must have relied on the direct transfer or adaptation of the foreign-made technology. For most of the post-1945 period some 30 to 35 per cent of new machinery and equipment in industry has been imported, of which about a third came from the developed West.

The Polish leaders under Gomułka were apparently concerned that Poland, along with other small East European countries, had neither the resources of the USSR nor the innovation-inducing system of the West, with the implication that Poland could not compete internationally in technological change and might have to remain always significantly less developed. One possible way out was a much closer technological integration of Eastern Europe and the USSR. Such an integration is difficult to achieve under the present system without supranational planning and a near-complete economic integration. So far this course has been resisted, presumably mainly for political reasons, but perhaps also because economic benefits of the strategy are not certain. The other extreme option is to adapt a highly competitive economic system. That option has also been resisted so far. In the 1970s Poland (and most of Eastern Europe) chose instead a third option, that of large imports of western technology and technology-intensive goods in exchange for future exports of goods, to be produced under the old system on the basis of new technology imports. Exports to the West did increase, but far short of the levels required to sustain this strategy of import-led growth. The subsequent economic crisis is forcing Eastern Europe to reassess the feasibility of the two other options (or of their combinations) for the 1980s and beyond.

The many ways in which the centralised economic system influences the rate and direction of innovation at the enterprise level have been discussed recently by several authors, such as Poznański (1980) and myself (Chapter 3, this volume). Some of these discussions are based wholly or in part on Polish empirical material. However, little progress has been achieved in quantifying the influence. The high use of energy in industry per unit of net output, some 2–3 times as high as in the West, is possibly the single most telling indicator of the large overall impact of the system on the choice of resource-intensive technologies by enterprises. We have already drawn attention to the implications of such system-induced choices on the branch composition of industrial output and investments.

7. INDUSTRIALISATION AND SOCIAL CHANGE

(i) Changes in social stratification

Industrialisation of Poland's economy has brought with it the usual changes in the skill composition required and the types of actual employment. In particular, in the half-century from the 1930s to the 1980s, Poland has been transformed from a predominantly village-based society to one dominated by urban population. This is true especially if one compares populations living not on the same piece of land (post-war Poland) but under the same (Polish) administration. The key data for the latter comparison are given in Table 9.8.

Upward social mobility was high throughout the post-war period. It was associated initially with rapid promotion to new political, administrative, cultural and industrial élites, almost irrespective of education, and later with a gradual rise of the middle classes, the intelligentsia and related white-collar workers, a majority of whom were of peasant and worker origin. Since most villages were poor and overpopulated, a mere change to city life,

Table 9.8 Changes in social structure in Poland, 1931–81

Social category	1931	1950	1981
Agricultural population:	60.6	47.1	21.5
independent[b]	51.7	42.1	17.5
employed[c]	8.9	5.0	4.0
Non-agricultural population:	39.4	52.9	78.5
blue-collar workers[a]	19.8		42.2
white-collar workers	4.2		21.1
self-employed	12.1	0.7	4.1
undefined[d]	3.3	4.0	11.1
Urban population	26.6	36.7	59.1

Sources:
Data for 1931 are based on the census returns, 9 December 1931. Data for 1950 and 1981 are compiled by this author from *Rocznik Statystyczny*, various years; the data for sub-categories are rough estimates.
Notes:
The work which is the main source of income is the classifying factor. [a]includes cottage workers; [b]includes peasant-workers and retired peasants who have bequeathed their farms to a descendent; [c]includes members of agricultural cooperatives; [d]includes pensioners.

even if to become a blue-collar worker, was often considered an advance in social status. In the years 1945–55, 30.6 per cent of all new blue-collar workers were of peasant origin; by 1972 this percentage declined to 16.[11] It is conceivable that the support for the industrialisation policy has been greatest among the new working class and the new intelligentsia, the groups which gained much in social status. That support provided a degree of legitimacy for the new regime which radiated throughout the Polish society and which must have mitigated somewhat the opposition of these and other groups to the new regime for well-known political and ideological reasons.

Upward social mobility for individuals is also present when social stratification of a nation is frozen, similarly as individual income rises over time for all are consistent with no change of the average income. This seems to be the case in Poland of the early 1980s. However, the usually higher social status of the middle-aged generation now than in 1945 may limit the perceived gain of any social advance by the young generation. The rapid social advance in the past may have also produced expectations among all generations which in the new circumstances of more balanced social change cannot be fulfilled.

(ii) Economic policies as both causes and outcomes of political change

In the post-1944 period the tempo and the social content of industrialisation have been decided by circumstances outside Polish control. Nevertheless, the economic policy of accelerated industrialisation and modernisation was producing social changes and political responses of the Polish population which had some feedback effects on the content of the policy. The details of these modifications of policy—such as in 1955–56, following the ambitious six-year plan, and in 1971, following the December 1970 uprising—are well known. However, it may be useful to make two general interpretative remarks. One is that until the latest crisis of 1980–82, all previous modifications were relatively minor changes within the general strategy of continuing emphasis on industrial growth. This continuity of emphasis is indicated in Table 9.9 by the share of non-productive investment being not just low compared with that of industry, but also consistently low. The other remark is that the crisis 1980–82 may have ended this consistency, forcing a major and possibly lasting fall in the share of industrial investment.

Table 9.9: Investment shares in Poland: non-productive and industrial (% of total)

	1951–55	1956–60	1961–65	1966–70	1971–75	1976–80
Non-productive sector	28.7	35.1	30.4	26.0	22.2	24.5
Industry	42.7	35.8	36.6	36.3	40.8	37.6

Source: Compiled by the author from *Rocznik Statystyczny* (1978, 1982).
Note: Investment in 1 January prices.

8. LIMITS TO FURTHER ECONOMIC DEVELOPMENT

(i) Where Poland's economy stands internationally in the early 1980s

In the years 1950–80 not only the Polish but also the world economy was growing much faster than ever before. The relevant growth rates are presented in Table 9.10.

Based on these data, in the period 1950–80 GDP per capita would have increased 3.7 times in Poland against 2.4 times in both the developed West and in developing non-communist countries, and 2.8 times in Western Europe. However, cross-country comparisons of GDP per capita are known to be sensitive to the choice of prices. It is also unclear how much to discount the Polish growth rate on the grounds of hidden inflation. Nevertheless, it is probable that Poland's relative position in the world, in terms of the share of total world GDP, or GDP per capita, did not deteriorate in the years 1950–80. Any relative improvement, if there was one, could have been wiped out by the fall in Poland's GDP per capita by 20 per cent in the years 1981–82, to about 3 times the level of 1950. The corresponding figure for Western Europe is 2.9. Thus even if hidden inflation has not been higher in Poland than in Western Europe, which seems unlikely, the relative gap in consumption per

Table 9.10: Average annual growth rates, 1950–80 (%)

	GDP	GDP per capita
Developing countries*	5.4	2.9
Developed West	4.0	2.9
Western Europe	4.0	3.4
Poland	5.7	4.5

Sources: For Poland, Table A6; otherwise, *Handbook of International Trade and Development* UNCTAD, 1983.
*China, North Korea, Mongolia and Vietnam are not included.

capita between Poland and Western Europe is, in the early 1980s, about the same as it was in 1950. The absolute consumption gap, of course, would have increased about 3 times.

It is instructive to evaluate the relative weight of Poland's industry using the exchange dollar/zloty rate which Poland earns in her trade with the West. In 1982 that rate was 84.8 zl for the dollar. Poland's net industrial output would be, then, $25.5 mld., or about $700 per person of the total population. The corresponding number for some of the western countries in 1981 was as follows: $3250 for the US, $3590 for West Germany, $2900 for Japan, $2000 for the UK, $1500 for Italy and $900 for Spain. (The dollar rates assumed are DM 2.6, £1.6, 220 yen, 1500 lira, 150 peseta.) If these data are approximately accurate, Poland should be judged to be a country about as industrialised as Spain is, while remaining nearly as far behind the developed West as it was in 1950.

(ii) Serious constraints on further growth

There is growing evidence that the Soviet-type industrialisation strategy that has been pursued in Poland and elsewhere in Eastern Europe has exhausted its growth potential. The strategy relied on a merciless exploitation (some would say shortsighted plundering) of the countries' natural resources of land, water and minerals, on processing these resources in a rather wasteful way to produce poor quality products using methods of production which appear to have been significantly more capital- and labour-intensive than need be. Clearly such a strategy cannot be sustained when the labour reserve is exhausted, when the non-industrial sectors must be given more investment resources for technological or social reasons, and when the low-cost natural resources of minerals, land, wood and water are already, or about to be, depleted.

The recent crisis has prompted a number of Polish academics to take stock of Poland's economic position in the early 1980s. A particularly interesting series of studies have been produced by a group of environmental specialists of the Polish Academy of Sciences. The data reported by Stefan Kozłowski (1983) on the (mis-) use of Poland's natural resources are quite informative about the past and still continuing wasteful practices, and about the constraints to future industrial growth arising from limited stocks of natural resources. According to that source, in the years 1950–80 the total annual consumption of water for production and consumption needs has increased from 2.5 km^3 to 15 km^3. If the consumption was to increase at the same growth rate in the 1980s, it would stand at 27 km^3 by 1990. However, the maximum 'disposable' water supply is only 22 km^3 per year. The author notes that despite Poland's water resources per person of the population being only about one-third of the average for Europe, water is regarded as costless and its consumption per person in urban areas is higher in Poland than in Western Europe.

At present production levels, Poland's key mineral resources are expected to last as follows (in years): hard coal 110, brown coal 70, copper 50, zinc and lead 30, sulphur 30. Yet only about 40 per cent of the recoverable coal is mined, against about 70 per cent 'in similar geological circumstances abroad.'[12] Another important natural resource, Soviet oil, is similarly in limited supply. In addition to these natural resource constraints, there is the afore-mentioned great domestic pressure to upgrade the rank of social infrastructure and the technological necessity to upgrade the rank of productive infrastructure.

From this brief survey it is evident that a substantial structural break in Poland's economic development policy may have to take place. In future the Polish economy may not be able to meet both high internal expectations and the repayment of external debts at the same time. A radical change of its economic system would help to increase efficiency, and a return to a Stalinist-type dictatorship to control expectations cannot be ruled out. The recent crisis has been and is painful, but it may still prove to be helpful in one respect. Namely, similarly as the oil crisis has awakened the world to the need of husbanding energy, the Polish crisis has forced both the country's élite and the population at large to face head-on the question of finding an economic system that would be significantly more resource-efficient. (This problem is the subject of Chapter 14.)

NOTES

1. This assumption must bias somewhat the measure of industrialisation, but there appear to be no data that would indicate the size or direction of the bias.
2. While C* is an arbitrary extrapolation of C, both are percentages and therefore C* is likely to follow an S-type pattern. In the early 1980s the share of industrial employment has already begun to decline.
3. Misztal (1970), p. 202, Table 7.
4. In Szyr *et al.* (1964), p. 49.
5. Kuziński (1962), p. 10.
6. It should be noted that this estimate of the PRF is not intended to

include the contribution of education and technological change in that period. These factors, along with a capital stock increase by 45 per cent and an unknown employment increase needed to operate that new capital, are credited to increase output by 45 per cent. This creditation is based on the observation that in the period 1953–76 the growth rate of capital stock is a good proxy for the growth rate of output that is due to all factors other than changes in the factors' utilisation rates.

7. If expressed as a proportion of GNP, the investment effort in industry has been increasing. The measure used in the text gives the size of Poland's investment activity in industry from the viewpoint of the sector concerned, the recipient, while the ratio of *I* to GNP gives this size from the viewpoint of the nation, the contributor. Both measures may be used depending on one's purpose.

8. Should the imputed capital share be actually higher than 0.3, the contribution of the extensive factors would have been greater than the shares given in the text. Whitesell (1985) experimented with a variety of production functions for Polish industry, 1960–79, and found the Cobb–Douglas with constant returns to scale a preferred functional form. His estimate of the imputed capital share is 0.44, which if applied for the period 1953–80 gives 5.1 per cent as the contribution of the purely quantitative growth of capital and labour (two-thirds of the industrial growth rate). It may also be noted that the phrase 'predominantly intensive growth' means only that the share of the contribution of all qualitative improvements was high; the contribution itself may or may not be high.

9. The interactions between planners and producers have been and are very complex. One can argue, as Fallenbuchl does, that the views of Stalin and his planners on what types of industrial production should be given priority were so strong and definitive that they were imposing a particular pattern of investment allocations and the production of inputs, and that enterprises were forced to adjust their methods of production and the assortment of outputs to what inputs happened to be available. The counter-argument would be that central planners probably did exercise an influence of that kind in the early years of industrialisation, say 1928–45 in the USSR and 1949–55 in Eastern Europe. However, as the economies became more complex, enterprises more numerous and enterprise managements more sophisticated, the balance of influence in deciding how to produce and what inputs to use has been shifting from the top centre to lower levels of management, activating in the process the system of incentives that the centre has devised.

10. According to the data reported by Patel (1961), there is a general tendency for the share of producer goods in gross (or global) industrial output to rise over time, especially in the early and medium stages of industrialisation. However, this rise of the share in the USSR, from 39 per cent in 1928 to 67 per cent in 1940, was much faster than the more gentle rises that took place in the developed capitalist countries. For an interpretation of this tendency see Ellman (1979), pp. 119–22, and for a denial of its validity see Wiles (1962), pp. 286–8.

11. Krzysztof Zagorski, after Jałowiecki (1982) p. 47.

12. Stefan Kozłowski (1983) p. 10.

APPENDIX

Table A1: *Total population, urban population and industrial employment, 1860–1980, on lands within the boundaries of Poland post-1945*

	Total population (millions)	Urban as % of total	Industrial employment as % of total population	Industrial employment by branches (%)				
				1	2	3	4	5
1860–61	15.1	18.2	1.9	7.7	13.1	18.0	26.1	37.8
under Russia	4.9	14.8	1.6	2.2	8.1	12.8	38.7	40.2
under Prussia	8.0	22.2	2.3	10.3	15.9	19.1	20.9	33.8
under Austria	2.2	11.0	1.0	5.6	7.1	26.4	33.5	27.4
1880	19.5	23.0	2.6	11.6	13.1	19.8	30.9	24.3
1900	24.4	26.0	3.3	11.3	13.5	20.5	37.6	19.3
1910	27.6	28.8	4.3	12.6	13.4	27.6	34.5	13.1
under Russia	12.3	26.0	3.0	7.2	6.9	20.7	51.7	13.5

	(1)	(2)	(3)	(4)	(5)	(6)	(7)	(8)
under Prussia	11.7	35.3	6.4	15.1	16.2	26.9	27.6	14.2
under Austria	3.6	16.6	2.1	14.0	17.0	20.5	35.8	12.7
1925	27.2	34.3	5.0	17.7	10.6	24.8	35.8	10.8
1938–39	32.0	37.0	5.0	13.6	11.0	31.0	32.5	11.4
under Poland	23.0	34.0	3.9	12.3	9.9	34.6	32.6	10.6
under Germany	9.0	46.4	7.5	15.2	12.3	26.1	32.9	13.5
1946	23.8	32.8	6.0	22.0	7.1	29.3	29.6	11.7
1950	24.8	36.9	8.5	17.3	6.8	30.4	37.2	10.7
1960	29.6	48.0	10.6	14.1	7.9	36.9	27.7	12.4
1970	32.5	52.0	13.7	11.7	6.7	43.5	25.5	11.3
1980	35.6	58.4	14.7	11.7	5.7	46.0	23.1	11.4

Notation:
1 = energy and fuels; 2 = building materials, ceramic and glass; 3 = metallurgy, machinery and chemicals; 4 = wood, paper, textiles, clothing and shoemaking; 5 = food processing, tobacco and others.

Sources:
Misztal (1970) for all years except the post-1945 years. For these years the data are compiled by the author from *Rocznik Statystyczny*, and the branch shares are those of socialised industry. Misztal's data do *not* include establishments in which those engaged numbered five or less.

Table A2: Industrial growth 1860–1980, within the boundaries of Poland 1980
(1960 = 100, growth rates in percentage)

	L	g_L	Y	g_Y	K	g_K	I	g_I	$\dfrac{K}{Y}$	$\dfrac{\Delta K/\Delta Y}{(K/Y)_{1960}}$
1860	9.1									
		2.9								
1910	37.6									
		0.9								
1925	43.0									
		1.3								
1938	50.6									
		– 1.4								
1946	45.2		14.1		40.4		6.1		2.86	
		9.9		31.6		3.7		55.0		
1949	60.0		32.2		45.1		22.7		1.40	0.34
		12.5		18.0		4.1		64.5		
1950	67.5		38.0		47.0		37.3		1.24	0.32
		6.5		14.1		7.7		25.8		
1953	81.6		56.6		58.7		74.2		1.04	0.72
		4.5		9.4		7.9		– 2.7		
1955	89.0		67.6		69.6		70.3		1.03	0.98
		4.3		5.9		7.9		5.7		
1956	92.8		71.6		75.1		74.3		1.05	1.38
		1.9		8.7		7.4		7.7		
1960	100.0		100.0		100.0		100.0		1.00	0.93
		3.1		8.9		6.6		8.0		
1965	116.4		153.1		137.6		146.6		0.90	0.61
		4.2		7.8		7.8		7.7		
1970	143.1		222.5		200.6		212.2		0.90	1.11
		3.0		10.8		10.1		21.0		
1975	165.5		371.0		325.4		550.2		0.88	0.85
		– 0.4		2.6		8.5		– 7.1		
1980	168.6		422.0		488.4		381.3		1.16	

Notation:
All but last column are indices, with 1960 = 100. Industry is manufacturing and mining, private, cooperative and state-owned. L = employment (changes in man-hours per year are *not* taken into account); Y = net output (*produkcja czysta*), concept close to net value added; K = gross fixed capital assets; I = gross investment in fixed capital assets; g_x denotes the (average) annual growth rate of X; $X = K, L, Y$ and I, in periods between the neighbouring years listed in col. 1.
Sources:
Table A1 for the years 1860–1938; *Rocznik Statystyczny,* various years, for the post-1945 period.
Note:
Absolute values in 1960: L = 3.16 ml persons; Y = 201.5 mld.zl; K = 545 mld.zl; I = 46.4 mld.zl. Prices of 1 January 1977.

Table A3a: *Poland's industry: branch distribution of net output, inputs and profits, 1960 (%)*

i	Branch	Y_i/Y	K_i/K	L_i/L	I_i/I	Π_i/Π	I_i/K_i	Π_i/K_i
1	Energy & fuels	21.6	30.2	13.6	30.6	24.9	8.6	14.2
2	Metallurgy	6.1	10.1	5.5	11.8	5.4	10.0	9.2
3	Machinery	13.4	15.3	24.9	14.2	−0.6	7.9	−0.7
4	Chemicals	4.6	9.0	6.0	11.6	3.2	11.0	6.1
5	Building materials	4.0	8.0	7.5	10.2	0.7	10.9	1.6
6	Wood & paper	5.2	4.6	7.2	3.6	3.9	6.6	14.5
7	Textiles & clothing	17.7	8.3	20.9	6.7	18.4	6.9	38.5
8	Foodstuffs, incl. alcoholic beverages & tobacco products	30.1	13.3	12.1	10.0	52.8	6.4	68.3
9	Other	−2.7	1.2	2.3	1.3	−8.7	9.2	−118.5
10	Total industry	100.0	100.0	100.0	100.0	100.0	8.5	17.3

Note:
Absolute values in 1960 in 1977 prices: $Y = 201.5$ mld.zl; $K = 545$ mld.zl; $I = 46.4$ mld.zl; $L = 3.16$ ml. Net output (*produkcja czysta*) excludes amortisation. Profits are defined as follows: $\Pi_i = Y_i - 1.25\, w_i L_i$, where w_i is annual wage; 0.25 of the wage bill is assumed[1] as needed to cover non-wage labour costs, such as bonuses and insurance, and[2] as equal in all branches. Total $\Pi = 94.3$ mld.zl.

Table A3b: *Poland's industry: branch distribution of net output, input and profits, 1975 (%)*

i	Branch	Y_i/Y	K_i/K	L_i/L	I_i/I	Π_i/Π	I_i/K_i	Π_i/K_i
1	Energy & fuels	15.7	26.9	10.6	19.4	16.2	11.1	15.1
2	Metallurgy	5.9	11.1	5.2	16.9	5.9	23.4	13.2
3	Machinery	27.7	20.5	32.2	24.3	19.4	18.3	23.7
4	Chemicals	10.4	11.0	6.8	9.5	13.8	13.2	31.5
5	Building materials	3.5	6.6	6.3	7.0	2.1	16.3	8.0
6	Wood & paper	4.7	4.0	6.2	4.5	4.5	17.4	28.3
7	Textiles & clothing	17.3	6.8	18.0	6.0	20.3	13.6	74.7
8	Foodstuffs	14.0	11.6	11.1	10.7	18.0	14.2	38.8
9	Other	0.8	1.5	3.6	1.7	−0.2	17.4	−10.6
10	Total industry	100.0	100.0	100.0	100.0	100.0	15.4	25.1

Source:
Compiled by the author. Raw data from Polish official sources, mainly from *Rocznik Statystyczny Przemysłu, 1978.*
Note:
Absolute values in 1975 in 1977 prices: $Y = 748$ mld.zl; $K = 1722$ mld.zl; $I = 265$ mld.zl; $L = 4.73$ ml and $\Pi = 686$ mld.zl.

Table A4: Poland's economy: the growth of inputs, 1950–80 (L in ml persons; K and I in mld.zl; 1 January 1977 prices)

	Material sectors			Non-material sectors		
	L	*K*	*I*	*L*	*K*	*I*
1950	9.714	1148	35.1	1.424	1473	16.4
1955	10.786	1346	59.6	1.732	1562	27.4
1960	11.421	1635	85.3	1.647	1715	48.4
1965	12.300	2005	133.3	2.137	1927	51.9
1970	13.465	2672	200.0	2.578	2213	73.4
1975	14.847	3959	483.7	2.912	2521	129.4
1980	14.840	5790	382.5	3.267	3050	144.4

Notation:
L = employment; K = gross value of fixed capital assets; I = gross investment in fixed capital. Material sectors comprise the so-called productive sectors of the economy: industry, construction, agriculture, transport, communications and trade. The non-material sectors include housing, education and research, health services, government, insurance and banking.
Source:
Compiled by the author from *Rocznik Statystyczny* for various years. However, the employment in the non-material sector is augmented by 0.6 ml throughout, which is *assumed* to have been the number of the personnel of the armed forces, police and security services.

Table A5: Poland's economy: the growth of outputs, 1950–80 (In mld.zl, 1 January 1977)

	Material sectors		Non-material sectors			Total economy		
	NNP	GNP	*rK + wL*			GNP		
			$r = 6\%$	$r = 8\%$	$r = 10\%$	$r = 6\%$	$r = 8\%$	$r = 10\%$
1950	252	272	128	157	187	400	429	459
1955	381	410	142	171	204	552	581	612
1960	523	571	161	196	230	732	767	801
1965	706	772	197	236	275	969	1009	1047
1970	943	1034	242	287	231	1276	1321	1365
1975	1503	1658	326	376	427	1984	2034	2084
1980	1594	1829	398	459	520	2227	2288	2349

Notation:
NNP (net national product of the material sectors) is the official national product; GNP – NNP equals the difference between gross investment and net investment; $rK + wL$ is the imputed net output of the non-material part. The imputed capital rent includes capital amortisation.
Source:
Compiled by the author from *Rocznik Statystyczny* for various years and Table A3.

Table A6: Poland's economy: average annual growth rates, 1950–80 (%)

	NNP		GNP (material & non-material)		
			Total economy		
	Industry	Material sectors	$r = 6\%$	$r = 8\%$	$r = 10\%$
1950–55	12.2	8.6	6.7	6.2	5.9
1955–60	8.2	6.5	5.8	5.7	5.5
1960–65	8.9	6.2	5.8	5.6	5.5
1965–70	7.8	6.0	5.7	5.6	5.5
1970–75	10.8	9.8	9.2	9.0	8.8
1975–80	2.6	1.2	2.3	2.4	2.4
1950–80	8.4	6.3	5.9	5.7	5.6

Source:
Compiled by the author.

Table A7: Poland's economy: joint productivity residuals for industry and economy total 1949–80 (%)

	Industry (soc. and private)					Economy (material & non-material)			
				λ					λ
	g_Y	g_L	g_K	$\eta_K = 0.3$	$\eta_K = 0.5$		g_Y	g_K	g_L	$\eta_K = 0.4 \ r = 8\%$
1949–53	15.1	7.8	6.8	7.6	7.8					
1953–56	8.2	4.4	8.5	2.6	1.7	1950–55	6.2	2.2	2.4	3.9
1956–60	8.7	1.9	7.4	5.2	4.0	1955–60	5.7	2.9	0.9	4.0
1960–65	8.9	3.1	6.6	4.8	4.0	1960–65	5.6	3.3	2.1	3.0
1965–70	7.8	4.2	7.8	2.5	1.8	1965–70	5.6	4.4	2.2	2.5
1970–75	10.8	3.0	10.1	5.7	4.4	1970–75	9.0	5.8	2.1	5.4
1975–80	2.6	0.4	8.5	−0.2	−1.9	1975–80	2.4	6.4	0.4	−0.4
1953–80	7.7	2.7	8.2	3.4	2.2	1953–80	5.8	4.4	1.5	3.1

Notation:
g_Y for industry is the growth rate of industrial net output (*produkcja czysta*); g_Y for economy total is the growth rate of GNP. The productivity residual, λ, is defined as the difference: $g_Y - \eta_K g_K - (1 - \eta_K)g_L$, where g_K and g_L are growth rates of capital and labour, respectively.

Source:
Compiled by the author.

REFERENCES

Ehrlich E., 'An International Comparison of Infrastructural Development', in Levick, F. (ed.), *International Economics—Comparisons and Interdependencies,* Springer-Verlag, 1978.

Ellman, M., *Socialist Planning,* Cambridge: Cambridge University Press, 1979.

Erlich, A., *The Soviet Industralization Debate 1924–1928,* Harvard University Press, 1960.

Fallenbuchl, Z. M., 'The Communist Pattern of Industrialization', *Soviet Studies,* **4,** 1970, pp. 458–84.

Fallenbuchl, Z. M., 'Industrial structure and the intensive pattern of development in Poland' *Jahrbuch der Wirtschaft Osteuropas,* **4,** 1973, pp. 233–54.

Feiwel, G., *Industralization and Planning under Polish Socialism* vol. 1(2), New York: Praeger, 1971.

Herer, W. and Sadowski, W., *Migracja z rolnictwa, efekty i koszty (Migration from Agriculture: Effects and Costs),* Warsaw: PWE, 1975.

Jałowiecki, B., 'Strategia uprzemyslowienia a proces urbanizacji; Studium socjologiczne' (Industrial strategy and urbanisation; A sociological study'), *Biuletyn KPZK (Komitetu Przestrzennego Zagospodarowania Kraju),* PAN, **119,** pp. 9–116, 1982.

Jędruszczak, H. (ed.) *Wizje gospodarki socjalistycznej w Polsce 1945–1949 (Visions of the Socialist Economy in Poland 1945–1949)* Warsaw: PWN, 1983.

Jezierski, A. and Petz, B. *Historia gospodarcza Polski Ludowej 1944–1975 (Economic History of People's Poland 1944–1975),* Warsaw, 1980.

Karpiński, A. *Twenty Years of Poland's Economic Development 1944–1964,* Warsaw, 1964.

Karpiński, A. *Gospodarcza pozycja Polski w swiecie (Poland's Economic Place in the World),* Warsaw, 1973.

Komorowski, S.M., 'Przestrzenna organizacja gospodarki polskiej; Proba analizy krytycznej' ('Spatial organization of Polish economy; Critical Analysis') *Biuletyn KPZK PAN,* vol. **117,** 1981.

Kozłowski, S., 'Wstepna ocena gospodarki zasobami przyrody' ('Preliminary evaluation of the husbandry of natural resources), *Biuletyn KPZK PAN,* **116,** pp. 13–33, 1981.

Kozlowski, S., 'Ocena gospodarki zasobami naturalnymi' ('Evaluation of the husbandry of natural resources'), *Biuletyn KPZK PAN,* **123,** 1983, pp. 7–27.

Kurowski, S., 'Model a cele gospodarki narodowej' ('The model and the aims of the national economy'), *Zycie Gospodarcze,* no. 7, 1957.

Kuziński, S., *O czynnikach wzrostu gospodarczego Polski Ludowej (Sources of Economic Growth in People's Poland),* Warsaw, 1962.

Kuziński, S. *Polska na gospodarczej mapie swiata (Poland on the Economic Map of the World),* Warsaw, 1976.

Lewin, M., *Political Undercurrents in Soviet Economic Debates,* London: Pluto Press, 1975.

Lissowski, W., *Capital–Output–Employment Ratios in Industrial Programming,* Oxford: Pergamon Press, 1965.

Misztal, S., *Przemiany w strukturze przestrzennej przemyslu na ziemiach polskich w latach 1860–1965 (Changes in the Spatial Distribution of Industry on Polish Lands 1860–1965),* Warsaw, 1970.

Montias, J. M., *Central Planning in Poland,* New Haven and London: Yale University Press, 1962.

Nasilowski, M., *Analiza czynnikow rozwoju gospodarczego PRL (Sources of Economic Growth in People's Poland),* Warsaw, 1974.

Patel, S. J., 'Rates of industrial growth in the last century, 1860–1958', *Economic Development and Cultural Change,* 1961.

Poznański, K., 'A study of technical innovation in Polish industry', *Research Policy,* vol. 9(3), 1980.

Roman, Z., *Productivity and Economic Growth,* Budapest, 1982.

Slama, J., 'Gravity model and its estimations for international flows of engineering products, chemicals and patent applications', *Acta Oeconomica,* 1983.

Spulber, N., *Soviet Strategy for Economic Growth,* Bloomington, Ill., 1964.

Szyr E. et al. (eds), *Twenty Years of Polish People's Republic,* Warsaw, 1964.

Wellisz, S., *The Economies of the Soviet Bloc: A Study of Decision Making and Resource Allocation,* New York: McGraw-Hill, 1964.

Whitesell, R. S., 'The Influence of Central Planning on the Economic Slowdown in the Soviet Union and Eastern Europe: A Comparative Production Function Analysis', *Economica,* 1985.

Wiles, P., *The Political Economy of Communism,* Oxford: Basil Blackwell, 1962.

Zauberman, A., *Industrial progress in Poland, Czechoslovakia and East Germany 1937–1962,* Oxford: Oxford University Press, 1964.

10 Growth and the Import of Technology: Poland 1971–80*

1. INTRODUCTION

The view that new technology is primarily embodied in new equipment, and not generally available throughout the economy in already existing capital stock, has led to the development of a class of growth models in which gross investment is the main agent of the diffusion of new technology, as new generations (or 'vintages') of machines are introduced in the economy. This type of model, associated primarily with the work of Johansen, Salter, Solow and Kalecki, can be extended to illustrate also the international diffusion of technology in a world where technical knowledge is embodied in the equipment produced by countries at different stages of technological development. The method of acquiring foreign technology through the import of equipment is of course not new. Recently, however, it has been rapidly gaining importance in the development policy of many countries, such as the oil-producing countries and the economies of Eastern Europe.

The purpose of this paper is that of investigating the impact of importing foreign technology on the growth rate of labour productivity, with reference to the Polish case, and of quantifying the order of magnitude of the growth effect that can be expected from large-scale application of this policy of 'import-led' growth.

The plan of the paper is as follows. Section 2 describes the particular form of the strategy which has been adopted in Poland. The concepts of 'subvintage' and the 'diffusional effect' are

*An earlier version of this paper was presented to the NASEES Annual Conference (Cambridge, 1977). I would like to thank Mario Nuti, the paper's discussant at the conference, an unknown referee, and the editors of this journal for useful comments and suggestions. Reprinted with permission from Stanislaw Gomulka, *Cambridge Journal of Economics*, 1978, **2**, pp. 1–16.

introduced in Section 3. An estimate of the diffusional effect, as well as the underlying data and key assumptions, are reported and commented upon in Section 4. The question of the extent to which embodied diffusion can serve to stimulate economic growth in the countries of the Soviet bloc area, in view of our estimates for Poland, is taken up in Section 5. The model and the description of the estimation procedures, as well as the data used in the paper, are all given in the Appendices.

2. TWO PHASES OF THE STRATEGY: THE ECONOMIC BACKGROUND

While the strategy of import-induced growth always presupposes a high ratio of machinery imports from technologically advanced countries to total machinery investments, it may vary in the length of the transitional period in which this ratio is attained. Two variants deserve particular attention.

One is to increase that ratio so gradually that exports can always catch up with imports. The transition to a path of faster growth then takes place in conditions of equilibrium in the balance of payments. However, acceleration of growth is likely to be low and hence the transitional period is likely to be long.

The other variant has two phases, A and B. In phase A, a sharp increase in machinery imports takes place. It is financed partly or wholly with credits, which in some cases may be repaid in the form of certain quantities of goods being produced with the imported machinery. But sooner or later there comes a point when the increase in the accumulated debt must be stopped. At that point phase B begins, in which exports exceed imports until eventually the debt is repaid. Hopefully the high ratio of machinery imports to total machinery investments, achieved towards the end of phase A, is thereafter maintained.

The second variant was adopted in Poland. There were two important factors which influenced this decision. One was external: the signing of a 'normalisation treaty' with the German Federal Republic in December 1970, followed by the Soviet–American détente of the early 1970s. This external development created a climate conducive to large-scale imports from the West on credit terms. But possibly it was the internal factor which pushed the government to take full advantage of the new option. Following a rise in food prices in December 1970, a large-scale confrontation took place between workers and the government. As a result, by the end of December a new government was installed. However, despite the change in government, workers continued to take industrial action and to demand both an increase in wages and the imposition of a freeze on food prices at the pre-December levels. With hesitation and delay, the latter demand was finally accepted, and higher increases in wages were soon promised too. These decisions ruled out acceleration in investment growth based on internal resources. Indeed the five-year plan for the years 1971–75, adopted by the Central Committee of the Polish Communist Party on 4 September 1971, envisaged an investment growth of exactly the same magnitude as that achieved in the years 1966–70. It was probably in late 1971 or early 1972 that the decision was taken to increase investment activity sharply through massive machinery imports from the West on credit terms. As may be seen from Figure 10.1, this policy resulted in an unusual case of parallel movement in the growth rates of both real wages and investment: increasing in the years 1972–75 and decreasing thereafter. In this paper we shall not discuss the wider issues, economic and political, of the Polish economy in the 1970s. [1] We shall instead limit ourselves to discussing a specific and rather technical question, of the contribution the increased imports of western machinery and technology made to the rate of technological change, and hence to the growth rates of labour productivity and output, in Poland's industrial sector.

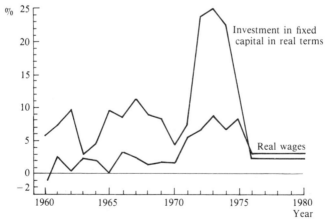

Figure 10.1: The Polish economy 1960–80. Growth rates of real wages and investment (prices 1971) in per cent, economy-wide: actual 1960–75, planned 1976–80.

3. ON THE CONCEPTS OF SUBVINTAGE AND THE DIFFUSIONAL EFFECT

The innovation of the capital–vintage model of the Johansen–Salter–Kalecki-type was to recognise the fact that both capital intensity and technology are essentially fixed in the case of existing machinery, but remain subject to choice for the new vintage of capital. The model assumes, however, that whatever that choice may be, each new investment vintage is technologically uniform.

This paper goes a step further by recognising the fact that the new investment vintage may also be technologically heterogeneous and that, therefore, a change in the technological composition of new machinery may affect the rate of technical change too, and hence also productivity and output growth.[2]

In the case in hand, we shall assume that machinery invested in Polish industry is made up of the following three 'subvintages': (1) machinery of domestic origin, (2) machinery imported from the socialist countries, and (3) western machinery. These and only these subvintages are assumed to be technologically uniform. Moreover, in actual calculations we shall assume that (2) is more advanced than (1), and (3) more advanced than (2). Increased machinery imports from the West after 1972 raised both the total volume of investment and the share of subvintage (3) in that volume. If labour is available to operate additional machinery, as has been the case in Poland, an increase in the volume of investment alone contributes to the growth of output. This may be called the vintage effect.

However, the vintage effect is only the most obvious and perhaps not the most interesting part of the story. There are two further effects of machinery imports. One is to increase incremental labour productivity, that is the average productivity of the labour employed at new machines, over and above what it would have been in the absence of the imports. This is called the *direct effect of embodied diffusion*. The effect clearly influences the level of average labour productivity, and, given the capital/output ratio, may also contribute to the growth rate of that productivity. (It should be intuitively clear that the latter contribution is absent if both the subvintage composition of new investment and the relative technological gaps between subvintages remain permanently constant. For details see Gomulka and Sylwestrowicz, 1976.) The other effect arises when part or all of the imported machinery is subsequently used in the home investment sector to produce more technologically advanced machinery. This spillover effect is extremely important in the process of reducing the technological (and productivity) gap, because given the capital/output ratio it influences the rate of increase of productivity of the workers employed at domestically-produced machines. This influence is called the *indirect effect of embodied diffusion*. It contributes to the growth rate of average productivity of the industrial worker. An estimate of the size of the total (direct and indirect) diffusional effect is reported in the following section.

4. DATA, ASSUMPTIONS AND THE ESTIMATION RESULTS

To be of significant and lasting consequence, the strategy of import-led growth presumes not merely an increase in the volume of investment and capital through a temporary injection of machinery imports, but a permanent change in the composition of new investment in favour of technologically more advanced subvintages. In the Polish case the strategy has meant, first, an increase in the share of machinery imports from the West and, second, maintaining a high share of these imports as long as the technological gap between Poland and the West remains significant. By 1975, the first part of the objective was achieved. However, strong internal political pressure to increase the supply of foodstuffs, and the great difficulties encountered in increasing

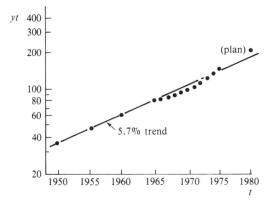

Figure 10.2: Value-added per worker in Polish industry, 1970 = 100 (total industry, socialised and private: all engaged, translated into full-time workers). $y_{1970}^{\text{trend}}/y_{1970}^{\text{actual}} = 107.6$

Table 10.1: Embodied diffusion and its estimated contribution to labour productivity growth: Polish industry 1971–80

	1961–70	Plan										
		1970	1971	1972	1973	1974	1975	1976	1977	1978	1979	1980
Ratio of gross fixed investment to gross fixed capital, at 1971 prices	0.100	0.100	0.095	0.118	0.136	0.147	0.157	0.160	0.145	0.130	0.115	0.100
Share of domestic machinery in total machinery investment	0.69	0.69	0.68	0.61	0.53	0.51	0.49	0.51	0.53	0.61	0.68	0.69
Share of eastern machinery imports in total machinery investment	0.20	0.20	0.20	0.20	0.20	0.20	0.20	0.20	0.20	0.20	0.20	0.20
Share of western machinery imports in total machinery investment	0.11	0.11	0.12	0.19	0.27	0.29	0.31	0.29	0.27	0.19	0.12	0.11
Labour productivity on newly produced domestic machinery[a]		100	105.7	111.7	117.8	126.4	138.7	153.3	170.0	186.7	202.2	214.9
Average labour productivity on newly-installed machinery[a,b]		115.3	121.9	129.7	143.9	163.8	179.6	198.4	213.1	228.0	233.2	237.8
Ratio of labour productivity on new eastern and domestic machinery	1.50	1.50	1.50	1.50	1.50	1.58	1.43	1.36	1.30	1.25	1.22	1.21
Ratio of labour productivity on new western and domestic machinery	2.50	2.50	2.50	2.50	2.50	2.47	2.38	2.27	2.17	2.03	2.04	2.03
Indirect diffusional effect, %[c]	2.9	2.9	2.9	4.5	4.5	6.9	7.7	8.1	7.0	5.5	3.3	2.5

Growth rate of average labour productivity on newly installed machinery[b]	5.7	5.7	5.7	6.4	10.9	13.5	10.0	10.4	7.4	7.0	2.3	2.0
Growth rate of net value-added		8.2	8.5	10.4	12.3	12.1	10.7	10.0	9.0	8.0	7.0	7.0
Index of average labour productivity,[d] trend level in 1970 = 100												
At trend rate of 5.7% per year		100.0	105.7	111.7	118.1	124.8	131.9	139.4	147.4	155.8	164.7	174.1
Actual index		92.9	98.5	105.2	115.1	125.8	135.7					196.1
Computed for $\beta = \gamma = 0$[e]		100.0	105.8	112.8	129.0	130.1	139.6	149.6	159.9	170.2	180.4	190.9
Computed for $\beta = \gamma = 1\%$[e]		100.0	105.8	112.4	119.9	128.4	137.6	147.4	158.0	168.6	179.5	190.4
Computed for $\beta = \gamma = 2\%$[e]		100.0	105.8	112.2	119.2	127.2	136.3	146.3	156.9	168.0	179.5	191.2
Growth rate of average labour productivity[d]												
Actual rate		4.7	6.0	6.8	9.4	9.4	7.8	7.5 (average annual)				
Computed for $\beta = \gamma = 0$[e]		5.7	5.8	6.6	7.3	7.9	7.3	7.2	6.9	6.4	6.0	5.8
Computed for $\beta = \gamma = 1\%$[e]		5.7	5.8	6.2	6.7	7.1	7.2	7.2	7.0	6.7	6.5	6.1
Computed for $\beta = \gamma = 2\%$[e]		5.7	5.8	6.0	6.2	6.8	7.2	7.3	7.3	7.1	6.8	6.5

Notes:

[a] Labour productivity on newly-produced domestic machinery in 1970 = 100.

[b] Regardless of origin.

[c] This is the contribution which the import of technologically more advanced machinery makes to the growth rate at which labour productivity grows on newly-produced domestic machinery every year.

[d] On new and old machinery regardless of origin.

[e] β and γ are parameters characterising disembodied technical change (see Appendix). They are the rates at which, respectively, labour employed with the existing capital is being reduced, and output increased, according to alternative assumptions.

exports of Polish manufacturing to the West more rapidly, forced the planners to envisage a swift return to, approximately, the 1970 composition of machinery imports. According to the new five-year plan, investment activity is to be almost frozen at the 1975 level and, consequently, the I/K ratio is also to return to a level close to what it was in 1970. My data in rows 1–4 of Table 10.1 for the years 1976–80 are in fact a stylised version of the plan. This version assumes a development which is exactly time-reversed compared with that of years 1971–75. (Details of these data are given in Appendix 1.)

The much increased level of investment activity has created a high demand for workers to operate new machines. Apart from a relatively high increase in the number of new workers, the pool of those who in 1970 were only nominally employed has been another potentially important source of supply. This pool was probably above 'normal', since in the years 1966–70 the gains in labour productivity were small, and in 1970 the productivity level was 7.1 per cent below its trend level. While it is not known how much of this 'labour reserve' was actually moved into operating new machines, there was apparently no need to increase the capital/output ratio with a view to saving labour; it actually declined by 6.6 per cent over the period 1971–75. In the post-war period in Polish industry, there has been a downward trend in the average capital/output ratio. This trend was reversed in the poor performance years 1966–70, and emphasised in the years 1971–75. This appears to indicate that the much better performance in the latter period could be due not only to a higher diffusional effect or a greater investment ratio, but also to an increased rate of organisational and other investment-free improvements.[3] These factors are often referred to as disembodied technical change. In our model, this technical change is characterised by two parameters, β and γ (see Appendix 2). They are, respectively, the rates at which labour employed with the existing capital is being reduced, and output increased. Since these rates are not known, the diffusional effect reported in Tables 1 and 2 was computed for the following three cases: (i) $\beta = \gamma = 0$, (ii) $\beta = \gamma = 1$ per cent, and (iii) $\beta = \gamma = 2$ per cent.

The key assumptions of the model
The estimates of the indirect diffusional effect and of the full impact of import-led growth upon labour productivity growth were made on the following assumptions.

Table 10.2: Control estimate of embodied diffusion[a]

| | 1970 | 1971 | 1972 | 1973 | 1974 | 1975 | Plan | | | | |
							1976	1977	1978	1979	1980
1. Indirect diffusional effect[c]	3.5	3.5	3.1	5.1	7.5	8.4	8.8	7.6	5.9	3.7	2.3
2. Growth rate of average labour productivity on newly installed machinery[b]	5.7	5.7	6.4	11.1	15.4	8.0	9.9	6.9	6.4	1.9	1.8
3. Computed index of average labour productivity[d]	100.0	105.8	112.4	120.0	128.5	137.9	147.8	148.0	168.5	179.1	189.9
4. Computed growth rate of average labour productivity[d]	5.7	5.8	6.3	6.7	7.1	7.3	7.1	7.0	6.6	6.3	6.1

Notes:
[a] For a 30 per cent share of eastern machinery imports, an unchanged share of western machinery imports (as in Table 10.1) and $\beta = \gamma = 1\%$ (see note (c), Table 10.1); [b], [c], [d], as in Table 10.1.

(1) The share in total machinery imports of machinery going to the investment sector, itself producing machinery, equals the share of gross investment in the gross national product. This assumption applies for machinery imported from socialist countries and, separately, for western machinery.

(2) The value-added lost because of scrapping the old capital remains a constant proportion of the total industrial value added.

(3) The capital/output ratios for new subvintages are all the same and constant over time. Actually, the incremental capital/output ratio appears to be approximately constant, or slightly declining, in the years 1971–75, but the plan expects it to rise somewhat in the years 1976–80. The effect of this rise on the growth of labour productivity, which Table 10.1 ignores, may well be significant in the years to come.

(4) The assumption about the productivity differentials is that in 1970 the average productivity of workers on new Polish machines was about 77 per cent of the productivity on new machines imported from the East and 46 per cent of the productivity on new Western machines. The empirical basis for these percentages is Table 5 in Gomulka and Sylwestrowicz (1976), itself a compilation of findings from several sources. The productivity comparisons are known to be notoriously imprecise, and the numbers here must essentially be regarded as the author's best guesses.

Comments on the results

The main characteristic features of the numerical estimates in Table 10.1 are as follows.

(i) In the years 1956–70 the average contribution of embodied diffusion to the 5.7 per cent trend rate of growth of labour productivity was about 2.9 per cent per annum, or about half the growth rate. In the years 1974–78 the size of the diffusional term rises to about 6–8 per cent, and, on average in the 1970s, to about 5.1 per cent. Its impact in the 1970s is to increase the average growth rates of the incremental and average labour productivity above their common trend rate of 5.7 per cent by, respectively, 1.5 and 1 per cent per annum.

(ii) While the above contribution of embodied diffusion in the 1970s is virtually independent of the extent to which technical change is of the disembodied type, this contribution will be somewhat greater in the first half of the decade and somewhat smaller in its second half, if the disembodied component of technical change is smaller.

(iii) Assuming that the apparent 'labour reserve' of 7.1 per cent of the labour force in 1970 had been fully activated during 1971–75, this in itself would have increased the average annual growth rate of labour productivity in the period in question from 5.7 to 7.2 per cent. Actually, the growth rate was 7.9 per cent. The combined effect of the full activation of the labour reserve and of the estimated impact of 'import-led growth' would be to make the growth rate of labour productivity equal to 7.9, 8.2 or 8.5 per cent, depending on whether the trend rate of disembodied technical change is, respectively, 4, 2 or 0 per cent. There are several factors which may account for this difference between the estimated and the actual growth rate: the labour reserve might not have been fully utilised; the productivity gaps between Poland and the West and/or the East could have been lower than assumed; the time-lags between machinery imports and their utilisation might have been longer than one year, industry's share in total machinery imports could have been lower than its share in total machinery investment, etc. But since the difference is relatively minor, I would take it as evidence that our method of estimating the growth effect of embodied diffusion is not evidently wrong.[4]

(iv) The technical capital/output ratio (the ratio of utilised capital to output) appears to have been approximately constant over the years 1971–75, but is expected to rise by about 2 per cent a year in the period 1976–80. Hence while the substitution effect (in the Harrod–Kalecki sense) was negligible in the first half of the decade, it may contribute to labour productivity growth by some 1 per cent per annum in the second half (assuming the imputed capital's share to be 1/3). The joint impact of this substitution effect and of the diffusional effect would be to raise the average growth rate of labour productivity in the years 1976–80 from the trend value of 5.7 per cent to about 7.7–8.0 per cent. The new five-year plan assumes this growth rate to be 7.5–7.8 per cent, implying an unusually high degree of agreement with our estimate.

(v) Table 10.2 indicates that the estimates reported in (i) to (iv) above would remain essentially unaltered, if the share of machines imported from the East were changed from 20 to 30 per cent. The only important difference would be that the trend component of embodied diffusion would be 3.5 per cent, instead of 2.9 per cent.

5. SOME GENERAL REMARKS ON THE STRATEGY OF IMPORT-LED GROWTH AS A POLICY ALTERNATIVE FOR EASTERN EUROPE

It is often argued, and there are good though not necessarily compelling reasons to support the argument, that, over time, a Soviet-type, centrally-run economy must find it increasingly difficult to assimilate technical and organisational innovations at a high rate, and that in order to maintain rapid growth it will be necessary to increase radically both the decision-making role of individual enterprises and the allocative role of the market. At the same time, however, it has become quite clear that the central bureaucracies of the countries in question are most reluctant to accept this view, partly because, rightly or wrongly, they appear to regard an economic decentralisation as a threat to the existing political structure, and partly because certain side effects of such decentralisation—e.g. higher unemployment, lower job security, increased price instability, higher income inequality, etc.—are thought socially unacceptable. Consequently, the central bureaucracies have been trying hard to improve the existing economic system and to find, if necessary, a suitable substitute for major economic reform. A substantial increase in the transfer of technology from the West, which in the early 1970s suddenly emerged as a practical policy alternative, seemed an avenue especially worth exploring.

In these circumstances, Poland's large-scale experiment with this policy must be, and probably is, looked at with great interest in the whole of Eastern Europe. While it is too early for a full evaluation of the policy's economic potential, two or three tentative remarks can already be attempted.

   (i) Empirical evidence available so far appears to be consistent with the following 'rule of thumb': a 1 per cent acceleration in the growth of industrial labour productivity (hence also after some time in growth of capital and output) requires an increase in machinery imports from the West by about 10 per cent of all machinery investment. This percentage could be lower for the Soviet Union, where the capability to imitate is probably high, and higher for the GDR, which is technologically more advanced than Poland and where, therefore, gains per unit of imports might be lower.

(ii) The policy will be only a limited success, or even an outright failure, unless the export sector is developed sufficiently rapidly so that an increased scale of machinery imports from the West can be maintained permanently. The Polish experience suggests that making manufactured goods to western standards of quality and performance still remains as difficult as ever, and that improvement in the capability to export to western markets may come about later and be slower than initially expected.

(iii) The growing need to be capable of selling large quantities of manufactured goods on the highly competitive western markets may lead to the development of dual-type economies in Eastern Europe, with the sector producing for the West being technologically the most modern and organisationally the most market-oriented part. This part may over time become the East European equivalent of the Soviet military sector. In Poland developments in that direction have already been taking place over the last ten years or so, although the degree of duality appears to be relatively low so far.

APPENDIX 1. THE DATA

According to Bączykowski, in the years 1960, 1965, 1970 and 1974 machinery imports in the socialised sector represented, respectively, 8.9, 11.5, 12.4 and 22.6 per cent of the sector's total investment, which represents about 85 to 90 per cent of the nation's total investment. Assuming that Bączykowski's percentages apply also to this national total, those imports would have amounted to, respectively, 28.6, 31.9, 32.6 and 49.9 per cent of total investment in machinery and equipment, as given in Table A1, column 7. From these data domestic production of machinery in the four years in question can be found. Assuming steady growth of this production from 1970 to 1975, the following is the distribution of total machinery investment between imports and domestic production (billion zl, 1971 prices):

	Imports	Domestic production	Share of imports (%)	Share of imports adopted in Table A1 (%)
1970	28.2	58.4	32.6	31
1971	28.2	66.9	29.7	32
1972	48.9	76.7	38.9	39
1973	70.4	87.9	44.5	47
1974	100.0	100.7	49.8	49
1975	120.6	115.4	51.1	51

The above data appear to be broadly consistent with the following figures for import shares in the two categories of investment expenditure (in percentages; prices current domestic):

	Machinery alone	Transport equipment	Source[a]
1971	32.0	20.4	1973, p. 59, Table 22
1972	48.3	17.6	1974, p. 59, Table 21
1973	57.5	20.1	1975, p. 45, Table 18

[a]*Rocznik Statystyki Handlu Zagranicznego.*

Finally, it may be worthwhile to note that differences in the value of machinery imports from both the East and West are minor, if, instead of CMEC's, the SITC classification is used. These imports from the East would then be higher in 1971 by 0.5 per cent, the margin increasing to 4.8 per cent in 1975, and from the West lower by 5 per cent in 1971, the margin declining to about 2 per cent in 1974 and 1975.

APPENDIX 2: THE MODEL AND THE ESTIMATION PROCEDURE

The following notation will be used (all symbols refer to industry in year t):

	Total industry	Vintage τ	Subvintage (i, τ)
Gross investment in fixed capital	I_t	$I_{\tau t}$	$I_{i\tau t}$
Net value-added	Y_t	$Y_{\tau t}$	$Y_{i\tau t}$
Employment	L_t	$L_{\tau t}$	$L_{i\tau t}$
Labour productivity	y_t	$y_{\tau t}$	$y_{i\tau t}$
Capital/output ratio	k_t	$k_{\tau t}$	$k_{i\tau t}$

Table A1: Poland's industry (socialised and private): basic data 1950–80

	1970 = 100					Annual percentage growth rates					Joint productivity residual (%)	
	Y	K	I	L		$g_{Y/L}$	$g_{K/Y}$	$g_{K/L}$	$g_{W/P}$	g_I	$\eta_K = 0.3$	$\eta_K = 0.5$
1950	17.10	23.24	17.57	47.32								
1955	29.47	34.30	33.10	62.88	1951–55	5.3	−3.0	2.1		13.5	4.6	4.2
1960	44.94	49.53	47.07	72.73	1956–60	5.7	−1.0	4.5		7.4	4.3	3.4
1965	68.80	68.85	69.02	84.44	1961–65	5.7	−2.0	3.7		8.0	4.6	3.9
1966	72.93	73.86	73.19	86.92		3.0	1.2	4.2		6.0	1.7	0.9
1967	78.11	79.23	81.64	90.96		2.3	0.1	2.5	1.7	11.6	1.6	1.1
1968	85.51	85.22	90.08	94.62		5.2	−1.7	3.4	1.8	10.3	4.2	3.5
1969	93.71	92.04	99.09	98.15		5.7	−1.5	4.1	1.5	10.0	4.4	3.6
1970	100.0	100.0	100.0	100.0		4.7	1.8	6.6	2.3	0.9	2.8	1.5
1971	108.5	108.2	110.4	102.4		6.0	−0.2	5.7	1.6	10.4	4.3	3.1
1972	119.8	117.3	148.6	105.8		6.8	−1.9	4.9	5.4	34.6	5.3	4.4
1973	134.5	128.0	188.4	108.7		9.4	−3.0	6.3	4.7	26.7	7.5	6.2
1974	150.8	143.0	230.2	111.4		9.4	−0.4	8.9	6.3	21.6	6.7	4.9
1975	167.0	156.0	266.8	114.4		7.8	−1.5	6.3	7.0	15.9	5.9	4.7
1980 (plan)	249	253	270	118	1976–80	7.5	2.0	9.7	10.4	0.2	4.7	3.8

Notation:

Y = Net domestic product originating in industry (manufacturing, mining, and gas and electricity), 1971 prices.
K = Gross fixed productive capital, 1971 prices, on 31 December 1970, annual averages since 1970.
I = Gross investment in fixed productive capital, 1971 prices.
L = Labour force engaged (annual averages, part-time employees converted into full-time equivalent numbers).
W/P = Real wage rate.
Joint productivity residual (λ) is a weighted sum of capital productivity growth and labour productivity growth, that is
$\lambda = \eta_K g_{Y/K} + (1 - \eta_K) g_{Y/L}$.
Source: Rocznik statystyczny for the years 1950–75, plan figures for 1980 as announced at the Party Congress in December 1975.

Table A2: Poland's imports of machinery and equipment 1950–75

	1	2	3	4	5	6	7	8	9
	Imports of machinery and equipment US $ m, current prices		Price index		Investment imports, zl billion, 1971 prices, M_{mt}		Total machinery and equipment investment, 1971 prices, M_t	M_{mt}/M_t	
	East	West	Machinery imports, 1960 = 100	All imports, 1960 = 100	East	West		East (%)	West (%)
1950	140	77	100	101.6	2.80	3.08	12.6	22	24
1951	207	106	100		4.14	4.24	14.4	29	29
1952	235	81	100		4.70	3.24	17.1	28	19
1953	259	62	100		5.18	2.68	19.7	26	13
1954	252	42	100		5.04	1.68	20.9	24	8
1955	249	39	100.0	102.8	4.98	4.56	23.4	21	7
1956	289	51	100		5.78	2.04	24.3	23	8
1957	231	66	100		4.62	2.64	25.4	18	10
1958	220	103	100		4.40	4.32	26.7	17	16
1959	269	121	100		5.38	4.84	31.2	17	16
1960	294	111	100.0	100.0	5.88	4.44	34.6	17	13
1961	375	116	100.0		7.50	4.64	37.6	20	12
1962	484	143	100.6		5.62	5.69	44.7	22	13

Year	1	2	3	4	5	6	7	8	9
1963	545	130		101.2	10.77	5.14	47.7	23	11
1964	534	100		100.6	10.62	3.98	47.8	22	8
1965	643	124	97.9	101.6	12.67	4.88	55.5	23	9
1966	695	180	96.7	103.8	13.60	6.94	60.7	22	11
1967	759	219	95.4	104.3	14.55	8.40	67.1	22	13
1968	761	264	94.9	105.4	14.44	10.02	73.2	20	14
1969	855	300	96.6	106.5	15.06	11.27	79.2	20	14
1970	1022	246	98.2	108	18.93	9.11	86.6	22	11
1971	1076	326	96.5	115	18.71	11.31	95.1	20	12
1972	1378	697	95.7	115	23.86	23.96	125.6	19	19
1973	1943	1286	103.7	121	32.13	42.47	158.3	20	27
1974	2216	1821	121.6	126	35.18	57.76	200.7	18	29
1975	2249	2439	130.6	134	33.58	72.80	236.2	14	31

Sources:

Cols. 1–4: *Roczniki Statystyki Handlu Zagranicznego* 1970, ..., 1975, and *Rocznik Statystyczny* 1976. East = socialist countries, West = non-socialist countries. The CMEC classification of goods is used. Numbers with decimal digits in cols 3, 4 are official; other numbers have been assumed by the author. (CMEC stands for Council of Mutual Economic Cooperation, often referred to as Comecon.)

Notes:

Col. 7: New (post-1971) classification applied.

Cols 5, 6: Half of machinery imports from the East are assumed to be military and consumer goods. Consumer goods represented, for example, 21 per cent in 1972 and 20 per cent in 1973 of total machinery imports from the East. The residual machinery imports from the USSR alone, believed to be military equipment, were 25 per cent in 1970, 21 per cent in 1971 and 23 per cent in 1972, of the same total. According to Bączykowski (1975), p. 32, Table 5, the ratio of M_m/M in 1974 in the socialised sector was 49.6 per cent. To be consistent with this figure, an exchange rate of 40 zl (of 1971) to 1 US $ (of 1960) was *assumed*. The above two assumptions are evidently somewhat arbitrary; high errors in cols 5–6 and 8–9 are therefore possible.

Vintage τ is the fixed capital introduced into operation in year τ. Since t denotes the current year, we have $\tau \leqq t$. $I_{\tau t}$ is the amount of fixed capital introduced in year τ that remains in operation in year t. It is assumed that the service life is u years, and that capital does not depreciate during its service, that is $I_{\tau t} = I_{\tau}$ for $\tau \leqslant t \leqslant \tau + u$, and $I_{\tau t} = 0$ for $t > \tau + u$. In the above notation $Y_{\tau t}$ is the vintage-τ's net value added in year t. Similarly, $L_{\tau t}$ is the number of workers operating vintage τ. Therefore Y_{tt} and L_{tt} are, respectively, net value-added and workers employed on vintage t, that is on new investment. Subvintage (i, τ) represents capital introduced in year τ from country (or level of technology) i.

It is assumed that, as a result of disembodied technical change (organisational and other investment-free improvements), employment on all vintages is reduced at a rate β per cent per annum and output is increased at a rate γ per cent. We expect β and γ to be positive, but in the case of any organisational regress they may well be negative. The 'internal' supply of labour is therefore $\beta_t L_t + L_{t-u,t}$, where $L_{t-u,t}$ are the workers released as a result of scrapping the oldest vintage. Since L_{tt} are the workers required to operate new machines, the demand for 'external' labour, denoted $\dot{L}_t$, is $L_{tt} - \beta_t L_t - L_{t-u,t}$. Hence:

$$L_{tt} = (g_{L,t} + \beta_t + b_t)L_t \tag{A1}$$

where $g_{L,t} = \dot{L}_t/L_t$ and $b_t = L_{t-u,t}/L_t$. From the balance equation for a change in output, $\dot{Y}_t = Y_{tt} + \gamma_t Y_t - Y_{t-u,t}$, we also have:

$$Y_{tt} = (g_{Y,t} - \gamma_t + a_t)Y_t \tag{A2}$$

where $g_{Y,t} = \dot{Y}_t/Y_t$ and $a_t = Y_{t-u,t}/Y_t$. On dividing (A2) by (A1) we get:

$$y_{tt} = \frac{g_{Y,t} - \gamma_t + a_t}{g_{L,t} + \beta_t - b_t}\, y_t. \tag{A3}$$

Technical progress parameters β_t and γ_t are likely to have changed (increased) in the years 1971–75, as a result of various organisational changes and new financial incentives for workers introduced by the new government. But since we want to separate the diffusional effect from the effect of a faster disembodied technical change, β and γ should be assumed constant in order to find the productivity of labour y_t which would have obtained had the diffusional effect alone been present. The unexplained difference between the actual y_t and the y_t thus found would then be attributed to other factors, among them to a change in β and γ.

However, the actual $g_{L,t}$ was probably lower in the years 1971–75 than it would have been in the absence of these other factors. So we have to replace $g_{L,t}$ in (A3) with $g_{Y,t} - g_{y,t}$. Hence:

$$g_{y,t} = g_{Y,t} + \beta_t + b_t - \frac{y_t}{y_{tt}}(g_{Y,t} + a_t - \gamma_t). \tag{A4}$$

Noting that $Y_{tt} = I_t/k_{tt} = s_t Y_t/k_{tt}$, and that:

$$L_{tt} = Y_{tt}/y_{tt} = (s_t Y_t)/(y_{tt}k_{tt}) = (s_t L_t y_t)/(y_{tt}k_{tt}),$$

equations (A1) and (A2) may also be presented in the form:

$$g_{L,t} = \frac{y_t}{y_{tt}}(s_t/k_{tt}) - b_t - \beta_t \tag{A5}$$

$$g_{Y,t} = s_t/k_{tt} - a_t + \gamma_t \tag{A6}$$

of which (A6) is Kalecki's familiar growth equation.

Now let L_{itt} be employment on subvintage (i, t) and let $L_{tt} = \sum_{i=1}^{N} L_{itt}$. By definition of y_{it} and k_{it} we have:

$$L_{tt} = \sum_{i=1}^{N} \frac{Y_{itt}}{y_{itt}} = \sum_{i=1}^{N} \frac{I_{it}}{k_{itt}y_{itt}} = I_t \sum_{i=1}^{N} \frac{\varrho_{it}}{k_{itt}y_{itt}}.$$

Hence:

$$\frac{L_{tt}}{Y_{tt}} = \frac{1}{y_{tt}} = \sum_{i=1}^{N} \frac{k_{tt}}{k_{itt}}(\varrho_{it}/y_{itt}). \tag{A7}$$

Assuming $k_{itt} = k_{tt}$, equation (A7) has the particularly useful form:

$$\frac{1}{y_{tt}} = \sum_{i=1}^{N}(\varrho_{it}/y_{itt}) \tag{A8}$$

that is, y_{tt} is a harmonic average of the productivities y_{itt}, $i = 1 \ldots N$, with ϱ_{it} being the weights. Three subvintages are distinguished: (1) domestic machinery, (2) eastern machinery, and (3) western machinery. The numbers assumed for the corresponding productivity levels in 1970 are as follows:

$$y_{1tt} = 1, \; y_{2tt} = 1.5 \quad \text{and} \quad y_{3tt} = 2.5, \; t = 1970. \tag{A9}$$

On this assumption, y_{tt} for 1970 is equal to 1.15, that is Poland's productivity would be about 77 per cent of the 'eastern' productivity and about 46 per cent of the 'western' productivity. The empirical basis for these percentages is Table 5 in Gomulka and Sylvestrowicz (1976), itself a compilation of findings from several sources. It is also assumed that y_{2tt} and y_{3tt} have been growing since

1970 at the trend rate of the average productivity of labour in Western Europe and the USSR, taken as 5.7 per cent per annum.

y_{itt} is given by a production function: $y_{1tt} = f(k_{1tt}, t)$. Hence the growth rate of y_{1tt} is as follows:

$$g_{y, 1tt} = qg_{k, 1tt} + \alpha_t \qquad (A10)$$

where q is the elasticity of f with respect to the capital/output ratio k_{1tt} and α is the Harrod–Kalecki rate of technical change. In our estimation we assume k_{1tt} to be constant. Hence $g_{y, 1tt} = \alpha_t$. By definition:

$$\alpha_t = \alpha_{h,t} + d_t \qquad (A11)$$

where $\alpha_{h,t}$ is the combined rate of home-produced (organisational and technological) change and of disembodied diffusion, while d_t is the contribution of embodied diffusion.

Derivation of the expression for d_t

At the beginning of year t, the technological level in the industrial sector of the importing country is θ_{1t}. In the absence of embodied diffusion the increase in θ_1 in year t would be $\Delta\theta_{1,h}$, and the actual increase is $\Delta\theta_1$. We treat $\Delta\theta_{1,h}$ as given, and we want to find the difference $\Delta\theta_1 - \Delta\theta_{1,h}$. Let M_t represent the volume of machines to be invested in the industrial sector in year t. We have $M_t = \sum_{i=1}^{N} M_{it}$, where M_{1t} represents home-produced machines and M_{it}, $i = 2 \ldots N$, represents machines imported from country i. The technological level of these machines is θ_i. These imported machines were produced in country i using capital stock incorporating technology inferior to θ_i. It is, in fact, always the case that the new vintage of more efficient machines is produced by older machines incorporating less advanced technology. However, in order not to overestimate the size of the diffusional effect, we shall assume that machines M_i incorporating technology θ_i will produce new machines incorporating the same technology θ_i.

Let $\mu = M_1/Y$. Since M_1 represents the flow of machines produced by the home industrial sector for its own use, μ is the proportion of the machine-building branch producing for the industrial sector in the total output of the industrial sector. In year $t - v$, where v is the construction time-lag, the imported machines $M_2 \ldots M_N$ were allocated partly to this branch and partly to the rest of the sector. We shall assume that the part allocated to the branch in question equals μ_{t-v}. In other words, we assume that imported machines are distributed among industrial branches in proportion to their output. Clearly, if the branch producing equipment for the industrial sector receives more machines from imports than its output share, the reported size of the diffusional effect will on this account be underestimated.

Let M_{it}^l represent the machines to be produced in year t on the machines $\mu_{t-v} M_{it,t-v}$. M_{it}^l is thus a fraction of M_{1t}. We have:

$$M_{it}^l = \mu_{t-v} M_{i,t-v}/k_t = M_{1,t-v} M_{i,t-v}/(k_t Y_{t-v}) \tag{A12}$$

where k_t is the machine/output ratio in the machine-building branch.

The increase in θ_{1t} in year t due to factors other than embodied diffusion was denoted above by $\Delta\theta_{h,t}$. This increase is assumed to apply to all new machines installed in the industrial sector in year t. But machines M_{it} are, in addition to assimilating $\Delta\theta_{h,t}$, assumed to inherit the level of technology of the equipment with which they were produced. This level is θ_i. Thus in year t among the home produced machines, we have some with the technological level $\theta_1 + \Delta\theta_h$, and some with the level $\theta_i + \Delta\theta_h$, $i = 2 \ldots N$. The former are in the volume $M_1 - \sum_{i-2}^{N} M_i^l$ and the latter in the volumes M_i^l, $i = 2 \ldots N$. The question is, what is the average technological level of the domestically produced generation of new machines for the industrial sector?

It is not clear what average to take. When technical progress is neutral in the Harrod–Kalecki sense and the capital/output ratio is the same for all subvintages and constant over time, then the harmonic average is the appropriate one. (In this case the level of technology is proportional to labour productivity, and from (A8) we see that aggregated productivity is a harmonic average of the partial productivities.)

In Gomulka and Sylwestrowicz (1976) an arithmetic average was taken, and we adopt the same procedure in this paper. We have:

$$(\theta_1 + \Delta\theta_1)M_1 = (\theta_1 + \Delta\theta_h)\left(M_1 - \sum_{i=2}^{N} M_i^l\right) + \sum_{i=2}^{N}(\theta_i + \Delta\theta_h)M_i^l.$$

Hence:
$$\tag{A13}$$

$$\frac{\Delta\theta_1}{\theta_1} = \frac{\Delta\theta_h}{\theta_1} + \sum_{i=2}^{N}\left(\frac{\theta_i}{\theta_1} - 1\right)M_i^l/M_1. \tag{A14}$$

The first term, $\Delta\theta_h/\theta_1$, is our α_h in equation (A11), and the second term is the sought for d_t. In view of (A12) we have:

$$\frac{M_{it}^l}{M_{1t}} = \frac{M_{t-v} M_{1,t-v} M_{i,t-v}}{k_t Y_{t-v} M_{1t} M_{t-v}}. \tag{A15}$$

But k is the machine/output ratio, so it equals mv, where m is the share of machines in capital and v is the capital/output ratio. Approximating k, by k_{t-v}, and assuming that both m and v for the machine-building branch also apply for the industrial sector as a whole, we have that:

$$\frac{M_{t-v}}{k_t Y_{t-v}} = \frac{M_{t-v}/m_{t-v}}{v_{t-v} Y_{t-v}} = \frac{I_{t-v}}{K_{t-v}},$$

where I is the industrial gross investment and K is the industrial stock of fixed capital. We also approximate the ratio $M_{1,t-v}/M_{1t}$ by unity. Eventually, $M_{it}/M_{1t} = (I_{t-v}/K_{t-v})\, \varrho_{i,t-v}$, where $\varrho_t = M_i/M$, and:

$$d_t = \frac{I_{t-v}}{K_{t-v}} \sum_{i=2}^{N} \left(\frac{\theta_{it}}{\theta_{1t}} - 1\right) \varrho_{i,t-v}. \tag{A16}$$

In the calculation reported in Tables 10.1 and 10.2 of the text, y_{itt} is used as a proxy for θ_{it}, and v is taken to be one year.

The depreciation parameters, a_t and b_t

By definition, $a_t = Y_{t-u,t}/Y_t = (Y_{t-u,t-u}/Y_t)\,(1+\gamma)^u = (k_t/k_{t-u,t-u})$ $(I_{t-u}/K_t)\,(1+\gamma)^u$. I assume $k_t = k_{t-u,t-u}$, and the service life of machinery u to be 20 years. The ratio I_{t-20}/K_t changes from 1.6 per cent for $t = 1970$ to 2.5 per cent in 1973 and 1.9 per cent in 1973 and 1.9 per cent in 1975; I take 2 per cent as an average for the period 1970–75. Hence, $a_t = 0.02\,(1+\gamma)^{20}$. Again by definition, parameter b_t equals $L_{t-u,t}/L = (y_t/y_{t-u,t})a_t = (y_t/y_{t-u,t-u})$ $(1+\beta)^{-u}\,(1+\gamma)^{-u}\,a_t = (y_t/y_{tt})\,(1+\alpha_0)^u\,(1+\beta)^{-u}\,(1+\gamma)^{-u}\,a_t$, where α_0 is the trend growth rate of incremental labour productivity. Hence $b_t = 0.02\,(y_t/y_{tt})\,(1+\alpha_0)^{20}\,(1+\beta)^{-20} \equiv b\,(y_t/y_{tt})$. The ratio y_t/y_{tt} is approximated by its trend value denoted by z^*, and calculated from equation (A4) at $g_{y,t} = 5.7$ per cent and $g_{Y,t} = 8.2$ per cent. It may be found that $z^* = (0.025 + \beta)/(0.082 + a - b - \gamma)$.

The diffusional effect is computed for the three pairs of parameters β, γ: (i) $\beta = \gamma = 0$, (ii) $\beta = \gamma = 1$ per cent, and (iii) $\beta = \gamma = 2$ per cent. Parameters z^*, a and b, calculated in these three cases, are as follows (in per cent)

	$\beta = \gamma = 0$	$\beta = \gamma = 1\%$	$\beta = \gamma = 2\%$
z^*	0.601	0.751	0.895
a	2.00	2.44	2.97
b	3.63	3.71	3.71

Eventually, the system of equations used to compute the full diffusional effect on productivity growth is as follows: (A16), with one year as the construction time-lag, equation (A8) and equation (A4). Moreover, the growth of incremental productivities is specified as follows: $y_{1,t+1,t+1}/y_{1tt} = 1 + 0.057 + d_t - d_{1970}$ $y_{2tt} = 1.5(1.057)^{t-1970}$ and $y_{3tt} = 2.5(1.057)^{t-1970}$, where $t = 1970$, ... 1980. The specification of the growth of y_{1tt} is based on the observation that, in 1970, $\alpha_h = \alpha - d_{1970}$, and α is approximated by the trend growth rate of labour productivity. This specification also assumes that the rate of home-originated technical change (of the embodied type) remains the same in the 1970s as it was in the 1960s.

NOTES

1. For such a discussion in English, see Fallenbuchl (1977).
2. The basic ideas of the model used in this paper were first developed in Gomulka (1976a) and Gomulka and Sylwestrowicz (1976). The general economic and political issues of West–East technological transfer are discussed particularly well by Hanson (1975, 1976).
3. Cf. Appendix 1, Table A1, cols 10 and 11, where the proportional rate of the joint factor productivity (of the Cobb–Douglas type) is given. It may be seen that at the assumed weights the productivity rate was higher in 1971–75 than in any five-year period since 1950, and in fact about double what it was in the years 1966–70. The greatest increase in the joint productivity was recorded in 1973, that is before the increased imports of Western machinery which began in 1972 could have had any significant impact. Better economic management in the post-1970 years is also reflected in the shortening of the average construction period, from 46.1 months in 1970 to 43.5 months in 1971, 40.1 in 1972, 38.4 in 1973, and 31.7 in 1974 (Baczykowski, 1975, Table 6). The construction period is defined as the interval between the completion date and the date when the construction site was handed over by the investor to the construction firm. It includes the time needed for the 'technological start' (*rozruch*).
4. Another way of expressing the contribution of import-led growth is to compare it with the difference between the actual increase in the labour productivity level of 46.0 per cent and its trend increase of 31.9 per cent, both referring to the years 1971–75. The difference to be explained is thus 14.1 per cent. The full diffusional effect as calculated in this paper contributed between 4.4 per cent and 7.7 per cent, depending on the assumed values of β and γ, that is between, approximately, 1/3 and 1/2 of the difference. The remaining 1/2 to 2/3 must be accounted for by increased organisational improvements, relaxation in the imports of intermediate outputs, and perhaps higher intensity of work. These are likely to be once-for-all gains associated with below 'normal' performance in the 1966–70 period.

REFERENCES

Baczykowski, A., 'Inwestycje i budownictwo w badaniach statystycznych' ('Capital Formation and Construction in Statistics Research'), *Wiadomości Statystyczne*, August 1975.

Fallenbuchl, Z., 'The Polish Economy in the 1970s' in *East European Economies Post-Helsinki*, submitted to the Joint Economic Committee Congress of the United States, Washington, DC: US Government Printing Office, 1977.

Gomulka, S., Investment Import, Technical Change, and Growth: a generalised vintage-capital model, mimeo, 1976a.

Gomulka, S., 'Do New Factories Embody Best Practice Technology?— New Evidence', *Economic Journal*, December, 1976b, and Chapter 11 this volume.

Gomulka, S. and Sylwestrowicz, J. D., 'Import-led Growth: Theory and Estimation', in Altman, Kyn and Wagener (eds), *On the Measurement of Factor Productivities: Theoretical Problems and Empirical Results*, Gottingen Zurich: Vendenhoesk and Ruprecht, 1976.

Hanson, P., 'The import of Western Technology', in Brown, A. and Kaser, M. (eds), *The Soviet Union Since the Fall of Krushchev*, London: Macmillan, 1975.

Hanson, P., 'International Technology Transfer from the West to the USSR', in US Joint Economic Committee, *Soviet Economy in a New Perspective*, Washington, DC: Government Printing Office, 1976.

11 Do New Factories Embody Best Practice Technology?—New Evidence*

The question of the empirical validity of the capital vintage hypothesis of the Johansen–Salter–Kalecki–type, according to which most of the technical changes (basically new goods and new methods of production) to be incorporated by the economic system require new investment, was revived by Gregory and James (1973). [1]

The primary purpose of this note is to reproduce, for the benefit of the western reader, the data on new factories which were published in 1969 in a Polish study (Gomulka, Tables 2 and 8), and which appear to support the vintage hypothesis.

The data on all factories existing in Poland in the year 1966 were obtained by the (Polish) Central Statistical Office through the General Census of Industrial Establishments. From the sample of about 10,000 establishments, 279 were built in the years 1961–65. These factories were regarded as the 'new vintage'. For this selected group of new factories we had, among other data, gross ouput, value-added, average employment and gross fixed capital stock, all for the year 1966. Unfortunately, not all of these data were published in the final report. Most of what was published is reproduced here in Table 11.1. I also reproduce a diagram showing individual factories in terms of capital per man and value added per man (Figure 11.1). In Table 11.1 a comparison of the labour/output ratio and the capital/output ratio for new and all existing factories is made, taking as ouput (a) gross production and (b) value added. The results are as follows:

(a) *Output = gross production.* The ratio of new factory to

*Comments by Professors W. B. Reddaway and R. G. Gregory have been very helpful in improving the exposition and sharpening the argument of this note. Reprinted with permission from Stanislaw Gomulka, *Economic Journal*, **86**, December 1976, pp. 859–63.

Table 11.1: Polish industry 1965: Labour/output ratios a_L and $\bar{a}_L$ (number of workers per 1 million zlotys per annum) and gross fixed capital/output ratios a_K and $\bar{a}_K$ for, respectively, new factories and all factories

No.	Industry	Output	New factories			All factories		Comparison		New factories' share in total output
			Number*	a_L	a_K	$\bar{a}_L$	$\bar{a}_K$	$a_L/\bar{a}_L$	$a_K/\bar{a}_K$	
1	Machinery and transport equipment	Value-added	41	1.51	2.44	14.97	1.65	0.10	1.48	—
		Gross	48	7.58	1.04	5.71	0.63	1.33	1.65	0.016
2	Chemicals	Value-added	16	2.56	1.00	10.30	3.09	0.25	0.32	—
		Gross	17	1.44	0.60	3.43	1.03	0.42	0.58	0.075
3	Construction materials	Value-added	40	10.55	4.10	23.70	5.85	0.44	0.70	—
		Gross	41	5.52	2.09	8.34	2.06	0.66	1.01	0.045
4	Wood products	Value-added	23	11.31	1.75	20.16	1.63	0.56	1.07	—
		Gross	26	5.82	0.90	6.39	0.52	0.91	1.73	0.044
5	Textiles	Value-added	11	6.32	0.86	13.00	1.33	0.49	0.65	—
		Gross	12	6.20	0.75	5.50	0.56	1.12	1.36	0.013
6	Processed foods	Value-added	48	2.42	2.46	7.58	1.21	0.32	2.03	—
		Gross	52	2.95	0.68	2.06	0.33	1.43	2.06	0.020
7	Industry total	Value-added	251	6.18	2.96	13.18	2.52	0.47	1.17	0.051
		Gross	279	3.41	1.38	4.38	0.84	0.78	1.64	0.035

Source: Gomulka (1969), Tables 2 and 8 for new factories and Rocznik Statystyczny (1966) for all factories.
Note: *The difference in the number of new factories relating to value added and to gross output are the factories excluded on the basis that they were not fully operational.

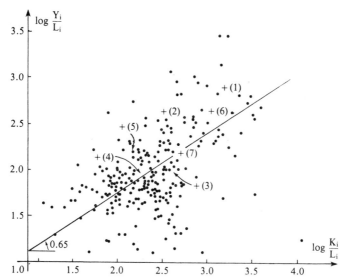

Figure 11.1: Each point in this diagram represents a single new factory in 1966. K_i, L_i and Y_i are gross fixed capital, employment and value added in factory i, $i = 1,2, \ldots, 251$. Crossed points, numbered from (1) to (7), are industrial averages for these new factories. The correspondence between these numbers and industries is the same as in Table 11.1. Arrows indicate the proper positions for crosses (3), (4) and (5).

average factory labour productivity for the industry as a whole is 1.28. The new factory capital/output ratio a_K is, however, higher than the average factory capital/output ratio $\bar{a}_K$. The ratio $a_K/\bar{a}_K$ is 1.64. The selected sample of new factories accounted for 3.5% of the total industrial gross ouput.

(b) *Output = value-added.* Value-added in 28 new factories, out of the original sample of 279 factories, was found to be either negative or close to zero. Further inquiry produced evidence which suggested that these factories were not yet fully operational. They were therefore excluded, reducing the size of the sample to 251 factories. The ratio of labour productivity in new factories to that in average factories for the whole of industry was 2.13. Labour productivity on the new capital vintage was found to exceed productivity in the average factory by 78 per cent in wood products, 106 per cent in textiles, 125 per cent in construction materials, 213 per cent in processed foods, 302 per cent in chemicals and (an unbelievable) 888 per cent in machinery and transport equipment.

Even if the last listed figure is wholly unrepresentative (which seems likely), the average differential of 113 per cent is still quite respectable. Moreover, the differential of 17 per cent in favour of the capital/output ratio for new factories is relatively small, allowing us to interpret the 113 per cent gain in labour productivity as predominantly a vintage effect.

The above remark needs a qualification. The differentials of 17 per cent and 113 per cent are biased by the fact that machinery in old factories is liable to require more maintenance labour, and, being more frequently out of commission, to have lower output per annum. Had the machinery been only technologically old, but physically new, the capital/output ratio for the average factory would have been lower and the output per worker higher. Therefore, if the effect of ageing is allowed for, the corrected labour productivity differential would be somewhat lower than the 113 per cent, while the corrected capital/output ratio differential would be somewhat higher than the 17 per cent, reducing thus the productivity gain to be explained by the vintage effect.

The fact that the 28 new factories which are included in (a) were not to be fully operational and therefore excluded in (b) makes these two cases not fully comparable. Generally, the inclusion of these 28 factories in (a) tends to understate the differential in output per worker and to overstate the differential in capital/output ratio. The size of the bias involved cannot be deduced from the data reported by Gomulka (1969). Since value added is also a better measure of 'output' than gross production, results (b) are probably of greater empirical value.

Our sample of 251 included all new factories from the period 1961–65. Yet they represented only about 11 per cent of Poland's total (gross) industrial investment in fixed capital in the five-year period 1961–65[2] and accounted for about 5 per cent of industrial value added produced in 1966. The remaining investment outlays were allocated to existing factories for the purpose of their extension and/or modernisation. Thus the selected sample was probably a superior subvintage, unrepresentative of the whole 1961–65 vintage of newly–installed machines. This point may be illustrated by an example which uses the fact that the average annual growth rate of labour productivity in Poland for the 10 year period 1956–65 was 5.6 per cent. Suppose that the average age of machines across Polish factories in 1966 was approximately seven years, and the average age of all the machines in the new factories was two years. Suppose further that for the moment we adopt the type of simplifying assumptions frequently used in growth economics, i.e. that all machines of all ages have the same capital/output ratio, while all machines of a given age have the same labour/output ratio. Then, even if all of the productivity gain of 5.6 per cent per annum can be ascribed to the vintage effect the differential between new and old factories would be about 31 per cent (since $(1.055)^{7-2} = 1.31$), and not the 113 per cent found for our sample. It is apparent, therefore, that at least one of the traditional assumptions must be radically wrong in the Polish case, and the most plausible explanation seems to be that it is quite wrong to assume that all machines installed in a given year, even in a single industry, have the same labour/output ratio. One can then go further and say that it is highly plausible that machines installed in wholly *new* factories will have a much lower ratio than those installed in existing factories, where all sorts of constraints (layout, compatability with existing machinery, etc.) restrict the entrepreneur's freedom.[3]

Poland in the period 1961–65 was not yet a modern industrial society. Labour productivity in industry was estimated to be between 15 and 20 per cent of US labour productivity, and about 30–40 per cent of the West European labour productivity. The scope for radical gains was therefore present. This 'extra' factor, which, I presume, was not present in Australia, might have produced a bias in favour of completely new factories. But whatever the cause of the bias, the evidence reported on new factories in Poland gives the vintage hypothesis fairly strong support.

NOTES

[1.] See also an interchange with Haig, Gregory and James (1975).
2. Assuming a two-year investment lag, the sample represented about 14 per cent of total industrial investment in the period 1959–63.
3. This point is not of course a new one: Salter (1969) discussed it in his Chapter VII, notably on pp. 85–7.

REFERENCES

Gomulka, S., assisted by S. Malecki, *Application of Production Functions to the Analysis of Economic Development.* Central Statistical Office, Research Laboratory in Economics and Statistics, Paper no. 16, pp. 1–68. Warsaw, 1969.

Gregory, R. G. and James, D. W., 'Do New Factories Embody Best Practice Technology?', *Economic Journal,* vol. 83, 1973, pp. 1133–55.

Haig, B. D., Gregory, R. G. and James, D. W., 'Do New Factories Embody Best Practice Technology?: An interchange' *Economic Journal,* vol. 85, 1975, pp. 378–88.

Salter, W. E. G., *Productivity and Technical Change;* Cambridge: Cambridge University Press, 1969.

Part C

CRISIS AND REFORM

12 Specific and Systemic Causes of the Polish Crisis, 1980–82*

The Polish events of 1980–82 were triggered by causes belonging to three distinct categories. The first consists of international factors related to the world economic depression. Following the energy price rises initiated by OPEC in 1973 and 1979, the market-oriented developed world has significantly readjusted production, consumption and trade patterns in order to reduce its dependence on energy and to balance foreign trade payments. While the non-energy imports were also reduced, credit-financed export was strongly encouraged. Many semi-developed countries of Latin America, the Far East and Eastern Europe have taken advantage of these easy credits to continue their policies of fast economic development, and in the 1970s this growth strategy became a worldwide phenomenon. However, faced with the persistently deflationary policies of the developed world, with their emphasis on low imports and high interest rates, this import policy collapsed under the weight of rapidly mounting external debts by the end of the 1970s and early 1980s.

Among the developing countries, the centrally-planned economies were much less successful in increasing their dollar exports in the 1970s than the countries of the market-oriented type. The second category, therefore, includes the systemic causes related to the functioning of Soviet-type economies. The third category covers the specifically Polish causes, which explain why the crisis in Poland has been more acute than elsewhere in Eastern Europe.

This paper[1] mainly discusses the systemic and the Polish-specific causes of the Polish events. The discussion focuses on the economic and sociopolitical reasons for the failure of the government to preserve the two key macroeconomic imbalances, external (foreign

*Reprinted with permission from Stanislaw Gomulka *Slavic and Soviet Series*, Tel-Aviv University, vol. **5** (1–2), 1983, pp. 39–57.

debt) and internal (excess demand for consumer goods), within 'safe limits'. The implications of an over-centralised economy and of the workers' revolts in 1970, 1976 and 1980 are emphasised. Since the beginning of 1982 the Polish government has been making an attempt to reduce the macroeconomic imbalances by sharply reducing consumption, and to amend the post-1956 system by combining a substantial marketisation of the economy with a more firm control in the political and cultural domains.

1. IGNORANCE AND RESERVES AS FACTORS IN THE CYCLICAL PATTERN OF ECONOMIC GROWTH

Whatever the nature of the economic system, market-oriented or centrally-planned, a crisis situation is a sign that the existing pattern of development cannot be sustained any longer. There may be a variety of direct reasons for this: shortages of some categories of labour or intermediate products or both, bottlenecks in the physical infrastructure (energy and transport in particular), an increasing balance of payments deficit, insufficient demand. However, the indirect and more fundamental reason must surely be that economic agents, whether private investors or governments, make operational (and long-term) investment decisions under conditions of considerable uncertainty and in ignorance of the present, and especially future, economic environment. They learn of the need to readjust their decisions and policies when it is too late. Seen in this light, the crisis phenomenon may be viewed as the price society pays for the decision-makers' limited knowledge, a limitation that may be partly, though never wholly, avoidable.

Investment or output may change quickly, but this is not true of the labour force or capital stock. Downturns in economic activity tend to produce upturns in production reserves. During subsequent revivals in activity these reserves are partly or wholly activated, resulting in an above trend output performance. The latter, in turn, may stimulate above average investment growth and thus, according to the cycle theory, tend to drive the economy again onto an unsustainable growth path and toward a new crisis.

Although centrally-planned economies are generally resource-constrained rather than demand-oriented, resource reserves may also be present. When they are, they tend to give rise to a 'dash-for-growth' policy, to be almost inevitably followed by a period of growth slowdown, during which the planned economy can gradually cure itself of the imbalances and bottlenecks which have developed in the course of the boom period. The primary cause of what appear to be not random shocks, but endogenously produced (cyclical) fluctuations, is that some important resources, such as agricultural output, export earnings, or managerial and other labour skills, are also difficult for planners to know or reliably predict. Because of limited input substitutability, unforeseen severe shortfalls of some of these inputs may cause a growth slowdown. At the same time, some other resources are likely to continue to expand quickly, producing reserves and with them the conditions for a new sequence of prolonged boom, micro and macro imbalances, and enforced slowdown.

2. THE ACTIVATION OF RESERVES IN POLAND IN THE EARLY 1970s: A CASE OF MISINTERPRETATION

It seems that in the early 1970s the Polish central planners were highly impressed by the rapid expansion of agricultural and industrial output. Following the lean years of 1969 and 1970, the agricultural revival was probably due largely to the favourable weather conditions. However, at about the same time there were some changes in agricultural policy and the government used mass media to emphasise this factor as the main cause of the revival. The five-year output targets formulated in 1975 for agriculture, and especially for meat products, were highly optimistic.

The pre-1970 government under Wladyslaw Gomułka also bequeathed considerable reserves in the industrial and foreign trade sectors to its successor. As can be seen from Table 12.2, labour productivity in industry was some 7 per cent below its trend value, as a result of the poor performance in the second half of the 1960s. Some Polish economists argue that this situation was due to restrictions on imports of intermediate inputs, especially those of western origin. Indeed, total imports from non-socialist countries were, in the 1960s, rising somewhat slower than Poland's total industrial output, and considerably more slowly than exports to those countries.

The relaxation of import restrictions and export targets which took place in the early 1970s probably activated these latent industrial reserves, raising the output and productivity performance almost immediately. But again, Polish party and government leaders and the mass media tended to interpret this performance as being due to 'positive internal developments', such as a better new incentive system, improved management, and a measure of popular support for the new government, while at the same time playing down or ignoring the role of the external inputs in activating the reserves that were present in 1970. Consequently, the point that the spectacular growth improvement of the early 1970s could not be anything but a short-lived transitory phenomenon was conveniently overlooked. This self-serving misinterpretation of the improvements' causes inflated consumer expectations and prolonged the life of the dash-for-growth policy of the government, leading to a high level of credit-financed (consumer, material and investment) imports from the West in the years 1975–80. This prolongation eventually had the effect of dramatically increasing the severity of the shortages in domestic markets and the social price of the radical contractionary measures of 1980–82, such as the reduction of state investment by half and private consumption by about 30 per cent.

This Polish crisis of 1980–82 was deeper, and in many aspects different from that of 1970. However, the accumulation of very considerable reserves is one feature they both share. It is important to identify these reserves so that, when the constraints on growth are gradually relaxed in the course of the 1980s, their activation should not unduly inflate the claims of success made by the government of the day and the expectations of the nation (see Section 4).

In the winter of 1981–82 and the following spring, when the crisis reached its peak, the main question for Poland was how to halt the continuing contraction of the economy, which essentially represented an adjustment of domestic output to the falling dollar imports. The process of adjustment was also affected by the complex interaction of domestic and international economic and political factors. However, although these new factors came into play in August 1980, it seems that the key mechanisms which produced the crisis in the first place continued to function after that date, especially until the declaration of military government on 13 December 1981. These mechanisms are discussed in Section, 3.

3. THE ANATOMY OF THE POLISH CRISIS: AN OUTLINE

The system of economic and political institutions in Poland was, in the 1970s, quite similar to that prevailing in the other Comecon countries, of which only Hungary is something of an exception. It is well known that under such a system market competitiveness and financial discipline are low and allocative inefficiencies are large and widespread. Moreover, enterprises tend to resist innovation, especially if it saves material and enhances quality.

Low price and quantity flexibility result in persistent micro disequilibria: shortages of some goods and surpluses of others. Yet it could also be said that, despite these important deficiencies, the system has served the USSR relatively well, at least until recently.

What then happened in Poland in the 1970s? What is Gierek's own contribution, apart from misinterpreting the reasons for the early successes, and what are the Polish nation's characteristics that have put Poland in the forefront of change?

It may be recalled that Gierek came to power following the December 1970 workers' uprising, an event that in terms of size and political consequences was already unique in the whole Soviet bloc. However the workers did not merely change the government. They also won a freeze on food prices at the pre-December level and a promise of high increases in real wages. The politically convenient and economically important freedom to set prices and real wages at levels which the centre thought fit was thus partly lost. A bid to regain this control was made later on, in June 1976 and in the summer of 1980, but, as we know, was not successful. Even this partial loss of control over the economy was sufficient to rule out any acceleration of investment growth based on internal resources. This was confirmed by both the plan for 1971–75 and subsequent events. The investment rate in 1970 was already high, having been geared up in the 1960s to a level thought necessary to absorb the 3 per cent annual increase in the (non-agricultural) labour force in the years 1965–75.

However, the new leader and his associates were keen to accelerate Poland's economic development. They were looking for ways of making a technological 'great leap forward', of turning Poland into the Japan of Eastern Europe. A bid was made to build a 'second Poland' and double the gross national income and consumption in the course of the 1970s. After the solid but dull and ascetic policies of the 1960s, the new leaders seemed to the man in the street to be offering an exciting new venture. As it happened, the signing of a 'normalisation treaty' with the Federal Republic of Germany in December 1970, followed by the Soviet–American détente of the early 1970s, conveniently opened Poland's access to external resources. The idea of using western credits and technology to modernise Polish industry fast, and build an export sector capable of repaying the credit later on, proved irresistable. Accordingly, late in 1971 or at the beginning of 1972 the decision was taken to increase investment activity sharply through massive machinery imports from the West. An unusual case of parallel movement in the growth rate of both real wages and investment—increasing fast in the years 1972–75 and decreasing even faster thereafter—can be traced to this decision, as well as to the factors already mentioned: the activation of reserves in industry and agriculture in the early 1970s, and the political pressure to improve living standards.

The key to understanding the events of the 1970s is the development of internal and external imbalances. The former, which represents the excess purchasing power of the population over the supply of consumer goods, already started to emerge in the early 1970s, and was of course not planned. The external imbalance was part of the plan, but the government must have been alarmed, in the second half of the 1970s, by its size and the immense difficulties encountered in reducing its further growth.

The main reasons for the failure of the government to keep the two imbalances within 'safe limits' can be grouped into three categories. One was economic mismanagement: many absurd investment projects were started; heavy dependence on imported components was permitted; severe bottlenecks in the supply of electrical energy and transport services were not anticipated; the private agricultural sector was not supplied with sufficient inputs and the heavy concentration of debt repayment for the years 1980–82 was overlooked. The second category comprises systemic economic factors: a low capacity to assimilate and improve advanced technology; an inability to respond fast to changes in demand and compete in quality and price in international markets; an emphasis on quantity rather than choice and quality and little regard for costs and financial constraints. The third category covers reasons of a political and socio-cultural nature, which include characteristics of the Polish society on the one hand and of the Polish party government élite of the 1970s on the other. It should be noted that the Polish nation was never informed about the size of the external debt for most of the 1970s.

The riots of June 1976 were uniquely Polish. They showed that the working class were determined to oppose the correction of the two macroeconomic imbalances at the expense of the standard of living. This opposition alone made it virtually certain that a major crisis was inevitable sooner or later. Following the riots the government did make an attempt to correct the imbalances at the expense of investment, but its actions were slow and proved ineffective. At the same time, in the years 1976–80, the government bought time by allowing money wages to rise more rapidly than the consumer supplies and by continuing to borrow abroad on a large scale, thus putting the economy off balance still further. This practice continued from August 1980 until December 1981 with remarkable consistency, and on a much larger scale.

The economic policy of the government since the summer of 1980, the performance of the economy in 1981, and in 1982 under conditions of martial law, are briefly discussed later in this paper.

4. UNDERUTILISATION OF INDUSTRY'S CAPITAL STOCK AND LABOUR FORCE

The tentative nature of the estimates and suggestions presented below should be stressed. They are intended to give only some indication of the extent of Poland's major macroeconomic reserves in 1981 and over the following few years.

Industry accounts for about half of Poland's material production and for some 80 per cent of total export earnings. Its performance is also a vital factor in determining the output of other economic activities, such as agriculture, construction, transport and domestic trade. Table 12.1 presents some of the basic industrial data for the years 1955–81. In the period 1950–65, the capital/output ratio had been declining, but it stabilised during the years 1966–70. However, in 1971–75, when imported inputs were more freely available, the ratio declined further by about 7 per cent. Since 1975 it has been increasing sharply, especially over the last three years. If we assume that in 1975 the capital stock was fully utilised, then excess capacity in 1980 may be put at 34 per cent of the output for that year. Or, to put it differently, in 1980 the capital utilisation ratio was, in the industrial sector, about 75 per cent of the 1975 ratio, and in 1981 it was about 60 per cent of the 1975 ratio.

Labour productivity, as measured in terms of net ouput per employed (changes in labour hours per year were minor until 1981), was moving along the 5.7 per cent trend in the years 1956–65. However, productivity increased slowly in the 1966–70 period, to reach a level of 7 per cent below the trend in 1970. Following the relaxation of import controls in 1971 and subsequent large-scale imports of materials, machinery and know-how, the pace of labour productivity gains increased significantly, and in 1977 productivity reached a level of 7 per cent above the (long-term) trend. Assuming that this 7 per cent gain represented the impact of the improved technological composition of the capital stock, the productivity level in 1980 should also approximately have equalled 107 per cent of the trend level for that year. However, the actual level in 1980 was about 88 per cent of the trend level, and assuming that labour was fully utilised in 1977, it follows that the labour utilisation ratio in 1980 was about 82 per cent.

In the years 1981–82, industrial employment declined by about 5 per cent while net output in 1982 was some 25 per cent below the 1980 level (see Section 9). Over these two years both the capital stock and the trend level of labour productivity should have increased by about 10 per cent. On the other hand, the introduction from February 1981 of 24 free Saturdays per year represents a fall in the supply of man-hours of about 10 per cent. The potential output effects of these two changes would thus approximately cancel out, implying that the utilisation ratios both of the capital stock and the labour force fell by the end of 1982 to about 60 per cent. Since Saturdays are again working days under the military government of 13 December 1981 it follows, therefore, that even if as much as 10 per cent of the labour force is made redundant, there would still be very substantial reserves of unused industrial capacity.

5. ENERGY AS A MACROECONOMIC CONSTRAINT

In the years 1955–70 electricity consumption by industry was almost precisely proportional to industrial output. However, as Table 12.2 indicates, the ratio of electricity input to industrial output was, in the 1970s, below its 1970 level; in the years 1974–77 it was in fact as much as 10–12 per cent lower. It seems plausible, therefore, that the supply of electrical energy had already become the main constraint on output by the years 1973–75, some three years before the proportion of hard currency imports to industrial output began to decline.[2] Only over the years 1979–82 did the ratio apparently return to its trend level, more than half of the change being accounted for by a fall in industrial output. The output of highly energy-intensive products, such as fertiliser (of the nitrogen type) and cement was especially reduced, the latter falling in 1981 to about 60 per cent of the 1977 level.

According to Polish press reports, the electricity plants had been overexploited in the 1970s, and consequently have been suffering from an unusually high incidence of major breakdowns over the last few years. Moreover, the electricity transmission network is reported to be outdated and suffering from underinvestment. On top of this, the supply of coal for power stations is extremely tight and may well have to remain so for many years to come. The outcome would appear to be that even if imports of materials and components had been adequate, industrial output would have fallen in 1981 in any case, and possibly in 1982 as well, with only moderate increases forecasted for the years 1983–85.

However, the imports of materials and parts were of course extremely inadequate in 1981, with a further disastrous fall in 1982 due to credit restrictions imposed by the West following the military takeover on 13 December 1981. Beginning in 1977, the ratio of total imports to industrial output (both in real terms) has been declining. Hard currency imports per unit of industrial output fell particularly sharply. Consequently, in the years 1981–82 industrial imports became the macroeconomic bottleneck, and will remain so for many years, preventing the activation of capacity reserves until the economy is converted from western supplies to domestic substitutes or Comecon imports.

6. POLICY MISTAKES AND POTENTIAL RESERVES IN THE AGRICULTURAL SECTOR

Agricultural output in the years 1976–80 was in the range of 5–15 per cent below the trend level of the 1950–75 period. Value-added had fallen particularly sharply to some 25 per cent below the trend. Only the sales of agricultural products to the state agencies had been moving broadly along the trend, partly reflecting the switch of farmers' households from food they produce themselves to subsidised food supplied by the state shops.[3]

Poor weather conditions notwithstanding, the government is now widely believed to have committed major policy blunders. First, it permitted a reduction in the ratio of the total of private agricultural income per employee (net of taxes and investment) to average net money income per employee in the total state sector to

84 per cent of the 1970 level of this ratio in 1975, and to 93 per cent in 1977. (In 1975 the ratio itself stood at 74 per cent. If all income in kind was assumed to benefit only the state sector, then this 1975 ratio would equal 61 per cent.) This worsening of the relative income position, combined with the revival of the 'socialisation' doctrine and severe shortages of basic industrial inputs, induced potential young farmers to seek employment in the towns. The share of the arable land which remained in the private farm sector consequently declined from 75.1 per cent in 1970 to 70.5 per cent in 1975, and to 68.8 per cent in 1977.

The price of such land had been more or less constant in the 1970s, but it must have declined significantly in real terms, while the price index of agricultural output more than doubled in that period. The size of the socialised farm sector (mainly the state farms) had thus been expanding. This sector uses about twice as much fertiliser and animal fodder per unit of land as the private farm sector. The consequent and inevitable decline in the provision of these two industrial inputs for the private farm, combined with a 10 per cent decline in their total supplies over the three years 1977–79, must have hit the private farm considerably with predictable consequences. As if this were not enough, in 1980 came the disastrous crop failures in potatoes and sugar beet, and both crops fell by about 40 per cent due largely to exceptionally poor weather conditions. The result was the food crisis of 1981.

Another interesting aspect of the agricultural sector is the fact of unusually high production costs incurred by the non-private farms. While private farms managed to increase the net normal income (a concept close to value-added in current prices) per hectare from 10.2 in 1960 to 12.2 in 1975 and 13.6 in 1979, the socialist farms registered the following income: 5.1 in 1960, 5.0 in 1975, and 1.7 in 1979 (in thousand zlotys).[4] This is in fact a major reason why total net agricultural product in real terms shrank in the year 1979 to about 75 per cent of its (long-term) trend value.[5]

The above analysis indicates the presence of considerable reserves also in Poland's agricultural sector. The key move required to activate these reserves would appear to be the dissolution of those socialist farms which are persistently making a loss, and the introduction of a second land reform. The private sector would benefit immediately from higher deliveries of all sorts of industrial inputs. The move would also make the farmers more confident and secure, by removing the risk of socialisation from their investment calculations. Both implications, coupled with appropriate rises in farm prices and a substantial increase in the supply of industrial goods and services for the sector as a whole, would probably be sufficient to keep the enterprising talent on the land and motivate the owners of private farms to become more modern and efficient.

In the early 1980s the major reserves are similar in kind to those of the early 1970s but by now they are larger in size and much more difficult to activate. The vitality of the private agricultural sector is probably still intact, and a suitable government policy could, weather permitting, lead to a substantial upturn within the next two to four years. The industrial sector however is another matter. The net transfer of resources from the West was, in the early 1970s, instrumental in quickly activating the industrial reserves of the time. Today, however, western imports are and will have to continue to be extremely tight for several years yet, thus putting off the full activation of the reserves until the later years of the 1980s.

7. TRENDS IN DOLLAR EXPORTS AND IMPORTS AND DEBT PROSPECTS

In the four years from 1976 to 1979, Poland's trade with non-socialist countries was already geared to the task of closing the gap. The average annual growth rates were 2.3 per cent for imports and 9.3 per cent for exports (trade in current prices). Industrial net output in that period was increasing at the still respectable rate of 4 per cent.

One of the key questions now concerns the prospect of import and export growth in the coming years.

The ratio of dollar exports to industrial output, both in real terms, is given for the years 1970–81 in Table 12.2. It is remarkable that despite the strong emphasis on dollar exports, this ratio actually fell in the period 1973–77, and in 1977 it stood at only 85 per cent of its 1973 level. In real terms, dollar exports increased in that period by approximately 3 per cent, which was less than the increase in industrial production. Most of this fall took place in the years 1974–75, when total world exports (in real terms) also suffered a decline. In the present world trade environment, and with the recent fall in the production of coal, fertiliser, cement and other exportables, it would probably be unduly optimistic to expect dollar exports in real terms to expand faster than industrial production. In fact, in 1981 the total volume of exports fell by 19 per cent and the volume of dollar exports by 22 per cent, while industrial value-added fell by 15 per cent. Significantly, the ratio of total exports to industrial output returned in 1980 to the 1970 level. The trade gap in 1981 reached about $2 billion, totally from trade with the Comecon group. In 1982 the dollar imports fell by about 30 per cent, while dollar exports remained at the 1981 levels, resulting in a trade surplus of about $1.4 billion. However, since interest payments on western debts run now at about $3 billion per annum, the total dollar debt increased in 1982 by $1.5 billion and is expected to increase by a further $1.5 billion in 1983. In addition, the Polish debt to the USSR reached the equivalent of $5 billion by the end of 1982.

Over the years 1976–79, dollar exports in nominal terms rose at an average annual rate of 9.3 per cent, which is less than the present average interest charge, reported by the Polish (Central) Commercial Bank to be 11.5 per cent in 1980. Industrial output and dollar export earnings are now severely restricted by limited dollar imports, while interest rates in the West are still on the high side. However the military takeover did suppress consumption and consumer expectations, the first necessary steps toward bringing external imbalances under control.

8. SYSTEMIC FACTORS IN THE POLISH CRISIS

Joseph Schumpeter once argued that capitalism would fall under the weight of its successes.[6] A somewhat similar view was held by Marx himself, who noted that the more successful the capitalists are in their efforts to accumulate capital and expand factory production, the faster they create a political force—the proletariat— that would take capital and political power from them. Today these utterances may not be acceptable without substantial qualifications. Even so it seems still meaningful to inquire whether the present developments in Poland are the effects of a similar sequence of causality at work. The proposition would be that the successes of the communist élites in the modernisation and industrialisation of their countries also breed economic and social changes that are contrary, and in the long run possibly deadly, to the élite's own interests.

Obviously the major difficulty in looking at Polish events in this light lies in singling out and assessing the contribution to the crisis of the systemic factors, listed below, from the influence of specifically Polish circumstances. The latter include the powerful Catholic Church, wide cultural and family links with the West, and historically-rooted democratic traditions, together with startling economic blunders and corruption under Gierek's government. It would indeed be difficult to overestimate the significance of macro-economic mismanagement, especially in explaining the particular timing of the crisis. Equally it would seem to be wrong to view the crisis as being a uniquely Polish phenomenon. There are, in fact, good grounds for interpreting certain systemic factors and economic and social trends, common to all industrially-advanced economies of the Soviet-type, as important causes of the crisis.

Among the many systemic factors that are common to Poland and her Comecon partners, the following four are particularly significant: (i) central control over the wages of workers and prices of consumer goods; (ii) the low level of entrepreneurship on the part of local managers and the limited disciplinary role of markets; (iii) persistent shortages in home markets; and (iv) slow innovation and the low non-price-competitiveness of manufactured goods produced for export markets.

Apart from these systemic factors, we have also to consider a number of key social and economic trends. These trends are all associated with the gains in the industrialisation process that have been made in the post-war period. These are as follows: (i) a change in the composition of the population from peasants to town-dwellers and, among them, to workers in large factories; (ii) a change in the composition of production from primary activities, such as agriculture and mining, to manufacturing and services; (iii) a change in the composition of needs (and consumption), from the most basic to more sophisticated material and non-material needs, such as high-protein food, better housing, cars, travel abroad, and so forth.

These three trends are of course not system-specific; they are in fact common to all countries that undergo rapid industrialisation. However, when these trends occur in a country where both economic and political power are highly centralised, and where economic well-being depends strongly on success in trade with the competitive West, then, I shall argue, the likelihood of serious economic difficulties and consequent political tensions tends to increase with time, unless substantial reforms are introduced in the direction of increased marketisation of the economy and, more gradually and subtly, political democratisation of the state.

The argument runs as follows. A less-developed country of the

Soviet-type, such as Poland or Romania in the 1950s, initially had a sizeable trade surplus in agricultural products and minerals which was used to pay for net imports of 'technology-intensive' goods. However, with the progress of industrialisation and urbanisation, the domestic demand for minerals and basic materials for industry and for agricultural products has increased faster than domestic supplies.

Two systemic factors have accentuated this trend. One was that the choice of techniques and innovations tends to be heavily biased towards a high material intensity, with a consequent high consumption of energy, steel, cement and so forth per unit value-added, and a corresponding bias in the composition of investment outlays.[7] The other factor relates to the apparently increasing difficulties caused by the traditional way of controlling workers' wages and consumer prices. Although workers under any system insist on high wage increases and resist price rises, the implications for economic and political stability are system-specific.

In a competitive economy prices are set by the impersonal market and wages are constrained by the threat of unemployment. The former insures that micro-economic disequilibria between demands and supplies do not arise, or tend to disappear quickly, while the latter ensures that the possibility of hyperinflation, which has the potential of destabilising the economy as a whole, is not very likely. Consequently, price increases and unemployment tend to be viewed as externalities; as certainly unwelcome, but perhaps inevitable, by-products of economic activity. The blame for them is also spread throughout the economy, rather than focused exclusively on any single part of it.

On the other hand, in centrally-planned economies the responsibility for price increases rests solely with the government. Hence price increases are not seen as inevitable. They may still be necessary, but this has to be supported by argument. Alas, the Soviet political system is singularly ill suited for seeking consent. In fact, price rises have always come as a surprise to the population, the authorities at times offering a justification *ex post facto*. Moreover, for reasons that are not quite clear—although administrative convenience is certainly one of them—government price rises are usually not gradual, but sporadic and sudden. The authorities must of course be aware that their price decisions send shock waves among the consumers, and that the resulting political cost probably increases as industrialisation proceeds. Consequently, the authorities in the USSR and Eastern Europe appear to be increasingly reluctant to impose the price rises for basic consumer goods that are required to maintain a market equilibrium at home and a sizeable surplus for export. In fact the two largest countries of the Comecon group, the USSR and Poland, became food importers on a big scale in the 1970s.[8]

The turnabout in the trade balance for food and other primary products would not be so serious if the dollar exports of other manufactured goods, especially technologically more advanced products, had risen sufficiently fast. The foreign trade data indicate, however, that the sales of centrally-planned economies on the primary international markets for mass-produced consumer goods, components and investment equipment continue to be marginal. Consequently the balance of payments constraint to growth is looming large, and especially so for the smaller East European economies, which are much more dependent on imports and less endowed with natural resources than the USSR.

In the 1970s an attempt was made to overcome this by borrowing in the West and modernising the export sector. This policy permitted a high level of investment activity and relatively fast industrial growth throughout most of the decade, but it has clearly failed to stimulate manufactured exports to the levels expected in the early 1970s. Faced with a net debt of about $80 billion and a continuing large balance of payments deficit of some $10–15 billion per annum, the Comecon countries are now being forced to curtail their dollar imports severely, reduce industrial growth and often accept high underutilisation of the facilities that were built with the help of western suppliers in the earlier years.

Summing up, the major barriers to growth and the areas of conflict appear to be as follows. First, the planners' ability to control consumer prices and workers' wages effectively is under increasing strain; in Poland it was repeatedly challenged in the 1970s, and from the summer of 1980 until 13 December 1981 it was practically lost. The pressure is thus probably building up to broaden the narrow political base of present communist governments, so that their decisions concerning prices and wages will appear to command wider support. Alternatively, central planning may have to be replaced by a regulated market mechanism of the Yugoslav variety, or at least of the Hungarian-type, so that the consumer price rises become less of a factor integrating workers against the government. If this latter course is adopted, the pressure for political democratisation may be containable for some time yet. An increase of repression is the third option.

Secondly, the common western view that the present Soviet system is not conducive to fast innovation or successful competition in international markets now seems to be accepted in Eastern Europe more widely than ever before as being a major systemic weakness. This failing may well be serious enough to prevent the industrially-advanced and centrally-planned economies from making any further gains in closing the (still large) technological gaps between them and the West. What is, in this respect, merely a possible outcome as regards the USSR, seems a probable one as regards the small East European economies which have neither the large quantities of minerals needed for exports to finance technological imports nor large R & D resources for effective inventive and imitative activity at home. These smaller countries are consequently faced with a disturbing dilemma: they must either sharply increase the allocative role of markets and competition at home, probably at the expense of some long-standing socialist objectives such as job security, or else sharply reduce technological imports from the West and accept their own present technological inferiority as something more or less permanent. The urgent need to restrain the large dollar debt from rising still further must give this dilemma an added emphasis, as must the prospect of the small Comecon countries having to increase their imports of oil from the dollar market in the course of the 1980s and beyond.

A third powerful factor that now acts to decelerate growth is the policy, pursued by all these countries in the past, of concentrating on investment in industry at the expense of the infrastructure. Consequently, the transport and communication sectors are now so underdeveloped that they are widely considered to be serious bottlenecks. These sectors are, however, highly capital-intensive. Other underinvested sectors, such as housing and agriculture, are also highly capital-intensive, and hence likely, in the future, to attract a significantly greater share of investment resources than they have in the past.

The growth slowdown in the USSR and Eastern Europe, which set in during the middle of the 1970s, continued in the years 1980–82. This was happening at a time when the workers were already numerous and the population was becoming more educated. The combination of these two trends has proved to be explosive in Poland, where the working class has apparently also become more self-confident after the events in 1970 and 1976. It is conceivable that these trends will have no such dramatic effect in other East European countries, especially in the immediate future.

However, after Polish events the communist élites may be justified in thinking that the risk of a serious attempt to make them accountable is probably on the increase in all communist countries. This perception alone, if it spreads widely, could have a significant influence in enlarging the political base of the governments of Eastern Europe, and making the economies of the region more efficient. However, the Polish events of the years 1980–82 also indicate that while significant economic reforms are conceivable in Eastern Europe before they are attempted in the USSR, the pace of the political democratisation is likely to be decided largely in the factories and towns of the Soviet Union.

9. EVENTS IN 1981 AND 1982: THE REMARKABLE INTERLOCK BETWEEN POLITICS AND ECONOMICS

In Section 8 we were concerned with the wider, long-term and systemic aspects of the Polish crisis. In this concluding section we return to the domestic scene to consider developments since the summer of 1980.

The establishment of the trade union movement 'Solidarity' raised expectations of radical reforms but, it seems, not many expected an early improvement. Yet the population appeared stunned by the extent of the economic deterioration in Poland in the course of 1981, a fact that must have helped the government to contain the popular resistance against the December 1981 crackdown. Without going into details, it would be instructive to note the actual extent and the main causes of this deterioration. This should also prove useful for the primary purpose of this section, which is to comment, albeit briefly, on the internal dynamics of the crisis.

The main economic indicators for 1981 (in comparison with the performance in 1980) were as follows: industrial production down by 19 per cent, electrical energy down by 5.7 per cent, meat sales to the state down by 22.3 per cent and nominal wages up by 25 per cent. Agricultural output in 1981 was estimated to be some 10 per cent less, and GNP to be 13 per cent less than in 1980. Real exports and imports in 1981 were both 18 per cent less than in 1980. Despite severe cuts in the import of machinery and current inputs the balance of payments gap widened from about $3 billion in 1980 to $5 billion in 1981, of which about $3 billion was in hard currencies.

The internal (consumer) imbalance also increased sharply. In the first three quarters of 1981 the gap between private disposable income and all private expenditure was zl 134.7 billion, or 9.6 per cent of the disposable income. This difference used to be, in the 1960s and 1970s, in the range of 2 to 5 per cent. Assuming that this represents the ratio for voluntary savings, forced savings in 1981 were some 5 to 8 per cent of disposable income. However, the stocks of consumer goods were depleted in the first three quarters of 1981 by zl 76.5 billion or 5 per cent of the income. The underlying (trend) ratio of forced savings was equal, therefore, to some 10 to 13 per cent. The data for September 1981 confirm this, as the total (voluntary and forced) savings ratio in that month reached a level of 15 per cent. By the end of 1981 the accumulated forced savings appear to have been about zl 500 billion, which was three times the value of the consumer goods that still remained in stock. Consequently the queues were getting longer, the rationing system was spreading, and the social cost of obtaining goods was rising. There were also signs that Polish currency was becoming unacceptable as a means of payment, and that the volume of transactions in hard currency and on a barter basis was rising sharply.

The immediate major causes of this economic deterioration in the aftermath of the summer strikes of 1980 are not difficult to identify. The fall in meat supplies was largely the delayed effect of the potato disaster of 1980. The fall in coal output by about 40 million tons per annum, worth about $2.5 billion, was almost entirely due to the miners no longer being willing to work on all Saturdays and some Sundays. This fall, in turn, affected the supplies of energy and export earnings. As these two inputs limit the overall level of industrial activity, the supplies of industrial products for domestic and export markets duly declined. Since employment remained unchanged labour productivity fell sharply, by some 15–20 per cent. At the same time the Gdansk agreement resulted in wages increasing faster than state-controlled prices. The consequent surplus of purchasing power over output has created havoc in the domestic market. The government felt it needed to buy time, so it responded to the acute shortages of basic consumer goods in state shops by reducing exports and increasing imports of these goods. The inevitable effect of this policy was a further reduction of the import of current inputs for industrial production.

The rescheduling agreements of 1980 between the Polish government and western parties simply acknowledged that Poland could not repay the principal on the dates initially promised. However,

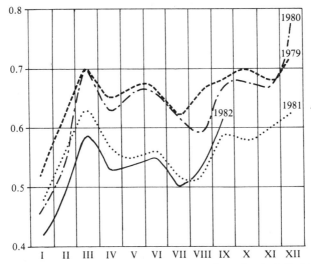

Figure 12.1: Global monthly industrial output in Poland 1979–82
Note: Socialised sector, output sold, in 1982 prices. The value unit is 10^6 million zlotys
Source: Życie Gospodarcze, no. 36, 1982.

the agreements also stipulated that Poland would continue to pay the interest, an obligation which it proved impossible to meet in 1982 and which cannot be met for several years yet. Dollar exports were \$7.5 billion in 1980, but fell to about \$5.4 billion in 1981.

From this brief survey it is quite clear that Poland, by the end of 1981, was on the brink of economic chaos and political unrest that could have been much worse than anything seen before. Under these circumstances it was legitimate to ask, as many did, whether there was any non-violent way out of the crisis engulfing Poland.

The key difficulty has been widely recognised as political in nature. It lay in part in the determined opposition of the population, articulated through the 'Solidarity' movement, to the admittedly very large increases in consumer prices which were necessary to equilibrate markets, and to other austerity measures. Possibly this opposition would have been much weaker had institutional changes been introduced that, in the eyes of the population, would reduce both the widespread inefficiencies in factories and costly macroeconomic blunders at the centre, and so make the 'sacrifice' worth while. The institutional changes insisted on by 'Solidarity', such as all-powerful workers' councils in enterprises, wide access to the mass media, much restricted censorship and free elections to parliament and local councils, would, however,

Table 12.1: Basic growth data: Poland 1971–82

	1971	1972	1973	1974	1975	1976	1977	1978	1979	1980	1981	1982
Domestic output, NN(M)P	8.1	10.6	10.8	10.4	9.0	6.8	5.0	3.0	-2.3	-6.0	-12	-5.5
Investment in fixed capital	7.5	26.0	25.9	24.2	15.2	2.8	3.4	0.6	-5	-12.3	-22.3	-12.1
Industrial gross output	8.8	10.2	11.0	11.3	11.0	2.3	6.3	3.6	1.9	0.0	-11.8	-2.1
Agricultural gross output	3.6	8.4	7.3	1.6	-2.1	-1.1	1.4	4.1	-1.5	-10.7	3.8	-2.8
Exports (in real terms)	6.2	15.5	11.6	12.3	8.3	4.4	8.0	5.7	6.8	-4.2	-19	+8.7
Imports (in real terms)	14.0	21.8	22.8	14.9	4.4	9.6	-0.1	1.5	-0.9	-1.9	-16.9	-13.7
Real wages	5.7	6.4	8.7	6.6	8.5	3.9	2.3	-2.7	2.4	4	?	-25
Productivity of fixed capital	1.8	3.8	3.0	1.0	-1.1	-2.6	-4.3	-5.6	-9.6	-11	-20	-10
Productivity of labour	6.9	8.6	9.0	8.2	8.3	7.7	5.0	3.3	-1.5	-4	-12	-5

Sources: Report on the State of the Economy, July 1981; *Życie Gospodarcze*, 25 October 1981; Report of the Central Office of Statistics, *Trybuna Ludu*, no. 36, 12–13 February 1983. (Data for 1980–82 corrected to conform with *Rocznik Statystyczny* 1983.)

Table 12.2: Poland's industry (socialist and private) and foreign trade 1955–81: basic data

	1970 = 100		Annual % growth rate		1975 = 100	trend = 100	1970 = 100	Constant prices		1970 = 100	
							Electricity input	*per unit of net industrial product*			
	Y	K	gᵧ	gₖ	K/Y	Y/L		Total exports	Dollar exports	Total imports	Dollar imports
1955	29.47	34.30			123	100	102	83			
1960	44.94	49.53			118	100	103	84			
1965	68.8	68.85			107	93	101	93			
1970	100.0	100.0			107		100	100	100	100	100
1971	108.5		8.5	6.3			98	98	103		
1972	119.8		10.4	9.0			96	96	107		
1973	134.5		11.6	9.3			93		106		
1974	150.8		12.0	12.6			89		100		
1975	167.0	158.5	11.4	11.2	100	103	88	100	95	122	193
1976	182		9.3	10.6		106	88		99	124	198
1977	196	190.9	7.7	12.2		107	90		92	115	164
1978	200	215.4	2	9.5		103	85			115	
1979	195	230.8	−2.5	7.4	118.4	94	90	108	100	114	152
1980	190	241.2	−2.6	4.5	126.9	87	89	107	100	114	149
1981	162	249.1	−14.7	3.3	153.8	70	96	101	92	114	120

Notes:

Y = net product (approximately value-added), 1971 prices.

K = gross fixed productive capital, until 1970 in 1971 prices, from 1971 in 1977 prices.

(Y/L) trend = at trend rate of 5.7 per cent per year, which is the average growth rate of (Y/L) in the years 1956–65.

Electricity use to output ratio given for the socialist industry only. (Data for 1979–81 corrected to conform with *Rocznik Statystyczny 1983*.)

amount to transferring economic and political power from the communist leadership to the elected representatives of the nation. Such demands were, naturally enough, strongly opposed by the communist élite. This opposition became particularly vigorous in August 1981, following a relatively successful Party Congress in July 1981 on the one hand and anti-communist 'hunger marches' in Kutno, Lodz and Warsaw on the other. By October the Party leadership apparently realised that the propaganda war with 'Solidarity' was not particularly successful. Moreover, the industrial administration and civil service, caught between the two sides, began to adapt a wait-and-see attitude, which rendered central directives increasingly ineffective. There were also indications that rank-and-file membership of the Communist Party was falling at an increasing rate, and that most of those remaining were unwilling to defend the leadership in political confrontations at the local level. The time had come to use other means to defend the communist power structure.

10. CONCLUDING REMARKS

Poland in the years 1976 to 1981 resembled a social laboratory, demonstrating vividly how major economic problems breed mass political unrest, which then helps to spread dissent and promote new leaders. These leaders in turn attempt to channel this unrest into social pressure for immediate policy changes and longer-term institutional reforms. The rise of 'Solidarity' had clearly put at risk the stability and the very survival of the traditional communist system. The threat to communist rule from political democratisation and in particular 'Solidarity's' insistence on free elections to the Polish parliament, was very real. For these reasons it had to be removed. The military takeover was, in this sense, the system's act of self-defence, even if desperate and crude.

Following the takeover, the communist élite under Jaruzelski's leadership still seemed ready to identify and gradually introduce those economic and political reforms that might be thought capable of meeting the main economic problems without, at the same time, endangering the élite's nearly absolute power. Since the beginning of 1982 an attempt has been made to amend the traditional system by combining some ideological flexibility and what eventually is promised to be a far-reaching marketisation of the economy with continuing firm control in the political and cultural domains.

The response of the Polish communist élite to the crisis may well be indicative of the kind of systemic changes that may be adopted throughout the region. If one overlooks the ideological content of the state propaganda and the question of ownership of the productive assets, the system that emerges would be similar to that prevailing in Spain under Franco or in Greece under the colonels, with comparative freedom in the economic domain but strict control in any other field as its essential features. However, the level of repression, actual and potential, needed to sustain such a system in a modern and well educated society may have to be high. This must be so especially in Poland, where an inevitable further steep decline in national production in 1982 is likely to be followed by a period of slow recovery and high inflation at a low level of per capita consumption.

Moreover, Poland's inability to pay interest for a number of years introduces an element of uncertainty in East–West economic relations, since now Poland may be declared, or declare itself, in default at any time. This would possibly trigger off severe credit restrictions for the whole of Eastern Europe and hence increase the risk of further defaults. Whether or not a chain-reaction of this kind actually happens, some of the countries may well follow Poland in adopting a mixed economic system that combines limited decentralisation and marketisation with some form of direct military control.

NOTES

1. An earlier version of the paper was presented at a conference on Poland organised by the Russian and East European Research Centre Tel Aviv University in January 1982. It was written when the author was a Fellow of the Netherlands Institute for Advanced Study in Social Sciences and Humanities, Wassenaar. Helpful criticism and useful comments by Tamas Bauer, Michael Ellman, Jan Rostowski and Hans Wagener are gratefully acknowledged. The final version was prepared in January 1983.
2. According to an official Polish source, there was a major shortage of electric power for the first time in the winter of 1975–76, when it was estimated at 4550 MW, or some 30 per cent of the power supplied. The shortage remained about the same, in percentage terms, until 1979. Wlodzimerz Wodecki, 'Atomowy bałgan', *Życie Gospodarze*, no. 3, 1983, p. 1.
3. By 1980 bread was no longer baked in villages, and home-made butter and cheese had practically disappeared.
4. R. Manteuffel, *Polityka*, 21 February, 1982, p. 4.

5. If value-added per hectare in the socialist sector had moved, in the years 1960–79, in parallel with that in the private sector, total agricultural value-added in 1979 would have been 11 per cent higher than it actually was. If the former had reached the level of the latter in 1979, the total value-added would have been 20 per cent higher than it actually was.

6. J. Schumpeter, *Capitalism, Socialism and Democracy*, London, 1976.

7. An aggregate indicator of the material (primary and intermediate) consumption is the use of energy per dollar of the national product. This was in 1979 (in kg coal equivalent) 0.48 in Japan, 0.56 in West Germany, 0.6 in Austria, 0.89 in the UK, but 1.5 in Poland (Jerzy Kleer, *Polityka*, 13 March 1982). The Soviet and other East European figures are close to the Polish one. The difference in these data between East and West appears too large to be explained away by reference to various measurement errors, climate, or differences in energy endowments.

8. In Poland the trade imbalance in food and food products represented, at $4.3 billion, 24.4 per cent of the total dollar trade imbalance for the decade.

13 East–West Trade and the Polish Experience, 1970–82*

The matters to be discussed in this paper are indicated by the following questions we shall address:

(i) Does the effective collapse of the import-led strategy of growth, in its form practised by Eastern Europe and the USSR in the 1970s, suggest that the ultimate factors keeping East–West trade flows at low levels are not, or no longer, the trade-restricting policies of governments, both eastern and western, but rather the inherent export-restricting characteristics of the centrally planned economies (CPEs)?

(ii) The western premise behind the 1970s policy of economic détente would appear to have been that net economic gains to the East from trading with the West might be large enough to act as an effective incentive for communist governments to improve East–West relations in human and other aspects. If so, how large, in fact, were the net benefits of the policy for Poland in the period 1971–82?

(iii) Does the Polish experience suggest that, unintentionally, economic détente has turned out to be a policy of western economic pressure? Whatever its past effects, can the policy be effective in promoting economic reform in the East in the future? In view of the debt crisis and the somewhat different economic interests of the USSR and Eastern Europe, what might be an 'optimal' eastern trade policy for the West?

*This was an invited paper presented at the Transatlantic Conference on East–West Trade, held at the Hoover Institution, Stanford, 24–26 August 1983. I wish to thank Melvyn Kraus, the main organiser of the conference, for his invitation, and the Hoover Institution for its financial assistance and the permission to include the paper in this volume. The present version benefited much from criticisms and suggestions of the following colleagues: George Blazyca of the South London Polytechnic, Włodzimierz Brus of Wolfson College, Oxford, and Peter Wiles of the London School of Economics.

(iv) What is the post-1982 Polish trade policy towards the West? What, in the circumstances, might be an optimal western trade and credit policy towards Poland?

Each section of the paper is concerned primarily with one of these four questions, the order of sections following the sequence above. Another description of the sections would be that (1) is introductory, (2) gives an economic assessment of the Polish experiment, and (3) and (4) deal with policy issues concerning, respectively, East–West trade in general and Polish–western trade in particular.

1. SYSTEMIC FACTORS VERSUS POLICIES IN EAST–WEST TRADE

In 1980 the world total exports were $2000 mld., of which the trade between the Seven accounted for $90 mld., while the exports of the Seven[1] to the West, meaning all non-Comecon countries except Communist China, Yugoslavia and North Korea, were valued at about $60 mld. If we take $1910 as the size of the world dollar market in 1980, the Soviet share of that market was 1.8 per cent, while the combined share of the remaining Six was 1.4 per cent. The total dollar purchasing power of the Seven is thus relatively quite minor, about the same as that of Belgium and Luxembourg ($64.6 mld. in 1980), or Canada ($64.3 mld. in 1980).

It is interesting to compare the relative export share of each of the Seven in 1980 with that in 1970, and to note how the change of this export share compares, in turn, with corresponding change for some of the medium developed, market-based countries, especially those which have also attempted, in the 1970s, to stimulate dollar exports through much increased technology imports. The relevant data are given in Tables 13.1 and 13.2. With the exception of the USSR and Romania, the only significant Comecon exporters of oil, natural gas and petroleum products to the West, the joint share of the dollar market of the remaining five East European countries declined from 1.58 per cent in 1970 to 1.08 per cent in 1980, the latter percentage equal to the share of Spain alone. The relative decline of the share, at 32 per cent of its initial size, contrasts rather sharply with usually stable or increased, sometimes much increased, market shares of the newly-industrialised countries of the Far East, Latin America and Europe, also those which were net energy importers.

Table 13.1: Exports of the Seven: absolute and relative, in 1970 and 1980

	1970 (in $ mld.)		1980 (in $ mld.)		Percentage share of the $ market	
	Total	Dollar	Total	Dollar	1970	1980
1. USSR	12.5	4.4	76.4	35.0	1.51	1.83
2. Poland	3.5	1.3	13.2	5.4	0.44	0.28*
3. Romania	1.9	0.8	12.2	6.9	0.27	0.36
4. GDR	4.6	1.2	17.3	5.4	0.41	0.28
5. Czechoslovakia	3.8	1.1	13.7	4.0	0.38	0.21*
6. Hungary	2.3	0.8	8.7	3.6	0.27	0.19*
7. Bulgaria	2.0	0.4	10.7	2.2	0.14	0.12*
Total Six	18.1	5.4	75.8	27.5	1.85	1.44
Total Seven	30.9	9.8	152.2	62.5	3.35	3.27
Total world	313.4	292.3	2000.0	1910.0	100.00	100.00

Notes: The intra-Comecon trade for 1980 is probably significantly over-valued, due to the use of overvalued transferable roubles (TR) for exchange purposes. For example, in Poland, in 1981, the cost-based exchange rates were 86 zl for the dollar and 69 zl for the TR. But one TR equals 1.34 accounting dollars (^{a}). Hence $1 = $^a1.67$, or $^a1 = 0.6. Similarly a large discrepancy between the actual dollar and accounting dollar can be found in Hungary and Romania, and it may well be present in all the other East European countries.

*1981

Source: Rocznik Statystyczny, 1982, Tables 947, 949 and 952.

Table 13.2: Dollar exports in 1970 and in 1980, absolute and relative, and percentage change in the relative share in the 1970s

	1970	1980	Share of the world $ market in %		Change of share (%)
	(in $ mld)		1970	1980	
Argentina	1.8	8.0	0.61	0.43	−30
Brazil	2.7	20.1	0.94	1.05	12
Mexico	1.3	15.3	0.44	0.80	82
Spain	2.4	20.7	0.82	1.08	32
Finland	2.3	14.4	0.79	0.76	−4
South Korea	0.8	17.5	0.29	0.92	217
Hong Kong	2.5	19.7	0.86	1.03	20
The Six	5.4	27.5	1.85	1.44	−22
USSR	4.4	35.0	1.51	1.83	21

Dollar exports of the Seven are not only relatively minor, but their commodity composition indicates that some 85 per cent of these exports are minerals, agricultural products, metals and simple textiles and chemicals, some 5 to 10 per cent are arms, and only the remaining 5 to 10 per cent represent somewhat more technology-intensive investment and consumer goods. Exports of the latter category, at some $3 mld. to $6 mld. in 1980, may be estimated to represent about 1/2 to 1 per cent of the world relevant export market (taking the size of the latter in 1980 as $600 mld; or 30 per cent of the world total export market).

The continuing inability of the Seven to do well in their manufacturing sales in world markets seems to be one of the most telling pieces of evidence indicating that rapid innovation and fast adjustment of supplies to the income-and-innovation induced changes in demand do require, among other things, the kind of managerial entrepreneurship and organisational flexibility that are neither present in CPEs nor really feasible under Soviet-type socialism.[2] No doubt the western prolonged recession has made things harder for eastern exporters. It was in order to reduce the influence of the recession factor on our international comparisons that we emphasise the changes in market shares rather than in the level of exports. These comparisons seem to support the view that 'attempts to explain away the troubles by this factor are either clumsy propaganda devices or self-deception, since long before the present recession began there was not much to penetrate western markets with, nor is much in sight when and if the recession ends, especially in view of the growing competition from some of the Far East countries and new prospective members of the EEC' (Brus and Kowalik, 1983).

That limited ability to innovate fast at home and compete successfully abroad may represent two key systemic weaknesses of the CPEs has, in Eastern Europe, long been suspected, but it was seldom if ever before the recent debt crisis discussed openly in the academic literature. One could argue that, in the 1950s, the industrialisation of the East had not yet progressed far enough and that, in the 1960s, the East–West trade was restrained on both sides for non-economic reasons. However, the 1970s have seen a major change of policy, as Eastern Europe received Soviet agreement for an all-out effort to raise the East–West economic cooperation to its seemingly maximum sustainable level, including such anathema as joint ventures and direct private investment. Moreover, in the 1970s the accumulated experience of a number of market-based countries, at the level of development similar to or lower than that of the Six, such as Spain, Finland, the Far East and some Latin American countries, has become sizeable enough to be of use for comparative purposes. The period since the early 1970s may still be too short to draw firm conclusions, but what comparative evidence we have does seem to suggest that the systemic weaknesses mentioned above are indeed very serious.

In this respect the small East European countries appear to be much more vulnerable than is the USSR, since they have neither the large quantities of minerals needed for exports to finance technology-intensive imports nor large R & D resources needed for effective inventive and imitative activity at home. Consequently, the communist élites of the Six, much more than the Soviet élite, are faced with what must be for them a truly disturbing dilemma: they must either sharply increase the allocative and disciplinary role of markets at home—probably at the expense of some long-standing socialist principles, such as high job security, low income inequality, tight political control over managerial appointments and decisions—or else keep technological imports from the West low and accept present technological and standard of living inferiority as something more or less permanent. It may be assumed that the dilemma and its gravity have been noted widely throughout Eastern Europe, although only in Poland and Hungary is open discussion on these matters permitted. The need to restrain the rise of, and/or to reduce, the large dollar debt gives this dilemma an added emphasis, as does the prospect of the Six, with the exception of Romania, having to increase their purchases of oil in the dollar market in the 1980s and beyond.

It is this difference in vulnerability between the Six and the USSR, and its potentially powerful economic and policy implications, which we shall make a starting point in our discussion further in the paper, particularly in section 3.

2. NET BENEFITS OF GIEREK'S POLICY, 1971–82

There is by now a substantial body of the English language literature on the causes and dynamics of the Polish crisis 1980–82. The fact that the experiment in import-led growth ended in such a major economic disaster is, in this literature, usually taken as sufficient for judging it a failure. Even if the judgement is correct or even self-evident, it is nevertheless instructive to have an assessment of the size of net economic benefits (or costs) of the experiment to Poland in the period 1971–82.

Estimating net costs of this kind involves comparing the actual with what would have been if a policy of 'balanced growth' were followed. Guessing the latter is clearly always hazardous, hence the outcome of our comparisons has to be treated with due caution.

The technique used for our 'guesstimates' is very simple. In the period 1955–70 several key variables were changing at approximately constant growth rates. I assume that, under 'balanced growth' (BG), these growth rates would continue until 1975. Thus, the officially calculated net material national product (NMNP) would grow at 6.3 per cent per annum, investment in fixed assets at 7.2 per cent and total consumption at 5 per cent. We note that these rates differ, so the economic growth along such a path would not really be balanced. However, and this is the defining characteristics of our BG path, the trade with the West would (continue to be) balanced. In view of the low level of this trade in 1970, and the fact that the Polish terms of trade both with the East and the West have remained almost unchanged since the post-1973 energy price rises, the impact on Poland's economy of these rises would have, under the BG policy, probably been minor. But the economy would have become (as it actually did, along with the Soviet and other East European economies) subject to several other growth-reducing factors, such as underdeveloped agriculture, housing, transport and communications, all of which are very capital-intensive sectors. In the USSR, in addition to these, there have also been some other factors which resulted in a slowdown in the industrial labour-productivity growth. Consequently, the Soviet (official) growth rate of the N(M)NP fell from 6.6 per cent per annum in the period 1961–75 to 4.3 per cent in the years 1975–80, and to about 3 per cent in the years 1979–82. Guided by this Soviet experience, I assume a fall in the BG (trend) growth rate of the Polish N(M)NP from 6.3 per cent in the period 1970–75 to 3.3. per cent since 1975. I also assume that both investment and consumption would grow, since 1975, at a common rate so that investment share would have remained unchanged.

The implications of these assumptions are shown graphically in Figure 13.1, and precise data are given in Table 13.3. Compared with the BG case, the actual total output, investment and consumption—all three as officially reported—were significantly higher in most years of the 1970s. The consumption gain accumulated until 1981 represented nearly two years' consumption. This implies that

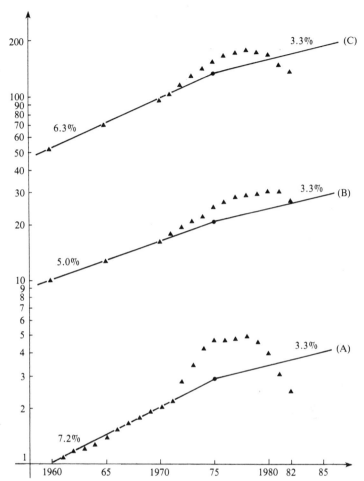

Figure 13.1: Poland's economy: (A) Total investment in fixed capital. (B) Total material consumption. (C) Net material national product. *All data as officially reported.*
Δ–actual observation, heavy line indicates BG path as defined in the text.

the consumption enjoyed by the Polish population in the 1970s was, on average, about 20 per cent above the BG level. It is interesting that in the crisis year of 1980, the actual (official) consumption was higher than the one implied by the BG scenario by as much as 23 per cent. This would seem to suggest that what produced the political crisis in 1981 was not low consumption as such, but low in comparison with what the population expected.

The consumer expectations in the second half of the 1970s were

Table 13.3 Polish national product and consumption: comparison of the actual outcome under import-induced growth policy with a hypothetical outcome under balanced trade policy

	N(M)NP		Total consumption		GNP (Alton)		Private consumption (Alton)	
	(in mld. 1977 Polish zlotys)				*(in mld. 1978 US dollars)*			
	Actual	*BG*	*Actual*	*BG*	*Actual*	*BG*	*Actual*	*BG*
1971	1020	1020	756	741	77.1	77.1	42.9	42.9
1972	1128	1084	821	778	82.8	80.6	45.0	44.5
1973	1250	1153	892	817	88.8	84.2	47.5	46.1
1974	1380	1225	953	858	94.1	88.0	49.5	47.8
1975	1504	1302	1059	901	98.5	92.0	53.5	49.6
1976	1606	1345	1151	931	102.6	94.7	56.9	51.1
1977	1686	1389	1226	961	105.5	97.5	58.9	52.6
1978	1737	1435	1240	993	109.6	100.5	59.4	54.2
1979	1697	1483	1280	1026	109.5	103.5	61.3[2]	55.8
1980	1639	1531	1308	1060	102.9[1]	106.6	62.6[2]	57.5
1981	1441	1582	1308	1095	90.4[1]	109.8	62.6[2]	59.2
1982	1325	1634	1151	1131	83.2[1]	113.1	53.2[2]	61.0
Accumulated difference act. − BG	zl 1230 mld.		zl 1853 mld,		− $2.8 mld.		+ $31 mld.	

Notes:
[1]Assuming the same rate of change as actual for N(M)NP.
[2]Assuming the same rate of change as actual for official private consumption.
Sources:
Official N(M)NP and consumption data come from *Rocznik Statystyczny* (1982). The Estimates by Alton and Associates are from Alton (1981). The assumptions stated in the notes above are by this writer. The way the balanced growth (BG) data are generated is explained in the main text.

presumably formed, to a large extent, by the import-induced economic boom of the years 1971–76. An extrapolation of the consumer growth path in that earlier period for later years does result in a gap of some 20 to 25 per cent of underconsumption in terms of the level actually achieved, in the years 1979–80. The consumer frustrations that resulted from this gap may have been compounded in the years 1980–81 when, under pressure, the government adopted the policy of buying time by permitting the purchasing power of the population to rise rapidly, producing as a consequence large shortages. These shortages depressed the perceived standard of living further below the expected one, by the welfare losses due to massive queueing and forced substitution.

However, Gierek's attempt of seeking to benefit from economic détente should not be judged only by the painful shortages of the years 1980–82 and a crippling debt of $30 billion. After all, the consumer did gain in the 1970s, and it is interesting to find by how much that gain exceeded the debt by 1982.

As seen in Table 13.3, the net consumption gain accumulated until the end of 1982 was, in 1977 prices, zl 1853 mld. or, if the past gains were discounted on 1982 at, say, 5 per cent rate, zl 2320 mld. In terms of the 1982 prices the gain would amount to zl 8000 mld. Bearing in mind that the average resource cost of obtaining 1 dollar in exports was about 80 zl in 1982, the dollar value of the gain would seem to be $100 mld. a sum seemingly much larger than the $30 mld. debt. The consumption may need to drop below the BG level for many years to come, thus changing the ultimate outcome of the policy's cost-benefit analysis. But it is interesting that if one abstracts from the post-1982 losses in consumption, Gierek's strategy would appear to have produced, in the years 1971–82 a net consumption benefit of a quite substantial size.

It is also interesting that the financial assessment of the strategy would be not much different qualitatively if one used estimates of the Polish personal consumption, for the years 1965 to 1978, made by Alton and Associates (1981). Even assuming only a small fall in the BG annual rate, from 3.7 per cent until 1975 to 3 per cent thereafter, one comes up with an accumulated consumer gain by the end of 1982, of some $30 mld. in terms of the 1978 prices, using the exchange rate suggested by Alton for consumption comparisons. Applying again a 5 per cent time preference rate, to express earlier consumption in terms of 1982 consumption, the gain increases to $38 mld., or to some $50 mld. in terms of 1982 prices. This is only half the estimate based on official consumption data, yet still comfortably above the $30 mld. debt level.

Our calculations of the net benefit do not take into account on the benefit side the gains in fixed capital and technology that the import-led growth strategy has brought to Poland in the years 1971–82 nor, on the cost side, the losses in output that the deep cuts in western imports are likely to bring about in the post-1982 years, both gains and losses referring to the differences between the real path and the BG one. The omitted gains are not all real, since some of the additional productive assets are likely to remain idle during their service life. On the other hand, the future output and consumption losses may prove so substantial that the past net gain may become an eventual loss.

The above qualification notwithstanding, the calculation that

claims a substantial net consumption benefit from Gierek's policy
in the period 1971–82 may be judged counter-intuitive by many
Polish consumers in 1983. A closer analysis of the commodity composition of Poland's personal consumption and imports from the
West helps to understand the apparent paradox. It is clear that
Poland, in the 1970s, did make a quantum jump, with the help of
western imports, in a number of key areas of consumption, such
as meat and meat products, private cars, household appliances,
consumer textiles and chemicals. For example, the consumption of
meat and meat products per person increased from 53 kg in 1970
to 74 kg in 1980, despite a 10 per cent increase in the population.
In order to maintain this much increased consumption, in the second half of the 1970s Poland imported from the West about half
of the total animal feed needed. Consequently, by 1980 Poland
became a major net importer of food and agricultural products.
The trade imbalances in these products accumulated in the 1970s
amount to $4.3 mld., or as much as 24.4 per cent of the country's
total dollar trade imbalance for the decade.

Clearly, the communist leaders of the Six, especially of Poland,
underestimated seriously both the supply (particularly export)-
constraining and demand (particularly import)-inducing features of
their centrally-run economies, as well as the political dangers of
pursuing a highly unbalanced consumption growth. The conclusion
would appear to be that significantly larger East–West trade, in
terms of the share of the world dollar market, is not sustainable
without the two economic systems becoming more compatible,
presumably by making economies of the East much more competitive than they are at present, as the alternative, economies of
the West ceasing to be market-based, can probably be ruled out for
the foreseeable future.

3. CAN EAST–WEST TRADE INDUCE REFORMS IN EASTERN EUROPE?

The East European experience, especially in Poland, provides am-
ple evidence for judging the outcome of economic détente as much
different from that originally intended. Paradoxically, some of the
unexpected results may now be welcomed by the original opponents
of the policy. It is useful to list these results.

(i) The communist governments of Eastern Europe did obtain
   resources to play with. In Poland the policy helped Gierek to

consolidate his power after the December 1970 uprising. However, these resources proved to be also a powerful inducement to embark on a highly unbalanced growth path. Consequently, the policy became recipe for a crisis.

(ii) The population of Eastern Europe did enjoy a significantly higher consumption for a while than otherwise possible, but in the wake of severe difficulties later on the early gains became less relevant. Capital investments were much higher, but due to self-imposed import cuts many projects cannot be completed or properly used. On the other hand, the debt is there to be repaid. Since it cannot, or cannot quickly be paid, the interest payments will stay high to burden the East European economy for long. (In 1982 they stood at about a fifth of total East European exports to the West.)

(iii) The political crisis in Poland forced the international communist system to reveal openly its ruthless and non-democratic nature over a prolonged period. This has been a powerful (re-) educational experience, especially in Poland. The crisis in Poland and difficulties in other countries of Eastern Europe might have also disillusioned the élites in those countries about the quality of the Soviet-type economic system, thus promoting thoughts about, and actual attempts at, systemic reforms.

For the western policy-maker these results must seem significant. However, he may still ask if they are significant enough to outweigh the potential benefits to the West that one might associate with other policies, such as a more limited East–West trade or (even) the total embargo.

The question is too complex to this author to be answered in a definitive manner. Clearly, the aspect that needs to be looked at particularly carefully is the contribution of West–East technology transfer to the East's economic growth, and the part played in that transfer by trade. With respect to this matter, the reader may find it useful to consult Chapter 3 of this book, in particular section 4, where references to key studies of this topic can be found. The survey-type monograph by Nove and myself interprets the work on international technological diffusion and growth as implying

'that the policy of complete embargo for West–East technology trade would be capable of reducing the East's technological change and output growth significantly only if the Soviet and East European R & D sector were to be sealed off from the western R & D sector to a sufficiently high degree. The present almost free access to most of western old and new science, as well as a somewhat less free, yet still relatively easy and inexpensive, access to western old and new process and product innovation, makes it possible for any highly industrialized country with large R & D resources, to develop or imitate at a relatively low cost most of the things which have been in use for some time, that is all except the 'latest' technological vintage.' (1984:, pp. 32–3)

However, in Chapter 3 we also noted that, in contrast to the USSR, the smaller East European countries are in a weaker position for two reasons: (i) their R & D sectors are small, so that they have to import more machinery from the West; and (ii) they have to export manufactured goods rather than oil or gold to pay for these imports. A western policy of maintaining a high level of debt would let the burden of interest payments act as a further factor inducing these countries to undertake systemic changes that would promote exports. This policy of 'realistic détente' would not allow the debts to increase above the levels at which the burden of interest payments would be so high that these countries might be tempted to consider an indefinite moratorium on the debts repayments. Such a moratorium need not be politically unpopular, and might be a possibility worth considering even at the present level of debt, especially for Poland.

What would the critics of détente say about this 'realistic' version? Peter Wiles, a persuasive proponent of the total trade embargo, understands the (positive) argument for economic détente to be as follows:

The Polish/Czech/Hungarian infection will spread even into the USSR. It is an inner change which we did not begin from outside and hardly influence and, in the meantime, we must transfer technology because nations whose economies are closely involved with each other do not make war on each other, and in any case a fat communist is more peaceful than a thin one. (1983, p. 3)

Wiles dismisses this argument on the grounds that it has 'no basis in human experience, no scientific foundation'. I am inclined to agree. A realistic détente policy would be, however, an instrument of self-imposed pressure, not of appeasement. Nor does it rest on the hope that the East European infection, meaning economic and possibly other reforms, will spread into the USSR as a *direct result* of that policy.

Peter Wiles offers also a counter-argument for the policy of (total) embargo:

We have in the case of the Soviet Union to do with an ITTP (ideologised, totalitarian, territorial power). The Soviet Union will not disappear of its own accord, because of its inner ideological dynamics. Poland etc. are only difficulties, there are no signs of the spread of the political infection into the USSR nor for that matter into the DDR, Bulgaria, Cuba, Vietnam or on balance Romania. War and *coup d' état* are of course not permitted, but that doesn't mean that we have to be nice to the Soviets. The USSR— and communists in the general way—have all the same weak points: agriculture and technology. From this we draw the conclusion of the *primacy of foreign trade:* the correct non-military Ost-Politik is that of the embargo .... An embargo is naturally cold war. Everything that isn't what we have called 'new détente' (the essence of which is that you can buy peace) is plainly cold war. When we take into account the incontestable fact that the communists have made cold war against us almost every year since 1917, it is hard to understand why this concept applied to our policy here has an unpleasant ring about it. Anyone who has a permanent enemy, and is not seeking to soften him, is making cold war. (1983, p. 4)

There is little in this argument I should disagree with except the conclusion, in so far as it seems to apply to the USSR as well as Eastern Europe. I simply think that keeping the debt and collecting (at least a part of) the interest payments, while at the same time offering Eastern Europe (not the USSR) the prospect of increased trade—large trade is not possible at present for commercial reasons—may be more beneficial for the nations both of the West and the East than the total embargo. The reason is that the latter would imply not only the write-off of debt, but also closer economic integration of the Six with the USSR. An embargo policy would cause an economic crisis in Eastern Europe that could be as deep, if not deeper, than that in Poland. That option for the West may be therefore thought tempting in the short run, but its wisdom is less obvious in the long run. Economic crisis in Eastern Europe might bring about economic decentralisation as it did in Poland. However, such reforms would be unlikely if, in the post-crisis period, the option of trading with the West is foreclosed. Economic integration of the CMEA economies to be effective may require, instead, the establishment of supranational planning and management.

4. POLISH TRADE POLICY TOWARDS THE WEST AND WESTERN POLICY TOWARDS POLAND

In this section we come back to Poland, to consider the Polish–western trade and credit policy options. Our primary aim is to identify the major facts and considerations, economic and other, that must influence thinking on these matters on both sides, especially on the Polish side. We begin by examining Poland's key foreign trade data for the period 1978–82, as given in Table 13.4.

New western credits practically ceased to be available from 26 March 1981 in response to Poland's decision to suspend debt repayments. Western imports had to fall in consequence, reducing Poland's outputs and exports, thus necessitating further import cuts, which again reduced exports, and so forth. In 1982 an equilibrium of some sort was reached. Imports from the West fell to some 40 per cent of the 1978 level in real terms, and from

Table 13.4: Poland's foreign trade data in the period of crisis

		1978	1979	1980	1981	1982
Trade with West current prices in $ mld.	Exports	5.5	6.4	7.5	5.4	5.2
	Imports	7.4	8.0	8.5	5.4	3.8
Trade with East current prices Polish R/$ exchange rate in $ mld.	Exports	5.2	5.8	5.6	6.0	7.5
	Imports	5.3	5.6	6.2	7.8	8.1
Trade with West constant prices 1978 = 100	Exports	100	102.1	107.2	83.5	84.3
	Imports	100	95.5	88.6	60.7	46.0
Trade with East constant prices 1978 = 100	Exports	100	109.6	99.2	82.3	96.0
	Imports	100	101.7	104.1	97.6	92.1
Terms of trade 1978 = 100	West	100	99.3	98.2	98.2	101.5
	East	100	97.1	94.9	92.8	89.8

Notes:
Terms of trade reported in the table are defined as the ratio of the index of export prices to the index of import prices, both indices implied by the trade data in value and volume terms. Until 1982 the official trade statistics were given only in terms of 'devisa zlotys'. For 1981 this implied the R/$ exchange rate of 1.32 dollars for the (convertible) rouble. Since 1982 the actual zloty are used instead. The cost-based exchange rates were, on 1 January, 1982, 80 zl for the US $ and 68 zl for the R, giving 0.644 as the conversion rate from 'official dollars' to 'resource dollars'. In rows 3 and 4 of the table this conversion rate is applied for all the years 1978–82. Note also that here 'East' means CMEA (ten) countries plus People's Republic of China, North Korea and Yugoslavia. All other countries belong to the 'West'.
Source:
Rocznik Statystyczny (1983) for the years 1978–82. The values expressed in devisa zlotys, given on p. XLI, were converted into US dollars using the exchange rate for each year as given on p. 328. The trade in volume terms is as reported in Table 2 on p. 329.

$7.4 mld. to $3.8 mld. in nominal terms. Exports to the West also fell, but only to 84 per cent of the 1978 level in real terms. Consequently, a trade deficit of some $2 mld. in 1978 was converted, in 1982, into a surplus of about $1.4 mld., one-third of which in trade with the developed West.

Trade with the East, both imports and exports, also declined, but only by about 6 per cent in real terms. It is interesting that the East/West composition of Poland's exports did not change significantly: the contraction of exports was area-balanced. Another fact of interest is that Poland's terms of trade deteriorated significantly with the East, especially with the USSR. Consequently, despite not having become a greater drain on Soviet (and other 'eastern') resources than in 1978, if it was then, Poland has in the early 1980s began to accumulate sizeable trade deficits with the East, again mainly the USSR. The Polish economy is now called upon to meet resource claims from both sides, in the form of interest payments and debt repayments to the West and in the form of terms-of-trade losses to the USSR. Since neither claim can be met in full, the debt in real terms is rising; it stood at $24.8 mld. and R3.7 mld. by the end of 1982. In terms of the 1982 exports, the total dollar-denominated debt represents 4.9 years of exports to the West and the rouble-denominated debt equals 0.5 year of exports to the East. Interest payments on the dollar debt, assuming an 11 per cent interest rate, amount to $2.6 mld., or about half of Poland's total exports to the West in 1982.

By imposing martial law, the government clearly decided to accept the risk of the West declaring Poland in default, or even imposing the trade embargo. The former would have been an inconvenience, the latter a disaster of war-type proportions. In the event neither happened, thus forcing the authorities again to face the question of Poland's optimal economic exposure to the West, of evaluating the very complex earlier experience and the long-term economic and political benefits. The question is openly debated, and is unlikely to be given a clear answer for some time in view of the many uncertainties still present.

One of these uncertainties concerns the form of agreement about the rate of debt repayment and interest payments. Here the Polish aim is 'to work out a way of rescheduling our debt repayments over many years, and not over one year as has been the case so far, which would create more stable conditions for cooperation with capitalist countries' (J. Obodowski, in 1983 a Deputy Premier and Head of the Planning Commission).[2] The Polish government could have interpreted the western sanctions of December 1981 as an act of war by other means, and used them as an excuse to declare non-payment of debts. This it can still do, especially if and when the impact of such a move is judged, by Poland and other East European countries, less painful than the burden of servicing the debt.

However, it seems that despite the debt problem, the Polish authorities are attempting to maintain the opening to the West, partly in response to having found it difficult to shift trading relations in favour of the CMEA, but quite possibly also for long-term reasons, economic as well as political. A clear indication of the official reluctance to move away from trading with the West is contained in the 'middle variant' of the three-year plan for the 1983–85 period that was selected for implementation at the start of 1983. This plan predicts a shift, but back towards the West. It expects the share of Polish exports to the CMEA countries to fall from 49 per cent in 1982 to 45 per cent in 1985, and the share of imports from the CMEA to fall from 58 per cent to 54 per cent (the two time comparisons are in constant prices). András Köves, a Hungarian economist, may be right in arguing that 'in the present situation of the world economy, and mainly of the economies of the CMEA countries, a consistent import substitutive policy on the regional scale which would have developed cooperation within the CMEA at the expense of external relations, the policy that was envisaged by the CMEA countries during the 1950s, is absolutely unrealistic' (1982, p. 337). I would put it differently, but to much the same effect. A disengagement from large-scale trading with the West, probably in favour of a greater intra-CMEA cooperation, must be feasible, but at an economic cost that the countries in question are apparently reluctant to accept. This may also apply to the USSR, which along with East European countries is faced, indirectly, with the same trade-off between the security cost of the West obtaining a crisis-making capability in Eastern Europe and the economic cost to the CMEA from poorer access to western technology.

The utilisation of industrial capacity in Poland continues, in the years 1983–84, to be only some 60 per cent. Investment activity has been more than halved, investment imports from the West being virtually eliminated. The level and composition of investment to 1985, as envisaged by the three-year plan, reflects the 'living standards' orientation of the plan. The food and the agricultural complex is expected to take 30 per cent of investment spending, the housing 'complex' to take a further 30 per cent, and the fuel and energy complex 14.5 per cent. This leaves 25.5 per cent for all other sectors of the economy.

It thus seems to be the case that with or without 'Solidarity', the pressure to increase living standards continues to be strong. This internal pressure was also present in the 1970s, especially in its first half. At that time the authorities sought external resources to meet that pressure. This time the hope is that the economic reform of January 1982 will lead to much better use of the internal resources. However, the reform is not particularly radical and its implementation has been slowed down, first by the 'state of war' regulations, and now by the apparent reluctance of the central authorities to trust markets and market instruments for allocative purposes (see Chapter 14). It is conceivable, therefore, that a recourse to western resources may be attempted again, this time under the disguise of the need to increase imports first in order to repay the debt later.

To my mind, any (significant) giving in by the West to such attempts on the part of Poland is likely to reduce the incentive to put aside ideological principles that stand in the way of implementing serious, efficiency-enhancing systemic reforms. Since the debt would rise rather than fall as a result, a really 'soft' western response in the short and medium terms may also increase the likelihood of Poland's eventual default, and would therefore be against western, as well as Polish, interests in the long term. On the other hand, all the major western institutions engaged in financial negotiations with Poland—private banks, the Paris Club, the IMF and the World Bank—may become a forceful ally for the more reform-minded segment of the Polish authorities.

NOTES

1. The Seven are the USSR and the six East European countries listed in Table 13.1.
2. For a good discussion of this topic, the reader may consult H. Levine (1983).
3. After The Economist Intelligence Unit, *Poland,* no. 1, 1983:, p. 21.

REFERENCES

Alton, T. P., 'Production and Resource Allocation in Eastern Europe: Performance, Problems and Prospects', in Hardt, J. P. (ed.), *East European Economic Assessment,* Part 2, Joint Economic Committee, US Congress, 1981.
Brus, W. and Kowalik, T., 'Socialism and Development: Joan Robinson and Beyond', *Cambridge Journal of Economics,* 1983.

Gomulka, S. and Nove, A., 'Econometric Evaluation of the Contribution of West–East Technology Transfer to the East's Economic Growth', Paris: OECD, 1984.

Hanson, P., *Trade and Technology in Soviet–Western Relations,* London: Macmillan, 1981.

Holliday, G. D., *Technology Transfer to the USSR, 1928–1937 and 1966–1975: The Role of Western Technology in Soviet Economic Development,* Boulder, Colorado: Westview Press, 1979.

Holliday, G. D., 'Transfers of Technology from West to East: A Survey of Sectoral Case Studies', Paris: OECD, 1983.

Köves, A., 'Alternative Foreign Economic Strategies for the CMEA Countries', *Konjunnkturpolitik,* **28**(5), 1982.

Levine, H. S., 'On the Nature and Location of Entrepreneurial Activity in Centrally Planned Economies: The Soviet Case', in Ronen, J. (ed.), *Entrepreneurship,* Toronto: Lexington Books, 1983.

Portes, R., *The Polish Crisis: Western Policy Options,* The Royal Institute of International Affairs, 1981.

Wiles, P., 'Embargology', mimeo, 1983.

APPENDIX: THE RELATIVE AND ABSOLUTE SOLVENCY CONDITIONS UNDER BALANCED GROWTH, AND THE TILTING EFFECT

The Polish economy is at present so unsettled that it may not be useful to engage in forecasting the balance of payments position for the 1980s. But it may be worth while to recall the conditions which must occur if Poland is to repay the debt eventually. We shall limit our discussion of this question to a very simple yet hopefully instructive case of balanced growth, in which imports and exports in real terms are proportional to the gross national product (or to industrial output), also in real terms, and in which there are no terms-of-trade gains or losses.

We shall use the following notation:

D = external debt

X = exports in real terms

M = imports in real terms

p = price index for exports and imports

r = nominal interest rate

g = growth rate of the national product (or industrial output) in real terms

d = D/pX

i = $\Delta p/p$

Inflation rate i, interest rate r, and growth rate g are all assumed to be constant. The question we ask is this: Given the assumptions above, what would the ratio of the trade surplus to exports have to be for the relative indebtedness of the country, indicated by the ratio d, to remain constant?

From the definition of d, it follows that $\Delta D/D = i + g + \Delta d/d$.

But $\Delta D = pM - pX + rD = pX\left(\dfrac{pM}{pX} - 1\right) + rD$. Hence,

$$\frac{\Delta D}{D} = \frac{1}{d}\left(\frac{pM}{pX} - 1\right) + r.$$

On comparing the two expressions for $\Delta D/D$ we obtain that:

$$\Delta d = (r - i - g)d - \frac{p(X - M)}{pX} \tag{1}$$

The last term is seen to represent the relative trade surplus. Therefore, for the d ratio to remain constant, the relative trade surplus would have to be equal to $(r-i-g)\,d$. This is what may be called the 'relative solvency' condition for the long term. Clearly, if $g > r-i$ and $X > M$, then the debt would eventually be repaid. These two inequalities combined form thus a sufficient condition to ensure 'absolute solvency' in the long term.

In principle, the western banking community need not worry unduly about Poland's debts so long as the d ratio stabilises at a level that the community considers to be 'acceptable'. Whatever that level may be, it is worth noting the following two important (and perhaps somewhat paradoxical) implications which follow from the 'relative solvency' condition: $\Delta d = 0$ or, on substituting into (1), from

$$\text{trade surplus} = (r-i-g)D \tag{2}$$

(a) Maintaining the d ratio constant requires, in a balanced growth situation, that the debtor country runs a balance of trade deficit, if $g + i > r$, that is, if the common growth rate of exports and imports in current value terms exceeds the interest rate, and runs a balance of payments surplus otherwise.

(b) If actually $g + i > r$, then the higher the (constant) debt/exports ratio, the higher should also be the balance of trade deficit as a proportion of exports.

Over the years 1976–79, dollar exports were rising at an average annual rate of 9.3 per cent, which is less than the present average interest charge, reported by Bank Handlowy to be

11.5 per cent in 1980 (possibly more in 1981). However, industrial output and dollar export earnings are now, in the early 1980s, severely restricted by limited dollar imports, while interest rates in the West are rather on the high side. If a less restrictive credit policy on the part of western banks and an economic reform at home could result in growth rates of Polish exports and imports that would be about equal and yet higher than the interest rate, then the long-term aim of stabilising the debt/export ratio may be achieved even if the balance of trade remains permanently negative. However, in the short run the increase in nominal interest rates has produced the damaging *tilting effect* for Poland, since the fall in the real value of principal counts only in the long run.

14 The Reformed Polish Economic System 1982–83[*]

1. INTRODUCTION

In the post-1945 period the communist authorities in Poland considered introducing a comprehensive economic reform on two occasions, in 1957 and in the early 1970s. In each case a political crisis provided the major stimulus. The blueprint for the first reform was prepared by the Economic Council under Oskar Lange in 1957, the first document of this kind in the Soviet bloc. The blueprint was not particularly explicit on the details of the proposed new system, nor particularly radical where it was explicit. Nevertheless, two key principles were clearly outlined. One was to implement central plans by, predominantly, economic (parametric) instruments rather than by physical targets. The other was to promote direct industrial democracy by setting up workers' councils. These principles were, of course, not new; the Yugoslav economy was then already operating on that basis. The Council's document, however, despite being in practice rejected by the Polish authorities, helped to legitimise the two principles among (usually Stalin-trained)

[*]This article is based on two earlier papers, one by Gomulka, S., 'Polish Economic Reform: Principles, Practice, Prospects', presented at the NASEES Annual Conference, Cambridge, 26–28 March 1983, and the other by Rostowski, J., 'Economic Reform and the Prospects for Stabilization of the Polish Economy', mimeo, 1982. The authors are grateful for useful comments they received at the LSE Seminar in Comparative Economics and Planning and at the Cambridge Conference. The paper also benefited much from the authors' visit to Poland and from criticisms by a number of Polish economists. Especially detailed and helpful were the criticisms by Leszek Balcerowicz, Ryszard Bugaj, Marek Dąbrowski, Cezary Józefiak, Jan Mujżel, Jerzy Osiatyński, and Zdzisław Sadowski. Needless to say, the responsibility for errors of fact or interpretation that may still remain is ours alone.

Reprinted with permission from Stanislaw Gomulka and Jacek Rostowski, *Soviet Studies,* vol. XXXVI, no. 3, July 1984, pp. 386–405.

economists and policy-makers of Eastern Europe, thus in part preparing the intellectual and ideological ground for reform attempts elsewhere, above all in Czechoslovakia and Hungary in 1968, as well as for the current reform in Poland.

It was again an economic and political crisis that has resurrected the question of a radical reform in Poland in 1980–81. This has happened despite strong evidence for the view that the direct cause of the crisis was a particular macroeconomic policy of highly unbalanced growth, rather than the economic system as such. Nevertheless, much increased technology imports and the credit-financed investment boom failed to improve efficiency or stimulate exports to the West sufficiently and this failure gave weight to the argument that the old system caused the crisis, if only indirectly. A sharp growth slowdown throughout the Soviet bloc since about 1978 has also brought home the realisation that the era of extensive growth is at an end. Under such circumstances it became more pressing than ever to consider radical efficiency-enhancing measures to deal with the debt problem abroad and consumption pressures at home. There was also the experience of price increases triggering severe social unrest, which suggested that apart from economic efficiency reasons it might be advantageous also for political reasons to leave the socially explosive business of setting prices and wages to markets and/or decentralised bargaining.

The reform of January 1982 is still fluid. However, the dust is settling and a reasonably clear picture is emerging. In this context the purpose of the present article is twofold. One is to describe the main (parametric and direct) instruments which, under the new system, the centre uses to influence the economy. We pay particular attention to fiscal and monetary measures and price formation rules, as well as to instruments of direct influence, such as appointments and investment decisions, input allocations and output orders. It will be clear that the reformed economic system (RES) which is being introduced in Poland is a variant of market socialism, bearing a strong resemblance to the Hungarian New Economic Mechanism (NEM). The overall objective of any reform of this kind in a country dominated by a communist minority is to increase allocative efficiency and the innovation rate, improve export capability and eliminate shortages without, at the same time, excessively compromising both the traditionally socialist principles of full employment, low economic inequality and price stability and the communist principle of retaining the pre-eminence of the economic and political preferences of the centre. Our second purpose is to examine the effectiveness of the reform in meeting these objectives so far.

The coalition of pragmatic communist politicians and reform-minded economists who came to power in the course of 1980 and 1981 appeared aware of the risks involved in launching an economic reform, itself a major disturbance in the short run, in the middle of a crisis that was to reduce consumption per person by some 30 per cent and investment by about 50 per cent. As a safety net, the reformers envisaged that there would be a transition period of three to five years in which some essential elements of the old command system would be maintained. In the sections that follow we describe the system as it was in 1982–83, at the same time making clear which of its elements are intended to be more permanent and which transitional.

2. MAJOR PRINCIPLES AND THE TRANSITIONAL PERIOD

The key initial document, *Kierunki reformy gospodarczej*, prepared by a large government-appointed Reform Commission, was completed in June 1981, approved by the Party Congress in July 1981, and served as a basis for the new law on the state enterprise and self-management adopted in September 1981. The law came into force officially on 1 October 1981, but its implementation began from 1 January 1982 after specific laws were enacted in November and December 1981, and to the extent to which these laws were not in conflict with the martial law regulations of 13 December 1981.

The major principles of the reform may be summarised as follows:

(i) Enterprises were to be independent, self-financed and self-managed; the so-called 3-S principle. Independence meant that the choice of what and how to produce was, for the enterprise, no longer to be constrained by the centrally-imposed directive plan. Self-financing meant that workers' incomes would be based on their financial results alone, and self-management was to give large powers to the workforce directly or, where the number of workers was more than 300, to workers' councils.

(ii) Market disequilibria were to be phased out through increased price flexibility, and microeconomic efficiency to be increased through enhanced financial discipline (a harder budget constraint, in Kornai's terminology). In order to maintain financial discipline, competition would be encouraged through anti-monopoly laws (greater) freedom to import, and conservative credit policy. Bankruptcies would be allowed.

(iii) Central planning would be maintained, but it would be much less detailed. More importantly, the government would attempt to implement central plans indirectly, through the use of taxes, credits, interest and exchange rates, direct purchases, price and income regulations, some major investment projects, import and export controls, and so forth. Regulated competitive markets would be the main medium through which the government would attempt to implement its own macro plans and social policy aims.

(iv) Since the centre would retain much economic power, institutional arrangements were envisaged to ensure that central plans were not arbitrary, but reflected 'social preferences'. To this end the principle of socialisation of the central planning process was proposed; large policy matters would be debated openly in the mass media, the consultative role of the supposedly independent trade unions, professional bodies and individual experts would be enhanced, and the decision-making powers of the centre would be diffused to involve more fully the Council of Ministers and the Sejm. Admittedly such changes would not amount to adopting parliamentary democracy, but they would nevertheless imply a higher degree of political democracy than in Hungary or Yugoslavia. Apart from helping to achieve a social optimum, political democracy was thought to be important because meaningful participation in forming national economic policy would help in motivating employees to work hard, as well as being a means of winning over the population at large to the reform and overcoming any opposition to it from the bureaucracy.

In these four principles the reader may easily recognise the influence of ideas associated with Oskar Lange and Włodzimierz Brus. If they were implemented in full, in particular the principle of self-management, the Polish reform would be more radical than the Hungarian, and if bankruptcies were really allowed and domestic markets opened to foreign competition, it would be more radical even than the Yugoslav reform.

Government documents state openly, however, that principles (i) to (iii) cannot be implemented immediately, but that they would be introduced eventually. Principle (iv) however, has been effectively abandoned since the introduction of martial law. We shall have more to say about the key elements of the traditional system that are still in operation later. At this point it is enough to note that they include direct allocation of many essential inputs, including more foreign exchange earnings; extensive subsidies; central control of prices, which are often set arbitrarily below costs and/or below market-clearing levels; a much reduced role of workers' councils and trade unions; and restricted (much more than before the reform) freedom to change employment.

3. THE 3-S PRINCIPLE IN PRACTICE

This principle is mentioned above under (i). In this section we shall describe how it has been implemented during 1982-83.

Self-management

Following the imposition of the 'state of war', workers' councils were suspended and managers placed under the supervision of military commissars. For a while the authorities appeared uncertain about the role the councils should play once the commissars were removed. The matter was eventually decided by a government decree of December 1982. The councils in all 6500 state enterprises were to be reactivated or set up before 1 April 1983. The councils have a deciding voice in the size and use to which the social fund can be put. However, they have only consultative powers as far as policy matters (output, pricing, employment) are concerned. Furthermore in some 1500 enterprises, usually large-sized and/or providing essential public services (and employing about 80 per cent of the total labour force) they are not consulted on the appointment or dismissal of directors.[1] Thus, in the transitional period at least, the reform will be managerial, of the Hungarian-type, and only in smaller-sized and peripheral enterprises will the self-management rule be retained. Although all chief executive directors are supposed to be selected through some sort of open screening procedure, some 2000 have been appointed in the old manner by ministries and local authorities since the introduction of the RES.[2] It seems likely that the Communist Party *nomenklatura* will remain the principal instrument of appointments policy, especially in the 1500 key enterprises.

Managerial independence

Enterprises are supposedly free in making decisions on employment and output, except that the government can place orders for goods the supply of which is of 'national importance'. Such government orders have to be met.[3] The goods in question are military supplies, goods needed to meet international trade agreements and those under 'operational programmes'. The government is responsible for providing enterprises with centrally-distributed inputs, including foreign exchange, needed to meet these orders. Since access to these inputs is often essential to be in business at all, enterprises do not shy away from, but rather compete for, such government orders. Nevertheless the extensive use of 'operational programmes', intended to ensure the supply of essential consumer goods and inputs that would otherwise be in excessive shortage, indicates the judgement of the centre that without this strong administrative support the reformed economy could collapse. However, when it was decided to keep a large number of prices at levels far below equilibrium, extensive control over quantities, whether inputs or consumer goods, became inevitable. These price and quantity controls represent probably the most powerful administrative instrument, apart from the continuation of the *nomenklatura* system, to have been retained from the old system; they seriously limit managerial independence, and with it the scale and usefulness of the reform itself. It is also important that directors' salaries are determined by the central authorities and not at enterprise level.[3]

The main objective of the Polish enterprise under the RES would appear to be similar to that of the Yugoslav one: maximising after-tax wages and bonuses, including retained profits, per employee. The time preference rate is likely to differ considerably among employees, however, as must the weights attached to bonuses in kind and to investment. Employees with a higher time preference rate will attach less weight to enterprise expenditures, such as investment in fixed capital or the development of markets, designed to generate future income. Factory managers, on the other hand, may tend to associate their promotion prospects with output expansion and/or status-giving technological innovation. For these purposes a high investment expenditure would usually be necessary. Therefore the investment pressure from below may still be there, especially if the overall budget constraint of enterprises remains soft while the tax systems are effective in restricting wage rises.

Self-financing

One of the key factors likely to decide the effectiveness of the reform is the degree of financial discipline at the enterprise level or, to use Kornai's term, the hardness of the budget constraint. A soft budget constraint may or may not cause shortages (Kornai argues that it does), but it certainly removes the pressure from managers and workers alike to seek more revenue through greater cost-saving effort rather than simply higher prices and subsidies. Polish reformers appear aware of this crucial relationship between financial discipline and efficiency-enhancing pressures, as well as of the factors which influence that discipline. However, there is little disagreement among Polish economists, both in academia and government, that enterprises' budgets remain, in the second year of the reform, about as soft as under the old system. The original reform document made it clear that the disciplinary role of the budget could be increased only gradually in order to avoid massive bankruptcies and high unemployment (possible, in part, as a result of the immense disruption caused in the years 1980–82 by the sharp decline in western imports). Some of the otherwise 'strange' decisions taken in the areas of prices, taxes and credits have been, we shall argue in section 4 below, subordinated to this argument.

4. PRICE FORMATION, INTEREST RATES, EXCHANGE RATES AND WAGES

There are three types of prices: state-fixed, regulated and free. Table 14.1 below gives their percentage distribution by type of goods in 1982 and, in brackets, in 1983. The proportion of freely-determined prices is rather high, especially in inter-enterprise trade. These prices could be set at market-clearing levels. State-fixed prices are often set below cost, as in the case of coal and electricity, while a regulated price is one which may not exceed the industry's marginal cost, but may exceed (this is the 1983 innovation) the producer's own marginal cost.

Table 14.1

Prices	Consumer goods	Percentage of sales Industrial inputs	Agricultural procurement
State-fixed	37 (40)	19 (20)	72
Regulated	15 (15)	5 (5)	0
Free	48 (45)	76 (75)	28

Source: Cezary Jożefiak for 1982; Władysław Baka (*Życie Gospodarcze*, 19–26 December 1982) for 1983.

In general it is the prices of politically-sensitive goods, such as food, that are state-fixed. Basic raw materials are in the same category because of their importance for the price level. The Polish authorities are still unclear whether prices should be left to be determined by supply and demand or set (arbitrarily?) on a cost-plus basis. They would like to gain the greater efficiency in the allocation resources that market-determined prices would provide, but without risking an increase in inflation which they believe to be at least partly generated by the monopolistic practices of enterprises. The government's recent anti-inflationary programme, while stressing the need to move towards market-clearing prices, also froze the prices of all intermediate and investment goods for 1983.[4] This capacity for interference has now been made permanent: the authorities have the right to freeze any prices at will or to impose maximum rates of increase on prices by sector.[5] Another way in which the centre attempts to prevent increased costs from leading to increases in either state-fixed or regulated prices is the spreading over four years of the increase in depreciation charges that ought to have resulted from the 1982 price increases. By 1987, when the effects of the 1982 price reforms will have been fully integrated into costs, and therefore into controlled price calculations, prices are likely to have risen by a further considerable amount, so controlled prices will continue to be based on underestimated costs.[6]

Price control based on cost calculations may limit, but is unlikely to abolish, price increases—if only because costs can be artificially inflated or simply overstated. In many cases, therefore, officially rigid prices may be relatively free, whereas officially free prices may in fact be controlled by the state either invoking special powers or exercising indirect pressure on enterprise managements. What is clear is that a mixed system of free and controlled prices exists, and that the balance between the two is not only indistinct but changes as the attention of the authorities switches from questions of efficiency to those of social discontent and back again.

Goods for which there is excess demand have to be rationed in some way. Goods whose prices are set freely by enterprises, but which nevertheless are not at a market-clearing level because of informal government pressure or the lack of incentive to raise prices in the face of highly progressive taxes (see section 5 below), are rationed by suppliers' preferences, as are many goods with regulated prices. Essential raw materials on the other hand continue to be centrally allocated, as do inputs into priority areas such as pharmaceuticals. Inputs for these priority sectors are obtained through compulsory government purchases. Finally, very many intermediate inputs can only be sold by producers via the sectoral supply organisations *(Centrale Zaopatrzenia i Zbytu)* as direct trade between producer and customer is forbidden. Most of the sectoral supply organisations come under the control of their respective branch ministries, and thus provide ministries with an additional tool for pressurising enterprises. During 1983 the number of supply organisations granted exclusive trading rights in 'their' products rose from 19 to 29, and the proportion of inter-mediate inputs under their control rose from 25–30 per cent to 40 per cent.[7]

It may be worth noting at this point that we do not consider, as Kornai does, that soft budget constraints on enterprises are suffi-cient to lead to generalised shortages throughout the economy.[8] We maintain that micro disequilibria would be largely eliminated if prices were sufficiently flexible and that the primary implication of soft budget constraints on enterprises is low economic pressure to reduce costs through innovation or harder work. (This matter is discussed in Chapter 5, this volume.)

The interest rate is set by the central bank and, together with pro-ject appraisal by the banks, it is supposed to determine the alloca-tion of credit. The total amount of credit in the economy is the responsibility of the central bank which under the RES draws up an annual 'credit plan', which is supposed to be consistent with the annual central plan.[9] In fact, the central bank believes the demand for credit to be completely inelastic with respect to the rate of interest.[10] In this it is surely right, as the cost-plus formula that is usually used to determine both controlled and free prices means that in the presence of generalised excess demand increases in in-terest rates are just passed on to customers. Where prices are free, but below market-clearing levels because of the progressive wage and profits taxes (see section 5 below), an increase in the interest payments which are included in costs will lead enterprises to raise prices so as to maintain the level of (post-tax) profits and wages.

The exchange rate is set by the central authorities, and is one of those key parameters whose manipulation is intended to provide the centre with the ability to run what is supposed to remain even in the view of the most radical supporters of the reforms a 'planned economy'. The problem facing the central bank is that devaluation is necessary to stimulate exports in the marketised sector of the economy,[11] but that this will also lead to an increase in the costs of imported inputs and of domestically-produced raw materials whose prices are supposed to be set at world levels, and this cannot but raise the domestic average price level. Fearing that the rise in domestic prices would be so great as practically to nullify the export incentive effects of a devaluation, the Polish authorities have taken a number of *ad hoc* measures which involve abandoning, at least temporarily, the principle of a uniform exchange rate which was enshrined in the original reform proposals. On the import side most imports continue to be centrally purchased under the auspices of the Ministry of Foreign Trade and then distributed administratively to user enterprises. [12] On the export side differential exchange rates are offered to different exporters and for different goods. [13] Enterprise directors inform the Ministry of Foreign Trade (MFT) that they can only cover their costs on a particular good if they receive, say zl 110 or zl 140 per dollar rather than the official rate of zl 95. [14] Apparently the MFT often agrees. Such a system would have much to recommend it if the MFT behaved as an auctioneer, accepting the best (i.e. lowest) bids from enterprises in terms of exchange rates that allowed it to achieve a predetermined export target. The system would then be a way for the MFT to extract quasi-rent from exporting enterprises. There is, however, no evidence that this is the way the system actually operates. Rather, it makes possible central control of what is supposed to be the marketised part of the export sector, making an objective calculation of the profitability of exporting a particular good more difficult, and at the same time it may encourage influential enterprises to use their power to get hidden subsidies.

Enterprises outside the temporarily centrally administered sector are free to set their own wage scales subject to centrally determined relativities. [15] However, these centrally-determined relativities can be circumvented by enterprises through the well tried methods of reclassifying workers, and paying out large premiums and bonuses. It thus seems that central control of wage scales is little more than a polite fiction, with enterprises in the marketised sector being free to determine their own wage scales, and the burden of limiting the total national wage fund being left to the system of direct taxation.

The impact on the labour market of enterprises' freedom to set wages has been limited, however, by the introduction in 1983 of labour rationing. Workers looking for employment are directed to particular enterprises by provincial labour offices, supposedly according to priorities imposed by the centre. [16]

5. THE SYSTEM OF TAXATION UNDER THE RES

Under the RES Polish enterprises are subject to three types of taxes. First, there is the turnover tax, which is simply a percentage tax, at varying rates, on gross output. Secondly, there are taxes on the inputs the enterprise uses. There is a wage fund tax of 20 per cent, a land and buildings tax of 3 per cent, and an amortisation fund of which a proportion is paid to the state budget and is thus, in fact, a tax on capital.[17] The effects of the turnover tax and the taxes on inputs are fairly straightforward, and we shall therefore limit ourselves to an analysis of the third type, direct taxes. In this analysis we make use of the following definitions:

gross profit = sales − turnover tax + subsidies − own costs − costs of external inputs;

net profit = gross profit − profit tax + tax allowances;

bonuses + social fund + development fund = net profit − reserve fund − *FAZ*;

$$\text{rate of profitability} = \frac{\text{gross profit}}{\text{own costs}}$$

Before the introduction of the economic reform in 1982 there were no significant direct taxes in the socialised enterprise sector in Poland. With the reform two important direct taxes were introduced: the *'podatek dochodowy'*, literally 'income tax',but in fact a tax on enterprise profits,[18] and payments into the *'fundusz aktywizacji zawodowej'* (FAZ), literally a 'retraining fund', but in fact a progressive tax on payments made to employees. A third direct tax, the one-off 'stabilisation tax' (*'podatek stabilizacyjny'*) was also imposed on socialised enterprises in 1982. Apart from funding government-financed programmes, the purpose of all three taxes is, first, to reduce the amount of demand inflationary pressure in the economy and, second, to discourage enterprises from taking advantage, where there is one, of their power to raise incomes through price rises.

The enterprise profits tax was highly progressive in 1982, but the progressive element was softened for 1983, and is to be eliminated altogether (the tax is to be linear) in 1984. The tax takes an (increasing) proportion of enterprise profits as the rate of profitability rises. As noted above, profitability is defined as gross profit over 'own costs of production', which in turn are defined as total costs of production and sale, less the costs of materials, energy and 'farmed out production' (*'obròbka obca'*). By far the greater part of 'own costs of production' are usually labour costs, so that profitability can largely be defined as the ratio of profit to labour costs. When profitability thus defined lies in the interval 5 to 10 per cent then, in 1983, 40 per cent of profit would have been paid in tax, this proportion rising progressively to 90 per cent of profit when profitability exceeded 50 per cent (30 per cent in 1982).

Controversy has surrounded the enterprise profits tax since before its introduction. The tax was supposed to discourage Polish enterprises, many of which are monopolistic, from using their power to increase profits merely by raising prices. However, if as a result prices are kept below market-clearing levels, shortages persist. On the other hand, enterprises would also be discouraged from reducing costs if and when the price rises alone would bring them into high profitability brackets. For example, if profitability lies in the 25–30 per cent range, then in 1983 only 20 per cent of any savings on material inputs and only 11 per cent on labour would be retained by the enterprise.[19]

These considerations bring us to yet another main cause for the reform's apparent failure to serve, in 1982–83, as an effective efficiency-enhancing incentive system. For, in order to soften the blow of the government-imposed consumer price increases of February 1982, money incomes were raised in the course of 1982, through so-called compensatory payments, welfare payments and direct wage increases, by some 65 per cent. An increase in aggregate demand of this size, coupled with a fall in consumer supplies by some 25 per cent, produced a large excess demand for those goods whose prices were free. Consequently, these prices went up by some 80 per cent in 1982, and these rises alone raised profitability rates to levels at which the marginal post-tax benefit to employees from reducing costs, or for that matter increasing prices to equilibrium levels, was zero or near to it. As a result, the two key economic diseases which were associated with the old system, excessive costs and persistent shortages, have not been cured by the reform (in its first two years of implementation, anyway).

For the years 1982 and 1983 the demand curve in Figure 14.1 may be represented by D_1. In this case the rate of inflation, chosen by enterprises, would be insufficient to clear the markets. Therefore, there would be no incentive at all to reduce costs. Only when the price rises are capable of clearing the market (demand D_2 and equilibrium E_2^*) do enterprises begin to be interested in increasing their revenue through cost reduction, the incentive to reduce costs being higher the less progressive is the profits tax.

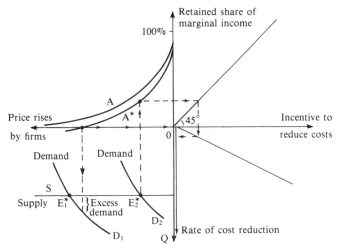

Figure 14.1: The relation between market equilibrium, tax rules, and economic efficiency under the RES. Dotted lines and arrows indicate the direction of causality.

Notation: Curve A in the NW quadrant is the relation between the percentage price rise and retained share of marginal income by the producer—the price-maker—taking into account the progressive profits tax and the *FAZ*. Curve A* adjusts this relationship by taking into account non-economic pressures from the government and the public against price increases. S and D in the SW quadrant denote, respectively, supply and demand curves. It must be noted that given the old price level, the rate of inflation defines a new price level.

This second direct tax is the wage fund tax (*FAZ*) paid, like the profits tax, by the enterprise. The nature of this tax was changed significantly in 1983, from taxing increases in the average wage to taxing increases in the total earnings of the enterprise workforce. Under the 1982 scale for the *FAZ* the rates paid rose from 0.25 per cent on the 4th percentage point of an increase in the average wage, to 4 per cent on each percentage point by which the average wage increased by more than 8 per cent. Such a tax encourages the hiring of workers who earn wages below the average paid by the enterprise concerned. This permits higher wage increases for the rest of the workforce. Such an effect was meant to be offset by an allowance which ensured that each 1 per cent reduction in the labour force employed by the enterprise raised the threshold at which the *FAZ* began to operate by 1 percentage point also up to a cut-off point of a 5 per cent reduction in the labour force. Nevertheless, this allowance against the *FAZ* failed as an inducement to shed labour, and 1982 was, in fact, characterised by the high degree of excess demand for labour.[20] Reasons for this failure included the pro-employment nature of the *FAZ* tax itself, the high profits (often due to subsidies) that enterprises made during 1982, the need to have a labour reserve to make up for highly irregular input deliveries and the fact that some 500,000 employees had accepted early retirement or gone on three-year maternity leave during the course of 1981. The introduction of the possibility of early or extended temporary withdrawal from the labour force was itself due to planners' fears that the RES might lead to large-scale unemployment—fears which proved totally unfounded in the event. The net effect was that employment in industry fell by only 3.5 per cent,[21] which cannot have gone far to remove the extensive over-employment that exists in many sectors.

The main purpose of the *FAZ* tax was, however, to prevent all enterprise profits from being passed on to the population in the form of increased incomes. Here also the results were not particularly satisfactory. This is indicated by the fact that the *FAZ* generated only zl 48 billion in 1982, which was just under one-third of the planned figure,[22] and this in spite of the fact that wages rose by 42 per cent compared with the planned 11.5 per cent.[23] The main reason seems to have been the authorities' fear of using fully the tool they had created. A whole series of exemptions from the *FAZ* was introduced in the course of 1982. Particularly important was the exclusion from the *FAZ* system in November 1982 of wage increases for work on officially free days and of wage increases for work on night shifts.[24] Additionally, enterprises had their *FAZ* scale shifted up by 0.5 to 0.8 per cent for each percentage point by which output in the second half of 1982 exceeded that in the first half of the year.[25]

These changes were introduced because, apparently, by mid-1982 the authorities became worried that the new taxes which they had created, the *FAZ* and the profits tax, were seriously inhibiting enterprises from increasing production through reduced use of inputs (Figure 14.1 above). Economists wrote of enterprises 'settling down at a low level of production' as a result of the system of taxation,[26] and indeed, industrial production rose by only 0.4 per cent in the course of 1983 (comparing output in December 1983 with that in December 1982).[27]

In 1983 further changes followed. The *FAZ* scale rates became more severe than those which operated in the second half of 1982.[28]

In order to act as an incentive to reduce labour input, the new rates were made applicable to the growth of total wages, bonuses and premiums paid by the enterprise, rather than to changes in their average level. A third important change was that opportunities for administrative decisions were introduced into both the *FAZ* and the profits tax. Most of these opportunities are linked to the system of allowances and exemptions from the two taxes (some 15 categories of exemption were introduced during 1983 alone).[29] As regards the *FAZ* system, the most important of the allowances and exemptions are: (a) the threshold at which the *FAZ* system begins to operate is moved up by 0.5 per cent of taxable labour costs for every 1 per cent increase in output; the branch ministry has the power to decide whether output is measured as value added or global output or in physical terms;[30] (b) the Planning Commission has the right to: (i) raise to 0.8 per cent the amount by which the *FAZ* threshold is raised for each 1 per cent increase in output; (ii) change the base of the *FAZ* system to changes in the enterprise's average labour costs i.e. to return to the 1982 system; (iii) to raise the *FAZ* threshold for a particular enterprise as it sees fit(!)[31]. These allowances are, moreover, being allocated administratively in lump sums to enterprises on quite a large scale. The Ministry of Chemical and Light Industries entered into binding contracts with its enterprises in 1983 in which the Ministry committed itself to allocate fixed amounts of zlotys in *FAZ* tax exemption, while the enterprise committed itself to exceed its output plan targets by fixed amounts of zlotys, as well as defining by what means it would achieve this additional ouput. Such an administrative allocation of allowances activates bargaining and leads enterprises to misinform the centre about their output plans in the old predictable manner.

A similar set of opportunities for intervention by central planners exists in the enterprise profits tax system. The Ministry of Finance can raise the enterprise profits tax threshold as it sees fit for those branches or particular enterprises which it considers to have a low ratio of 'own costs of production' to gross output, which are engaged in energy and raw materials-saving investments or are financing housing for employees out of their wages fund.[32]

The direct tax system, as amended in the second half of 1982 and in 1983, thus provides central planners with a whole panoply of devices for exerting direct financial pressure on individual enterprises. Consequently, the important principle of tax rules as parameters, that they be the same for all enterprises and not subject to individual bargaining, has been undermined. With this dilution of the parametric nature of taxes, direct administrative planning in disguise must reappear.

A further pitfall faces the Polish authorities. This is the temptation to change the tax system with every change in economic conditions, in which case the tax system itself will become part of the game between the centre and the enterprises. One symptom is the large number of changes that have occurred already in the first $1\frac{1}{2}$ years of the new system. Another was the use of a 150 billion *ad hoc* 'stabilisation tax' which was unexpectedly introduced in March 1982. The use of such taxes to cream off *ex-post* a major part of enterprise profits, if persistent, would clearly undermine any incentive role profit may still have. There is also the danger that the new 'variable' turnover tax will be used in just this way by the authorities. (From 1984 this tax is to be used to raise a free or regulated price near to its equilibrium level when it is not in the producer's own interest, because of the effect of other taxes, to fix the price at that level in the first place.)

This threat to the parametric role of the direct taxation system is all the more dangerous because of the extremely high level of subsidies that persists on the government expenditure side. Subsidies accounted for 44 per cent of enterprise profits in 1982 and for 40 per cent in 1983.[33] To this must be added an apparently very large, but as yet unquantified, amount of cross-subsidisation within the associations into which most Polish enterprises are grouped.[34] Moreover, there are over ten sectoral funds administered nationally which are supposed to cater for the development needs of their industries. These funds are financed by obligatory contributions from enterprises, and are then disbursed by the central authority controlling the fund (usually the branch ministry).[35] This widespread use of 'negative taxes' is probably seriously weakening the effectiveness of 'economic tools' for plan implementation (as opposed to 'administrative tools' in Polish economic parlance), and thus strikes at the very heart of the RES.

6. SIMILARITY OF DIRECT TAXES UNDER THE RES AND INCENTIVE FORMULAE UNDER THE *WOG* SYSTEM

There is a striking similarity between the incentive formulae of the Large Economic Organisations (*WOG*) system of the 1970s in Poland and the present system of direct taxation under the RES.

Not only do the two mechanisms attempt to achieve similar ends (see section 7), but they also use very similar means. Norm R, which was in force between 1973 and 1976 and from 1977 to 1980,[36] related the size of the wages fund increases in the *WOG* to value added increases. It thus functioned in much the same way as the mechanism which, under the RES, shifts the *FAZ* threshold up by a proportion of increases in value added (see above).[37] The introduction in 1977 of a progressive tax on unplanned increases in the wages fund made the *WOG* system even more similar to the 1983 *FAZ* structure, given the administrative allocation of lump sum tax exemptions mentioned above (section 5).[38] Moreover, during 1977 and 1978 there was a progressive 'excess profits tax' which was similar to the present enterprise profit tax.

Polish economists have noted some of the similarities between the two systems and have suggested that the undesirable effects experienced in the 1970s may reappear. Of particular concern are two aspects of the new system of direct taxation. The first is that the size of the wages fund is linked to output, the fear being that this will lead, as in the 1970s, to demand-pull inflation, open or repressed.[40] The second is that output may be measured in gross terms rather than by value-added, giving rise to an incentive to waste inputs.[41]

7. THE FINANCING OF INVESTMENT UNDER THE RES

Investment is divided into centrally-planned and enterprise-planned investment, with some 85 per cent of investment being administered.[42] There is still considerable confusion in the system, with electrification of the railways, for instance, officially classified as an enterprise-planned investment. Enterprises are free to determine their own investments as long as they have enough money. On the introduction of the RES many enterprises found themselves burdened with huge debts arising out of centrally-planned investments in them during the 1970s. Such enterprises are clearly dependent on bank credit for investment funds. The central bank claims that it intends to be very tight with investment loans to enterprises, but so far it has not had the opportunity to prove itself as the demand for investment loans by enterprises has been so low that net enterprise indebtedness with the bank actually fell in the first half of 1983.[43] This was probably as a result of the high profits earned by enterprises (which could not go into wages because of the *FAZ* tax) and because of the shortage of investment goods.

In the centrally-planned investments sector many of the old vices do persist. In spite of a 'verification' of investment projects there has been a further 'widening of the investment front' (i.e. increasing the number of investment projects and a lengthening of the average expected gestation period). Also the bias towards investment in building rather than machines seems to persist.[44] Furthermore, enterprise investment is to be limited in 1984 so that centrally-financed investment projects can be continued.[45] This probably reflects a real dilemma for the Polish authorities: whether to go for small-scale investments which will pay off quickly, or to complete larger ones with a much longer gestation period and uncertain profitability. The main disadvantage of the latter is that they will perpetuate the investment structure of the 1970s. This is because investment projects 'continued' from the 1970s constituted 88 per cent of the total investment in 1982 and 1983, and only 15 per cent of projects have been abandoned (as measured by the value of investment already committed). This leaves very few resources with which enterprises can undertake new investments. This policy is consistent with the official view of the central bank that structural changes in the economy can only be implemented through centrally planned rather than enterprise planned investment. At present, because of the economic and political crisis in Poland, the rate of investment is low, as priority is given to consumption. Therefore, if there were a recovery, the investment rate would increase and possibly centrally-planned investment would also rise as centrally-directed restructuring of the economy was continued.

8. CAN THE RES REDUCE THE MATERIAL INTENSITY OF THE POLISH ECONOMY?

Probably the primary aim of the authorities in introducing the RES was to encourage a more efficient use of inputs, particularly of material inputs. The new rights enterprises have gained should, in theory, facilitate the achievement of this goal. Four factors, however, appear to work against this achievement in practice. The first is the high level of subsidies and cross-subsidisation that still persists in Poland. The second is the highly monopolistic structure of Polish industry and the virtual absence of foreign (East and West) competition. The other two factors relate to the system of direct taxation that we have been discussing. One is that the central planners have the right to decide that for a given enterprise, for the purpose of determining the *FAZ* threshold, increases in output will be measured in gross output terms rather than value-added; 'if the circumstances justify it'.[47] The decision is up to the branch ministry 'after consultation with the Planning Commission'. When a number of criteria are available, enterprises are likely to press successfully for the one that suits them best. It may be assumed that in most cases this criterion will be gross output, as it will allow enterprises to inflate their achievements by using more, or more expensive, external inputs. Finally and this is our fourth factor, the various (formal and informal) ways that the centre can discriminate between enterprises through managerial appointments, taxation terms, investment credits, foreign exchange and other input allocations, if used really widely, would amount to a system of informal command planning. (Incidentally, the discretionary aspects of the direct taxation system would give the central planners an informal tool for plan implementation similar to the official French *agrément fiscal*). Where the tools of control are available, the control is likely to follow.

The influence of reforms on the attitude of enterprises to innovation has been the subject of an empirical study of 50 enterprises in the machine-building and steel industries.[48] The study found that the reform had introduced a number of changes which encourage innovation. These are, in order of importance, free markets for some inputs, the possible threat of bankruptcy, greater price flexibility, tax allowances for R & D activity and retention of a small part of export earnings in hard currency. However, other aspects of the RES discourage innovation. These are, in order of importance, the *FAZ* and profits taxes, restrictions on the use of the amortisation fund and of profits, and the central regulation of prices. The report concludes that, on balance, the reform is at best innovation-neutral. The most important pressure to innovate continues to be the need to compete on foreign markets, though this affects mainly those firms which export significant quantities to competitive western markets.

9. CAN THE ENTERPRISE PROFITS TAX AND THE *FAZ* CONTROL INFLATION?

At first glance the direct taxation system seems to provide an insuperable barrier to demand-pull inflation. Profit earned by the enterprise is taxed away on a rapidly progressive scale, and a second even more steeply progressive system of taxation, the *FAZ*, comes into operation when the enterprise tries to reintroduce its income into circulation by spending it on labour services. However, two factors work to lower this barrier. One is that bonuses and premiums become subject to the *FAZ* only when their value causes labour costs to rise by more than 7 per cent. The other is that the *FAZ* threshold is raised by between 0.5 and 0.8 per cent for each 1 per cent increase in output, in volume terms. This system may lead to an increase in inflationary pressure. In the short run this could occur if, to give an example, the coefficient relating the *FAZ* threshold to increases in output coefficient were 0.75 per cent on average while only 0.5 per cent of all ouput were sold on the consumer goods market. In that case, for each 1 per cent increase in national product income would rise 50 per cent faster than the supply of consumer goods. Although the output of groups A and B grew at the same rate, supplies of group A inputs to group B fell each year, and were only made up by imports financed through foreign borrowing.[49] Under the RES this should be less likely, given the increased power of the customer on the inter-industry market. It must be remembered, however, that many of the group A enterprises have been effectively excluded from the RES. Moreover, the inflation pressure of the 1970s may, in part, be attributed to just such a mechanism as that described above. Norm R, generally set at 0.5 to 0.6, related increases in the wages fund to increases in output, much of which was not marketed.[50] In such a system, moreover, additional inflationary pressure can also come from the welfare sector, the workers in (non-marketable) service industries and the private agricultural sector.

The *FAZ* does, however, have one great advantage. It discourages wage-push pressures on the part of the workforce, as beyond a certain rate wage increases would force the enterprise into total dependence on bank credit. In this way the *FAZ* stiffens managers' resistance to wage demands. In the absence of a steeply progressive tax, like the *FAZ*, managers, workers' councils and trade unions might believe that they could obtain the money to finance higher wages in some way. This might be by raising prices, if they ignore the fact that similar price rises would be made throughout the economy, or if they thought that the centre would validate the wage increases by relaxing credit terms. If such behaviour occurred throughout the economy, the centre would indeed be faced with the well-known choice of either validating the wage increases conceded by enterprises through monetary growth, producing inflation, or allowing certain enterprises to go bankrupt, thus producing unemployment. In the case of extremely strong social pressure for wage increases, the *FAZ* may not suffice to block them as managers may count on receiving sufficient credits to pay both the *FAZ* and the wage increases, but this is only likely in a situation of acute political crisis. Under normal circumstances the *FAZ* prevents wage-push inflation from developing and from forcing the government to choose between validating inflation and unemployment.

10. CAN THE RES STIMULATE NET EXPORTS?

Given Poland's large foreign debt both to the West and the USSR, and the importance of import bottlenecks in production, one of the main aims of the reforms has been to orient the economy more towards exporting. We have already seen that the exchange rate system leaves much to be desired in this respect. However, as the rate of inflation falls and the Polish zloty is slowly devalued, one can expect the price advantage from selling on the domestic market which apparently exists at present to be whittled away. This may lead with time to the use of a truly uniform rate of exchange.

The other main instrument to stimulate exports which was introduced under the RES is the scheme whereby enterprises are allowed to retain a proportion of their hard currency export earnings (*odpis dewizowy*).[51] The effect of this reform has been blunted, however, by the small amount of money that the centre has been able to put in the retained export earnings pool and by the fact that the proportion of export earnings retained tends to be linked to the import content of the exports of the enterprises concerned.[52] This, of course, encourages exporting enterprises to increase the import content of their output.

To correct these weaknesses in the system, the Consultative Economic Council (*Konsultacyjna Rada Gospodarcza*) set up under the RES has suggested that the exchange rate should be uniform and the proportion of retained export earnings linked to profits earned from exports. It remains to be seen whether these suggestions will be adopted. The system as it exists at present can be used to encourage gross exports, but it is harder to encourage net exports and difficult to encourage the economically most advantageous net exports.

11. INSTITUTIONAL REFORM UNDER THE RES

Like the second wave of economic reforms in Hungary[53] which began in 1979, the introduction of the RES in Poland has involved a large element of institutional reform. As in Hungary, the number of branch ministries was reduced (in Poland from 12 to 6) and the position of central functional bodies was strengthened relative to that of the branch ministries. We have already mentioned the considerably increased importance of the central bank in Poland; we can add here that the Price Commission and the Ministry of Finance have gained authority at the expense of the branch ministries. In the case of the Price Commission this is because it is now dealing with thousands of independent enterprises which are less able to oppose it than were the 12 branch ministries under the previous system. The strengthening of the Ministry of Finance has resulted partly from the realisation that the lax financial policy of the 1970s contributed considerably to the crisis Poland has suffered. As a result investment has been cut back sharply and the Ministry, as the dispenser of central investment funds and of the state budget, has been strengthened. These changes are likely to be helpful. Functional bodies are more likely to base their decisions on some conception of the national interest, whereas branch ministries are often accused of 'branch patriotism' and of being excessively influenced by pressure from individual enterprises.

One way in which the Hungarian reform differs from the Polish is that in Hungary the national supply agency (the Price and Materials Supply Office) was strengthened at the expense of the newly-created Ministry of Industry which succeeded the branch ministries. In Poland, on the other hand, the central supply organisations (*Centrale Zaopatrzenia i Zbytu*) for the various centrally-allocated goods have remained under the control of their respective ministries, whereas independent, self-financing, wholesaling enterprises have been set up for some of the non-centrally-allocated goods.

Another way in which the Polish institutional reform is similar to the Hungarian is the reduction in the number of trusts (*zjednoczenia*). In fact, officially in Poland trusts as such, which were merely links in the bureaucratic hierarchy linking the branch ministry with enterprise, have been abolished. They have, however, been replaced by associations (*zrzeszenia*) which are supposed to fulfil merely service functions for the enterprises which are their members. Moreover, the associations were supposed to be entirely voluntary, and to involve any imaginable combination of enterprises which believed that their cooperation, even on a temporary or functionally limited basis, would be mutually beneficial. In fact, many of the associations are compulsory, imposed via the use of reserve powers by the centre, and a standard complaint is that they continue to form part of the transmission-belt for instructions from the branch ministries to enterprises.[54] Until a detailed analysis of the powers of the associations is carried out, and each association has a different charter, the situation will remain unclear. Nevertheless, there are a number of indications that all is not as was initially intended. First, in the four main industrial branch ministries, out of 60 associations, 29 are officially obligatory.[55] Second, in very many sectors membership of associations is identical, or almost identical, to the membership of the previous trusts.[56] Finally, ministries have been accused of pressurising enterprises into joining associations.[57] Many associations, however, are truly voluntary. Aside from true economies which often clearly exist when producers in the same sector cooperate, the main motive behind truly voluntary associations seems to be the greater leverage they give their members *vis-à-vis* the centre, and the increased monopoly and monopsony power which the cartel-like organisation of the association gives them *vis-à-vis* customers and suppliers. It is distinctly odd that the authorities, who claim to be concerned with the threat which the highly monopolised structure of Polish industry poses to the success of the RES, have encouraged associations rather than putting obstacles in the way of their creation.

There is also the question of bankruptcy. In Poland the principle that the bankruptcy of socialist enterprises will be possible has been accepted and is enshrined in the new bankruptcy law. Even if this law is not watered down by the introduction of various periods of grace, or forced merger and thus forced cross-subsidisation, the indications are that whether enterprises are allowed to go bankrupt will always be a matter of policy rather than of institutions. So far, the single enterprise which was declared bankrupt in 1982 has still not actually been dissolved.[58]

Finally, institutional reforms in Poland have affected mainly the administrative levels from the ministry down; the role of the true centre is yet to be defined. Under the classic Soviet-type system there is no effective separation between the executive branch of the centre and the legislative branch. The group of top executives, usually the First Secretary of the Communist Party, the Prime Minister and the Chairman of the Central Planning Commission, could initiate and impose major investment and production changes almost at will, constrained by national resources or political considerations rather than by any law. Under the new system it is this true centre, and not just ministries, which must impose on itself an act of law that would limit its powers *vis-à-vis* enterprises if the rights that enterprises have been given are to be meaningful. Without such an act direct administrative intervention by the centre will not be obviously unlawful, and may therefore reappear that much more easily.[59]

12. CONCLUSION

What are the likely economic implications of these new instruments of indirect regulation? Do they encourage enterprises to reduce production costs and increase output? In the market place, do they reduce the power of the seller and enhance the power of the buyer? To what extent are these instruments capable of containing inflationary pressures? The experience so far is not particularly encouraging. Over the last year aggregate demand has continued to be excessive, mainly as a result of sharply increased wages, social welfare payments, large subsidies, and a large fall in consumer supplies. In many (most?) markets prices continue to be below equilibrium levels. Enterprises have not been keen to raise free prices to these levels since their net (after tax) marginal income to be gained from such rises would be negligible. Consequently, shortages prevail while at the same time enterprises continue to have virtually no incentive to reduce costs and indeed the 'material intensity' of production improved minimally during 1982 and 1983, even though production improved during 1982 as the economy recovered somewhat from the sudden unavailability of western inputs after the imposition of martial law. The insistence of the price-controlling agencies that prices reflect (average) costs is inconsistent with the aim of eliminating shortages. Consequently, the reform, it seems, has brought (so far) little change compared with the centralised system in the key areas of market equilibria, choice, innovation and allocative efficiency. This view is supported by the findings of a group of Polish economists from the National Economic Institute, who studied the efficiency implications of the reform in 44 industrial and construction enterprises. A summary of these findings by Urszula Wojciechowska[60] is (almost) dismissive of the effectiveness of the RES so far. The key recommendation is that the hardness of the budget constraint, which at present was found to be as soft as it was under the old system, be sharply increased.

In the course of 1982–83 the reformers have shown themselves ready to introduce changes that go against the reform principles. These changes may be categorised as follows: (i) A large number of general exceptions and reserve powers for the centre introduced from the start of the reform, such as the power to fire managers (almost) at will; (ii) subsequent adjustments weakening the moves already taken towards parametric planning, such as making relief from direct taxes enterprise-specific (see section 5); (iii) branch ministries have retained a wide range of powers to allocate both physical and financial resources to their subordinate enterprises, which leads to allocation by bargaining (as under classic Soviet-type planning) rather than according to efficiency criteria.

In any communist country of the Soviet-type there would be present what might be called *political and social limits to an economic reform* that involves a radical upgrading of competition. The political limits are clear enough; they arise from the opposition of those who are likely to lose influence in an ensuing redistribution of power from the intermediate levels to enterprises and from the party apparatus to enterprise managers and workers' councils. In (post-) 'Solidarity' Poland the relative position of factory organisations of the Communist Party versus workers' councils became a particularly sensitive issue. The centre seems to expect workers' councils to be dominated by (former) 'Solidarity' members. If such councils were given considerable powers, including the power to appoint managers, the Communist Party would effectively lose much of the influence it has in Polish factories. On the other hand, if workers' councils have consultative powers only, the communist-controlled bureaucracy would retain in its appointments policy a powerful instrument of influence and control. This would limit enterprise independence and hence the scope of the reform.

The *social limits* to economic reform are associated with the changes in the distribution of economic influence among citizens that an increase in efficiency and competitiveness would bring about. The new system could be expected to benefit particularly the innovator and entrepreneur, especially in the private sector. On the other hand, the risk of unemployment would increase sharply as would actual unemployment. These changes in income and status would go very much against the egalitarian ideals that the communist state and indeed the Catholic Church have propagated in the 40 years since the war and which the 'Solidarity' period showed to command strong support within Polish society.

In addition, the countries of Eastern Europe are rather too small to ensure a high degree of market competition at home without opening their borders to foreign producers. Such an opening would require the adoption of exchangeable currencies and the lowering of other barriers to the cross-border movement of goods and people, reforms that are clearly unlikely for some time yet.

To conclude, the Polish reform is, or rather is intended to be eventually, of the Hungarian-type, that is substantial but not particularly radical.[61] In the meantime, after two years of the reform, the actual economic system may be better described as one of 'informal command planning' rather than of indirect (market-regulated) central planning. Moreover, after the crushing of 'Solidarity' and the limiting of political freedoms there appears to be no social force capable of lifting significantly the political and social constraints on the reform.

NOTES

1. 'Informujemy', *Życie Gospodarcze,* no. 4, 1983.
2. This method of appointment has now been declared invalid for the future by the courts.
3. *Dziennik Ustaw,* no. 39 1983, p. 176.
4. 'Program Antyinflacyjny, Program Oszczędnościowy', *Rzeczpospolita* 19 March 1983.
5. *Dziennik Ustaw, op. cit.*
6. Dąbrowski, M., *Przeglad Techniczny,* no. 24 1983.
7. Skowronek, C., *Życie Gospodarcze,* no. 45 1983.
8. Kornai, J., 'Resources Constrained vs. Demand Constrained Systems', *Econometrica,* July 1979, See also his *Economics of Shortage* Amsterdam 1980, vol. 2.
9. Baka, W., *Polska Reforma Gospodarcza,* Warsaw, 1982.
10. Interview with S. Majewski, Chairman of the NBP, *Życie Gospodarcze,* no. 32 1983.
11. Olechowski, A.,*Życie Gospodarcze,* no. 13 1982.
12. Sobota, J., *Życie Gospodarcze,* no. 31 (1982), and *Monitor Polski,* no. 37, 1983.
13. Private communication to one of the authors by the director of an electronics firm.
14. On 1 July 1983 the official uniform rate was devaluted from the zl83 to the dollar, at which it had been set on 1 January 1982.
15. Szajnuk, J., *Życie Gospodarcze,* no. 45 1982. The mining industry has been effectively excluded from all the provisions of the reform, including the right of enterprises to set their own wage scales—see

Uchwala Rady Ministrow (199/1981) See also Walawski, A., *Przegląd Techniczny*, no. 16, (1983), Uchwala Rady Ministrow 135/1982, *Monitor Polski*, no. 17, p. 138, 1982, and Uchwala Rady Ministrow 60/1982 (unpublished).

16. *Życie Gospodarcze*, no. 48 1983.

17. *Dziennik Ustaw* no. 7, 1982, p. 55.

18 Law of 26 February 1982, *Dziennik Ustaw*, no. 7, 1982, p. 55.

19 If profitability exceeds 50% (30% in 1982) then any decrease in labour costs actually reduces profitability. J. Szumski, *Życie Gospodarcze*, no. 16, 1982.

20. According to official statistics, in June 1982, 280,000 vacancies were reported by enterprises, compared with 170,000 in June 1981, while 20,000 people were seeking work via labour exchanges. *Życie Gospodarcze*, no, 27, 1982.

21. *Życie Gospodarcze*, no. 4, 1984.

22. Wróblewski, A. *Życie Gospodarcze*, no. 8, 1983.

23. 'Aktualnosci', *Życie Gospodarcze*, no. 36, 1982; and 'Plan na rok 1983', *Życie Gospodarcze*, no. 47, 1982.

24 Directives Nos. 30/82 and 58/82 of the Ministry of Labour, Wages and Social Affairs.

25. Decision of the Council of Ministers No. 186/82. Decision No. 182/82 of the Council of Ministers introduced exceptions for enterprises engaged in exports.

26. Kabaj, M., *Polityka*, no. 26, 1982; and *Życie Gospodarcze*, no. 42 1982.

27. *Życie Gospodarcze*, no 4, 1984.

28. It is difficult to compare the scales applicable to 1983 with those for early 1982, as the latter, although they had a higher threshold, had fewer exemptions and a higher marginal rate.

29. Dąbrowski, M., *Życie Gospodarcze*, no. 49, 1983.

30. 'Informujemy', *Życie Gospodarcze*, no. 4, 1983, and Kierczynski, A. and Wiatr, M. S., *Życie Gospodarcze*, no. 8, 1983.

31. 'Informujemy', *Życie Gospodarcze*, no. 1, 1983.

32. 'Umowa zawarta w dniu ... pomiędzy Ministrem Przemysłu Chemicznego i Lekkiego a dyrektorem przedsiębiorstwa'. Blank form of such a contract in the possession of the authors.

33. Misiak M., *Życie Gospodarcze*, no. 45, 1982.

34. Jeziorański, T., *Życie Gospodarcze*, no. 31, 1982.

35. Dąbrowki, M., *Przegląd Organizacji*, no. 5, 1983.

36. Wanless, P. T., 'Economic Reform in Poland 1973–79', *Soviet Studies*, vol. XXXII, no.1, January 1980.

37. Wanless, *op. cit.*, Norm O, which was in force during 1976, related permissible increases in the *average* wage to increases in labour productivity and thus bore a family resemblance to the 1982 *FAZ* structure.

38. Wanless, *op. cit.*, under the *WOG* system the managerial bonus fund was also calculated in a very similar way to the wages fund now. It depended on net profit and was subject to a progressive tax (with marginal rates varying from 10 to 80 per cent) which increased as the ratio of bonuses to managerial basic pay rose compared with the preceding year.

39. Wanless, *op. cit.*, the 1977–78 tax differed from the present one in that it was a progressive charge on the *increase* in gross profits as a percentage of stocks and fixed assets. An increase in gross profits, so defined, of between 0–2 per cent lead to a 10 per cent marginal tax rate on the gross profit increase. This rate rose to 70 per cent the increase in gross profits exceeded 8 per cent.
40. Fiszel, H., *Życie Gospodarcze*, no. 1, 1983.
41. Kierczyński, A., and Wiatr, M. S., *Życie Gospodarcze*, no. 8, 1983.
42. Konsultacyjna Rada Gospodarcza 'Uwagi do Załozen, CPR na 1984', *Życie Gospodarcze*, no. 49, 1983, states that during 1982 and 1983 88 per cent of investment was on projects that were 'continued' from the 1970s. All of these are in effect centrally administered and financed. Moreover some new investments are probably also centrally administered, leaving very little indeed for enterprise determined investments.
43. Majewski, *op. cit.*, enterprise net indebtedness fell by zl50 billion, or some 5 per cent of total investment.
44. Majewski, *op. cit.*, and Kotowicz, J. *Życie Gospodarcze*, no. 48, 1983, who reports the findings of the third enterprise survey of the National Economic Institute, which found that in its sample of 54 enterprises 63 per cent of investment expenditure went on buildings.
45. Communicated to one of the authors by government sources.
46. Majewski, *op. cit.*
47. Informujemy, *Życie Gospodarcze*, no 4, 1983.
48. Ruszkiewicz, J., Monkiewicz, J., Hadyniak, B., and Oseka, M., *Perspektywy wdrażania innowacji w przmysle maszynowym i hutniczym w latach 1980-tych*, Warsaw Polytechnic, mimeo, 1983.
49. Szwarc, K., *Życie Gospodarcze*, 1983
50. Wanless, *op. cit.*
51. Sobota, *Życie Gospodarcze*, no. 31, 1982.
52. Konsultacyjna Rada Gospodarcza, 'Funkcjonowanie Gospodarki na obecnym etapie', *Życie Gospodarcze* no. 14, 1983.
53. Hare, P. G., 'The Beginnings of Institutional Reform in Hungary', *Soviet Studies*, vol. XXXV, no. 3, July 1983.
54. Jeziorański, T., *Życie Gospodarcze*, no. 31, 1983.
55. Dąbrowski, *op. cit.*
56. Jeziorański, *op. cit.*
57. Personal communication to one of the authors by the director of an electronics factory in Poland.
58. Mozołowski, A., *Polityka* no. 6, 1983.
59. In Poland Cezary Józefiak has written particularly widely and forcefully on this subject, e.g. 'W stronę Izby Gospodarczej', *Przegląd Organizacji*, nos. 4–7, 1982.
60. Wojciechowska, U. *Życie Gospodarcze*, no. 11, 1983.
61 Both Bauer and Kornai judge the budget constraint in Hungarian enterprises to be relatively soft and the reform there to be, for this reason, largely ineffective. Bauer, T., 'The Hungarian Alternative to Soviet-Type Planning', *Journal of Comparative Economics,* vol. 7 (3), September; 1983; Kornai, J., *Economics of Shortage,* Amsterdam, North-Holland, 1980.

Author Index

Subject Index